Rereading Appalachia

Rereading Appalachia

Literacy, Place, and Cultural Resistance

Edited by

Sara Webb-Sunderhaus

and Kim Donehower

UNIVERSITY PRESS OF KENTUCKY

Scholarly publisher for the Commonwealth,
serving Bellarmine University, Berea College, Centre College of Kentucky, Eastern
Kentucky University, The Filson Historical Society, Georgetown College, Kentucky
Historical Society, Kentucky State University, Morehead State University, Murray
State University, Northern Kentucky University, Transylvania University, University of
Kentucky, University of Louisville, and Western Kentucky University.
All rights reserved.

Editorial and Sales Offices: The University Press of Kentucky
663 South Limestone Street, Lexington, Kentucky 40508-4008
www.kentuckypress.com

Library of Congress Cataloging-in-Publication Data

Names: Webb-Sunderhaus, Sara. | Donehower, Kim.
Title: Rereading Appalachia : literacy, place, and cultural resistance /
    edited by Sara Webb-Sunderhaus and Kim Donehower.
Description: Lexington, Kentucky : University Press of Kentucky, 2015. |
    Series: Place matters : new directions in Appalachian studies | Includes
    bibliographical references.
Identifiers: LCCN 2015033892 | ISBN 9780813165592 (hardcover) |
    ISBN 9780813165615 (pdf) | ISBN 9780813165608 (epub)
Subjects: LCSH: Literacy—Social aspects—Appalachian Region. | Appalachians
    (People)—Social life and customs.
Classification: LCC LC152.A66 R47 2015 |
    DDC 302.2/2440974—dc23
LC record available at http://lccn.loc.gov/2015033892

ISBN 978-0-8131-7442-6 (pbk. : alk. paper)

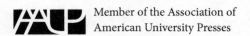

To the mountains
and their people

Contents

Introduction

Sara Webb-Sunderhaus and Kim Donehower

In *Something's Rising,* Silas House and Jason Howard write of the Appalachian activists whose testimonies they collect: "The people you will meet here are storytellers. They all speak of stories as a force that sustains them, just as the tradition of storytelling sustains the entire Appalachian culture. All of them know that one way to fight back is to tell a story in your own voice, in your own words."[1] Our collection features ten storytellers who are also trained as academics. In academic writing, storytelling is a particular form of resistance, disrupting genre conventions, and calling into question the value of stories as evidence. We have encouraged the contributors to this volume to experiment with mixing personal stories with more traditional forms of academic writing. For all of us, academic work on Appalachian literacies is deeply personal, and we do not wish to pretend otherwise. And we know that, for some of the audiences who may read our work, our stories might carry as much weight as our research, if not more.

Our goal in these pages is to consider Appalachian literacies outside the binary of us-versus-them, insider-versus-outsider literacies. The notion of Appalachia as a monolithic Other in opposition to mainstream American literacies, as portrayed in such works as *Storm in the Mountains* and described by Peter Mortensen in "Representations of Literacy and Region," conceals the diversity of literacies and groups within Appalachia.[2] It obscures the many complex relationships Appalachians have had with outside literacy purveyors and the ways in which Appalachians have deployed a variety of literacies to resist other Appalachians.

Why This Collection? Why Now?

While this is a collection about Appalachia and literacy, its roots lie outside the Appalachian region. Specifically, it began in Minneapolis, Minnesota, and Columbus, Ohio. Minneapolis is home to the University of Minnesota, where Kim earned her Ph.D. and wrote a dissertation on the literacy beliefs of her family's Southern Appalachian community. It was in Columbus that Sara, then a Ph.D. student at Ohio State, wrote her own dissertation on the literacy beliefs and practices of Central Appalachian student writers. At the time, there were few composition and rhetoric scholars whose research focused on Appalachia, and Peter Mortensen—whom Sara met when she was a prospective master's student—pointed her toward Kim's research. Knowing Kim was out there, doing similar work, helped Sara feel less alone during the sometimes-isolating experience of graduate school. Columbus is also where the idea of this particular collection was first formed. Beverly Moss, Sara's dissertation director, planted its seed by telling her that, since there were no edited collections on Appalachians and literacy, she should take on such a project.

It took several years, two successful tenure and promotion cases, and the birth of a couple of babies before this idea could come to fruition. In the intervening time, there was a surge of scholarly interest in Appalachia, its people, and their literacy beliefs and practices. Katherine Kelleher Sohn's *Whistlin' and Crowin' Women of Appalachia*, Katrina Powell's *The Anguish of Displacement*, and Erica Abrams Locklear's *Negotiating a Perilous Empowerment* were all published between 2006 and 2012, as was the *Community Literacy Journal* special issue on Appalachian literacies, which included articles by Sara Webb-Sunderhaus and Todd Snyder, the latter a contributor to this collection.[3] These years were an important moment in the fields of composition, rhetoric, and literacy studies as our scholarly conversations about literacy and identity finally brought the lives of Appalachians to the fore.

An uptick of interest in rural literacies also emerged during this time, as evidenced by Robert Brooke's *Rural Voices*, Charlotte Hogg's *From the Garden Club*, and Kim Donehower, Charlotte Hogg, and Eileen Schell's *Rural Literacies*. The latter authors' edited collection, *Reclaiming the Rural*, features two chapters that focus on Appalachia: Jane Greer's "Women's Words, Women's Ways" and Sara Webb-Sunderhaus's "Living with Literacy's Contradictions." Finally, several articles and book chapters have been published on Appalachian literacies, including Peter Mortensen's "Figuring Illiteracy," Casie Fedukovich's "Strange Exports," Katherine Kelleher Sohn's "Whistlin' and Crowin' Women of Appalachia," Katrina Powell's "Virginia Mountain Women Writing to Government Officials," and Sara Webb-Sunderhaus's "A Family Affair: Competing Sponsors of Literacy in Appalachian Students' Lives."[4]

Thus, while research on Appalachia was being published in composition journals and edited collections, a single-volume collection of scholarship did not exist. From our work on *Reclaiming the Rural*—Kim was the lead editor for Sara's chapter—we knew many young scholars in composition, rhetoric, and literacy studies were doing fresh work on Appalachia, and we wanted to pursue a project that would allow their voices—and their stories—to be heard.

Who Is Appalachian?

Many of the contributors to this volume met face-to-face in the Appalachian Composition, Rhetoric and Literacy special interest group for the Conference on College Composition and Communication. It was in meetings of that group that we saw evidence of the Appalachian diaspora: while several of us, including Kim and Sara, applied to Appalachian institutions, none of us was offered jobs at any of these universities. Instead, we ended up as displaced Appalachians, living in places like North Dakota, Indiana, Texas, and upstate New York, isolated from others who identify as Appalachian and/or share our research interests. As with any diaspora, Appalachian identity is a central concern. Each contributor to this collection is either of Appalachian heritage or strongly Appalachian identified, or both. Each interrogates how Appalachian literacies function and are represented in specific sites, and many reflect on the ways in which doing this kind of scholarly work intersects and interacts with their own Appalachian identities.

Issues of Appalachian identity are frequently debated within academic disciplines and Appalachian communities because they point to the rhetorical spaces in which Appalachian identity is composed. Perhaps, to borrow Benedict Anderson's phrase and apply it to a new context, Appalachia is an *imagined community,* one that has been created for various political purposes.[5] This point is the crux of Allen Batteau's argument in *The Invention of Appalachia*—that "Appalachia is a creature of the urban imagination" and that "the making of Appalachia was a literary and a political invention rather than a geographical discovery."[6] Jane Becker suggests that Appalachia was, in a sense, a political creation, noting that during the first half of the twentieth century, reformers looked to "traditional" Appalachian practices as a way in which to "transform an increasingly troubled American society."[7] This is not to say that Appalachians are not a real group of people or that there are not material markers and consequences of Appalachianness. This argument does suggest, however, that Appalachianness is largely a social construction that has been used for good and ill purposes.

Geographically, the Appalachian range stretches from Alabama to Newfoundland. Politically, the Appalachian Regional Commission (ARC) chops off the northern portion in southern New York, stretches the southern boundary all the way into the northeast corner of Mississippi, and draws the western boundary so that it just omits Cincinnati, home to a large population of Appalachian migrants. In her essay "Naming Affrilachia," Kathryn Trauth Taylor cites Frank X Walker and James Still, pointing out that the ARC definitions of Appalachia "exist as mythical boundaries that don't accommodate the nuances of self- and regional-identification with Appalachian culture or the region's vast history of out-migration."[8] Instead, the ARC primarily uses economic factors to determine what counts as Appalachia. "The Appalachian region's economy," the commission writes, "once highly dependent on mining, forestry, agriculture, chemical industries, and heavy industry, has become more diversified in recent times, and now includes manufacturing and professional service industries."[9] The ARC's focus and goals demonstrate one of the common designators of Appalachia and Appalachians: *poor.*

Trauth Taylor notes another: *white.* She observes: "Before Walker coined the term *Affrilachian,* even *Webster's* dictionary defined Appalachians as 'white residents from the mountains.'"[10] It is not only the dominant culture that depicts Appalachia as exclusively white; many Appalachian scholars have "whitewashed" the region as well, giving little critical attention to African American Appalachians, or Affrilachians, as well as other Appalachians of color. As a result, some would-be Appalachians do not recognize themselves in these all-white depictions and thus do not identify as Appalachian.[11]

So what constitutes Appalachianness? Sometimes it is viewed as a regional culture with a shared system of values, behaviors, beliefs, and attitudes. This view is suggested by such Appalachian studies scholars as Loyal Jones, William Philliber, Kathryn Borman, and Phillip Obermiller, whose work spans the social sciences and the humanities; these scholars also use the term *Urban Appalachian* to refer to the descendants of those who migrated from the region to nearby urban centers.[12] The anthropologist Kathleen Stewart and the folklorist Patrick B. Mullen, as well as projects such as the *Foxfire* publications, present people in the Appalachian region as a *folk group,* which Alan Dundes defines as "any group of people whatsoever who share at least one common factor": "It does not matter what the linking factor is—it could be a common occupation, language, or religion—but what is important is that a group . . . [has] some traditions that it calls its own."[13] In the poem "Affrilachia," Walker seems to echo Dundes's view, when he writes:

A mutual appreciation
for fresh greens
and cornbread
. . . .
makes us kinfolk
somehow.[14]

The anthropologist Susan Emley Keefe has identified a number of ways to think about Appalachian as an ethnicity. She argues: "The term ethnic identity is more usefully reserved for the symbolic dimension of ethnicity and must be analytically separated from the cultural and social dimensions in order to develop an informed understanding of their makeup and inter-relationship." In other words, cultural rituals, such as Appalachian food-ways and religious practices, as well as structural networks of kinship and friendship can stand apart from symbolic attachments, such as "Appalachian ethnic pride, Appalachian ethnic identity, lack [of] non-Appalachian ethnic pride, lack [of] non-Appalachian ethnic identity, [and] attachment to the mountains."[15] It is these symbolic attachments that mark the Appalachian-ness of many of the contributors to this volume, who might live far from daily contact with Appalachian relatives, and might not share the "appreciation for fresh greens and cornbread" that Walker notes, but nonetheless feel a strong attachment to the mountains.

It is the Appalachian Mountains themselves that are often at the center of Appalachians' self-identification. The term *Appalachian* is not widely used among many Appalachians themselves; many of our research participants did not call themselves *Appalachian,* and none of our relatives do. Instead, some prefer terms such as *country, hill people, mountain folk,* or *mountaineers.* These terms suggest, perhaps, what Keefe means by "lack [of] non-Appalachian . . . identity." A *mountain person* is not an *Appalachian*—with all that loaded term implies—but he is also not *not-Appalachian.* For the purposes of this collection, we use *Appalachian* as an umbrella term that includes rural, urban, and displaced Appalachians: those who, whatever cultural practices they embrace or relational networks in which they are embedded, maintain a physical or emotional attachment to the mountains and an Appalachian ethnic identity (or lack of a non-Appalachian ethnic identity). We believe that Appalachians share certain values, beliefs, and ways of knowing and being in the world and that these commonalities are what make up Appalachian culture. Yet we also realize that there is a specificity of experience that comes from living as a rural, urban, or displaced Appalachian. There are some characteristics that are unique to each Appalachian experience, and, in order to represent the specificity, we at times further identify Appalachians as *rural, urban,* or *displaced.*

What Do We Mean by *Literacies of Resistance*?

Literacy has been a broad term since its inception, meaning everything from "educated" to "knowledge of letters" to "knowledge of some body of stuff."[16] Appalachia is well known, and well researched, for its non-text-based cultural products—ballad singing, folktales, textiles. We focus in this collection on reading and writing—the practices by which Appalachia is typically judged illiterate. While recent work might permit us to include such activities as needlework as literacies,[17] we worry that such inclusion seems to indicate that one must stretch the definition of *literacy* to find enough literate activity in Appalachia to write about. When we were writing our dissertations, we both heard more than once a colleague's off-the-cuff remark that a dissertation on Appalachian literacy "must be a short one"—a comment whose casual bigotry relies on assumptions about Appalachians and print illiteracy. On the contrary, we have found that there is plenty of text-based literacy in Appalachia to write about, and part of the mission of this collection is to resist the idea that there is not.

But what sorts of activities with texts should count as literacy, beyond simple encoding and decoding? We begin with an understanding of literacy as a social practice, a foundational tenet of the New Literacy Studies. In the words of Brian Street: "Literacy is a social practice, not simply a technical and neutral skill. . . . It is embedded in socially constructed epistemological principles. . . . The ways in which people address reading and writing are themselves rooted in conceptions of knowledge, identity, and being."[18] Literate practices, then, take their nature from and facilitate and manage the relationships among individuals and groups.[19] But we must not overlook the relationships individuals have with the texts themselves. Since the advent of the New Literacy Studies, scholars have begun to highlight the importance of materiality in understanding literacy;[20] in chapter 3, Emma

M. Howes offers a way to understand literate practices through a material-ist feminist lens. In chapter 5, Gregory E. Griffey examines the intersection of his relationships with family, himself, his spiritual tradition, and his (and his family's) relationships with the biblical text.

While literacy is "not simply a . . . neutral skill," as Street notes, it is a skill or an ability and one that serves as a resource for a variety of pursuits, as Deborah Brandt describes: "Literacy skill [can be seen] primarily as a resource—economic, political, intellectual, spiritual—which, like wealth or education, or trade skill or social connections, is pursued for the opportuni-ties and protections that it potentially grants its seekers. . . . As a resource, literacy has potential payoff in gaining power or pleasure, in accruing infor-mation, civil rights, education, spirituality, status, money."[21]

That "payoff" can be realized only if literacy practices align with the "socially constructed . . . principles" of reading, writing, and doing things with texts within a particular group. James Paul Gee suggests that *literacy* should be defined as "control of secondary uses of language (i.e. uses of language in secondary discourses)," a "discourse" being in this conception "a socially accepted association of ways of using language, of thinking, and of acting" as practiced by "social institutions beyond the family (or the primary social-ization group as defined by the culture)."[22] The moonlight schools, analyzed in chapter 2, attempted to provide Appalachians with such institutionally sanctioned ways of using language, thinking, and acting. Chapter 9 questions the limits of Gee's model, but his central notion—that literacy increases as individuals or communities enlarge the number of social spaces in which they can do things with texts—is helpful, especially if those "things" help literates gain power or pleasure, accrue information, civil rights, spiritual-ity, status, and money, as Brandt describes.[23]

In the case of Appalachia, as with many other groups stigmatized for their literate practices, using literacy for the purposes Brandt lists requires the ability to open up rhetorical space. As Nancy Welch defines it: "*Rhetori-cal space*—that is, public space with the potential to operate as a persuasive public sphere—is created not through well-intentioned civic planning or through the application of a few sound and reasonable rhetorical rules of conduct. Ordinary people *make* rhetorical space through concerted, often protracted struggle for visibility, voice and impact against powerful interests that seek to deny visibility, voice, and impact. People *take* and *make* space in acts that are simultaneously verbal and physical."[24]

Creating rhetorical space is itself a literate skill and a necessary condition for exercising the full resources of literacy. Literacy, then, for the contributors to this volume, is the ability to do things with written texts for a wide range of purposes in a variety of social, cultural, and institutional settings. It includes the ability to create rhetorical space, when needed, for those activities to occur. We are particularly interested in the relational aspect of literacy: the use of written texts to explore, manage, and negotiate relationships among people and groups and people and texts themselves. Within the history of Appalachia and its association with the word *(il)literacy,* this relational focus brings us naturally to the idea of resistance.

We are interested in the term *resistance* for what it implies in multiple contexts. Seen as opposition to an invading or occupying force, *resistance* evokes the long history of literacy "missionaries" who came through Appalachia from the Protestant home missions in the mid-1880s to VISTA workers in the 1960s. Different groups offer different ways of valuing and practicing literacy; in Deborah Brandt's terms, these literacy sponsors "enable, support, teach, model, as well as recruit, regulate, suppress, or withhold literacy."[25] Collectively, they form a complex backdrop of "occupying forces" against which Appalachians must consider and make decisions about their own literacies.[26]

Resistance can also refer to an oppositional personal temperament, what is sometimes called *contrariness* in Appalachian terms; the Appalachian children's author Rebecca Caudill provides a classic example in her "Contrary Jenkins" stories.[27] We are intrigued by uses of literacy that resist internal as well as external cultural forces, by Appalachians using literacy to critique, challenge, or change local Appalachian culture, as exemplified by Griffey's chapter in this collection. Overall, we encourage readers to see Appalachian literacies neither as a defense against outsiders, nor as an expression of pure, untainted mountain culture, but as practices that continually resist and reshape the local, the nonlocal, and the relationships between the two.

Why These Essays?

Exploring the forms resistance might take in Appalachia, via literate practices, is the focus of this volume. In chapter 1, Kim Donehower describes how, as readers of research on Appalachian literacies, we must read with resistance to the standard narratives portrayed by both researchers and the researched themselves. In chapter 2, Krista Bryson examines how Cora

Wilson Stewart's mythic notions of Appalachians led her to make unsupportable claims about the powers of literacy, claims that Appalachian and literacy studies scholars are still battling today. In chapter 3, Emma Howes further complicates the difficult path Appalachian literacy researchers must tread as they attempt to avoid typical representations of Appalachian literacy workers as either saviors of the uncivilized or destroyers of local culture. She offers a contemporary look at an Appalachian literacy researcher—herself—as she encounters resistance from a local historian.

Collectively, the first three chapters call into question the reliability of many of our received notions about literacy in Appalachia and offer ways to interrogate and complicate past and future research on the region. Chapter 4 begins the process of asking readers to reconsider specific ideas about literacy and resistance in Appalachia and their connection to Appalachian identity. Todd Snyder examines how the socioeconomic force of extract industries shapes worldviews toward literacy and education—views that can conflict with the values and norms of the academy. In chapter 5, Gregory E. Griffey reveals the complicated role literacy played as he resisted and negotiated the tensions between his identity as a gay man and his identity as a fundamentalist mountain preacher. Chapter 6, by Kathryn Trauth Taylor, considers how performances of literacy and identity by Urban Appalachians of color resist and deepen typical understandings of Appalachian identity. In chapter 7, Nathan Shepley explores the literacy activities of students at one Appalachian university at the turn of the twentieth century. He argues that the students' writing resisted emergent harmful narratives of Appalachia and helped these non-Appalachians become Appalachian identified—an important step in creating coalitions to advocate for policies and programs that will ensure a sound future for Appalachian communities.

The final two chapters directly address the need for Appalachian advocacy and resistance. In chapter 8, Joshua Iddings and Ryan Angus describe a method of teaching English language arts in K–12 Appalachian classrooms that allows students to develop critical, resistant literacies and an understanding of language that appreciates the specific rhetorical powers of traditional Appalachian and Standard English discourses. In chapter 9, Sara Webb-Sunderhaus argues for a new theory of literacy for Appalachia, as current theories do not adequately address the lived experience of Appalachians' marginalization and resistance and its impact on their literacies and identities.

Notes

1. Silas House and Jason Howard, *Something's Rising: Appalachians Fighting Mountaintop Removal* (Lexington: University Press of Kentucky, 2009), 13–14.

2. James Moffett, *Storm in the Mountains: A Case Study of Censorship, Conflict, and Consciousness* (Carbondale: Southern Illinois University Press, 1988); Peter Mortensen, "Representations of Literacy and Region: Narrating 'Another America,'" in *Pedagogy in the Age of Politics: Writing and Reading (in) the Academy,* ed. Patricia Sullivan and Donna Qualley (Urbana, IL: National Council of Teachers of English, 1994), 100–120. For a much more nuanced analysis of the Kanawha County textbook controversy than *Storm in the Mountains,* see Carol Mason, *Reading Appalachia from Left to Right: Conservatives and the 1974 Kanawha County Textbook Controversy* (Ithaca, NY: Cornell University Press, 2009).

3. Katherine Kelleher Sohn, *Whistlin' and Crowin' Women of Appalachia: Literacy Practices since College* (Carbondale: Southern Illinois University Press, 2006); Katrina Powell, *The Anguish of Displacement: The Politics of Literacy in the Letters of Mountain Families in Shenandoah National Park* (Charlottesville: University of Virginia Press, 2007); Erica Abrams Locklear, *Negotiating a Perilous Empowerment: Appalachian Women's Literacies* (Athens: Ohio University Press, 2011); Sara Webb-Sunderhaus, "A Family Affair: Competing Sponsors of Literacy in Appalachian Students' Lives," in "Appalachian Literacies," ed. Katherine Vande Brake and Kimberley Holloway, special issue, *Community Literacy Journal* 2, no. 1 (2007): 5–24, reprinted in *The Norton Book of Composition Studies,* ed. Susan Miller (New York: Norton, 2009), 1600–1643; Todd Snyder, "The Webster County Blues: An Exploration of the Educational Attitudes of a Poor Appalachian Community," in Vande Brake and Holloway, eds., "Appalachian Literacies," 91–105.

4. Robert Brooke, *Rural Voices: Place-Conscious Education and the Teaching of Writing* (New York: Teachers College Press, 2003); Charlotte Hogg, *From the Garden Club: Rural Women Writing Community* (Lincoln: University of Nebraska Press, 2006); Kim Donehower, Charlotte Hogg, and Eileen Schell, *Rural Literacies* (Carbondale: Southern Illinois University Press, 2007); Jane Greer, "Women's Words, Women's Ways: Rural Literacy and Labor," in *Reclaiming the Rural: Essays on Literacy, Rhetoric, and Pedagogy,* ed. Kim Donehower, Charlotte Hogg, and Eileen Schell (Carbondale: Southern Illinois University Press, 2012), 90–106; Sara Webb-Sunderhaus, "Living with Literacy's Contradictions: Appalachian Students in a First-Year Writing Course," in ibid., 207–22; Peter Mortensen, "Figuring Illiteracy: Rustic Bodies and Unlettered Minds in Rural America," in *Rhetorical Bodies,* ed. Jack Selzer and Sharon Crowley (Madison: University of Wisconsin Press, 1999), 143–70; Casie Fedukovich, "Strange Exports: Working-Class Appalachian Women in the Composition Classroom," *Journal of Appalachian Studies* 15 (2009): 140–54; Katherine Kelleher Sohn, "Whistlin' and Crowin' Women of Appalachia: Literacy Practices since College," *College Composition and Communication* 54, no. 3 (2003): 423–52; Katrina Powell, "Virginia Mountain Women Writing to Government

Officials: Letters of Request as Social Participation," in *Women and Literacy: Local and Global Inquiries for a New Century* (National Council of Teachers of English–Lawrence Erlbaum Associates Research Series), ed. Beth Daniell and Peter Mortensen (New York: Routledge, 2007), 71–90; Webb-Sunderhaus, "A Family Affair."

5. Benedict Anderson, *Imagined Communities* (Verso: London, 1983).

6. Allen W. Batteau, *The Invention of Appalachia* (Tucson: University of Arizona Press, 1990), 1.

7. Jane Becker, *Selling Tradition: Appalachia and the Construction of an American Folk* (Chapel Hill: University of North Carolina Press, 1998), 4.

8. Kathryn Trauth Taylor, "Naming Affrilachia: Toward Rhetorical Ecologies of Identity Performance in Appalachia," *Enculturation* (2011), http://www.enculturation.net/naming-affrilachia.

9. "Appalachia's Economy," Appalachian Regional Commission, n.d., http://www.arc.gov/appalachian_region/AppalachiasEconomy.asp.

10. Trauth Taylor, chapter 6 in this volume, 120, citing Frank X Walker, *Affrilachia* (Lexington, KY: Old Cove, 2000), 92–93.

11. Unfortunately, this dynamic is apparent in our collection as well. While Trauth Taylor's chapter explores Urban Appalachian and Affrilachian identities, none of our contributors are people of color, and no Appalachians of color proposed chapters for this collection.

12. Loyal Jones, *Appalachian Values* (Ashland, KY: Jesse Stuart Foundation, 1994); William W. Philliber and Clyde B. McCoy, eds., *The Invisible Minority: Urban Appalachians* (Lexington: University of Kentucky Press, 1981); Kathryn Borman and Phillip J. Obermiller, eds., *From Mountain to Metropolis: Appalachian Migrants in the American City* (New York: Greenwood, 1993).

13. Kathleen Stewart, *A Space on the Side of the Road: Cultural Poetics in an "Other" America* (Princeton, NJ: Princeton University Press, 1996); Patrick B. Mullen, "Belief and the American Folk," *Journal of American Folklore* 113 (2000): 19–143; Alan Dundes, *The Study of Folklore* (Englewood Cliffs, NJ: Prentice-Hall, 1965), 2.

14. Walker, *Affrilachia.*

15. Susan Emley Keefe, "Ethnic Identity: The Domain of Perceptions of and Attachment to Ethnic Groups and Cultures," *Human Organization* 51 (1992): 35–43, 36.

16. David Barton, *Literacy: An Introduction to the Ecology of Written Language* (Oxford: Blackwell, 1994), 19–21.

17. See, e.g., Susan Frye, *Pens and Needles: Women's Textualities in Early Modern England* (Philadelphia: University of Pennsylvania Press, 2010); and Maureen Daly Goggin and Beth Fowkes Tobin, *Women and the Material Culture of Needlework and Textiles, 1750–1950* (Burlington, VT: Ashgate, 2009).

18. Brian Street, "What's 'New' in New Literacy Studies? Critical Approaches to Literacy in Theory and Practice," *Current Issues in Comparative Education* 5, no. 2 (2003): 77–91, 78.

19. See Kim Donehower, "Connecting Literacy to Sustainability: Revisiting *Literacy as Involvement*," in *Literacy, Economy, and Power: New Directions in Literacy Research*, ed. John Duffy et al. (Carbondale: Southern Illinois University Press, 2014), 97–110.

20. See, e.g., Christina Haas, *Writing Technology: Studies on the Materiality of Literacy* (Mahwah, NJ: Erlbaum, 1996); and Kate Vieira, "On the Social Consequences of Literacy," *Literacy in Composition Studies* 1, no. 1 (2013): 26–32.

21. Deborah Brandt, *Literacy in American Lives* (Cambridge: Cambridge University Press, 2001), 5.

22. James Paul Gee, "What Is Literacy?" *Journal of Education* 171, no. 1 (1989): 18–25, 23, 18, 22.

23. Brandt, *Literacy in American Lives*, 5.

24. Nancy Welch, "Living Room: Teaching Public Writing in a Post-Publicity Era," *College Composition and Communication* 56, no. 3 (2005): 470–92, 477.

25. Deborah Brandt, "Sponsors of Literacy," *College Composition and Communication* 49 (1998): 165–85, 166.

26. See Kim Donehower, "Choices about Literacy in an Appalachian Community," *Journal of Appalachian Studies* 9 (2003): 341–62.

27. Rebecca Caudill and James Sterling Ayars, *Contrary Jenkins* (New York: Holt, Rinehart & Winston, 1969).

1

How to Reread Appalachian Literacy Research

Kim Donehower

In 1990, as an about-to-be graduate student, I was asked by an Andrew Mellon Fellowship committee why I was not going to focus on Appalachian literature, given my "background." It was the one question that stumped me during the interview. It had never occurred to me that just because I was a first-generation college student from western North Carolina I ought to study Appalachia. It seemed like an offensive suggestion, as though I would not be equipped to do anything else. I mumbled something about not enjoying Lee Smith's *Black Mountain Breakdown* (1980), the committee laughed, and I did not get the fellowship. I went to graduate school anyway and floated among a variety of interests. Then I read James Moffett's descriptors of the "agnosis" of the Kanawha County textbook protestors in *Storm in the Mountains;* these include *passivity, forgetfulness, paranoia, self-contradiction,* and *prefascist authoritarian personality.*[1] It got me angry enough to write a dissertation.

What upset me so about *Storm in the Mountains* was the inexplicable (to me) return in the analysis section of the book to the standard attributes of Appalachians as willfully ignorant and cognitively and culturally unevolved, right after Moffett had reproduced transcripts showing the complex and savvy rhetorical sensibilities of those he interviewed. To offer such rich and site-specific data and then retreat into generalized explanations for Appalachian attitudes toward literacy—attitudes that have circulated since the region became distinct in people's awareness—seemed to me a massive analytic failure.

In "The Narrative Roots of the Case Study," Thomas Newkirk illuminates why such an analytic failure might be accepted by readers. He argues: "As readers of [case] studies, we find them true or convincing, not because of careful methodology (important as that is), or because of wealth of detail, but . . . because of the gratification we get from seeing cultural myths being reenacted."[2] This, I think, is what drove both the pleasure for Moffett of writing *Storm in the Mountains* and the pleasure many took in reading it. The book received glowing reviews on its release, and, as Sara Webb-Sunderhaus (chapter 9 in this volume) relates, it is still considered a bit of a sacred cow in the field.

How, then, ought we to read research on Appalachians and Appalachian literacy? Newkirk provides some advice when he writes: "Without some form of resistance, either in the construction of the text or in the act of reading, it is difficult to see how readers can avoid the seductiveness of deeply rooted and deeply satisfying narratives that place us in familiar moral positions."[3] Peter Mortensen documents the long-standing collusion of local-color writers, documentarians, educators, and academics to render Appalachia Other and to center that Otherness on Appalachians' literacy.[4] Since the late nineteenth century, many Americans have seemed to need Appalachia to be a certain way to justify their own worldviews and senses of heritage and to position them favorably within hierarchies of being.

But researchers and readers are not the only ones in this equation who might struggle to avoid narratives that place us in satisfying moral positions. In *Negotiating a Perilous Empowerment,* Erica Abrams Locklear demonstrates that, in Appalachia, the researched might edit their responses to literacy researchers to manage their status in light of the stigma of Appalachian illiteracy. In my Mellon interview, I got the committee off the topic of Appalachian literacy as it related to me as quickly as possible. I could not imagine it would be an advantage in seeking a graduate fellowship, and I disparaged Lee Smith in the bargain to try to demonstrate what I imagined to be the sort of superior taste the committee was looking for. Locklear also notes: "Mountain people are always aware of stereotypes and the dangers of reinscribing those if they discuss the pitfalls of becoming literate." In reference to Katherine Kelleher Sohn's *Whistlin' and Crowin' Women of Appalachia,* she writes: "The women's reluctance to discuss the costs of literacy attainment is closely bound with stereotypes of mountain illiteracy: Discussing those fears before going to school might be acceptable, but chronicling the costs of literacy attainment once they finished their studies would only support the fixed image of an illiterate, ignorant Appalachia, a perception most native Appalachians would prefer to avoid."[5] Locklear's fascinating study contrasts the prevalent theme of literacy as cultural loss in Appalachian authors' fictional works with the fact that, in interviews, these same authors seldom speak of the losses associated with literacy at all.

When it comes to qualitative research on Appalachian literacy, then, all participants in the equation—the researchers, the researched, and the readers of the research produced—are subject to strong sociocultural and psychological forces that might affect their abilities to write, speak, and read about Appalachian literacy in accurate and ethical ways. How, then, are we to read research on Appalachian literacy if we cannot trust the researchers, the researched, or ourselves as readers? In this chapter, I examine how this phenomenon plays out in Victoria Purcell-Gates's *Other People's Words*.[6] I argue that, for the researched, the cultural weight of the Appalachian literacy stereotype might lead not only to obfuscations of loss but also to other ways for the researched to provide data that reinforce researchers' and readers' moral positions and general worldviews. Ultimately, I assert that, given Appalachia's particular history in the construction of American identity narratives, we tend to read any research on Appalachian literacy—even quantitative research—in the ways Newkirk describes as pertaining to case studies.

Like many readers of qualitative research, what I remember of what I read tends to be based on the narrative aesthetics of the piece. So many readers of Shirley Brice Heath's *Ways with Words,* myself included, became attached to the "character" of Lem that Heath addresses the requests for an update on him in her subsequent work.[7] The aesthetics of qualitative narrative are both memorable and persuasive, and Newkirk argues that aesthetic persuasion is the primary way in which case studies convince their readers. He details the process of a writer constructing "a case study that works," by which he means one that persuades:

> The writer needs to see the data in terms of one of a variety of culturally grounded narratives. The writer "author-izes" the data, and in doing so faces the same problem that confronts the biographer or the historian who, according to Scholes and Kellogg, "is looking for aesthetically satisfying patterns in the people or events he considers as potential subjects for his work." To create these aesthetic patterns, the writer must also assign moral weight to the actions of characters. . . . [T]he case-study writer draws on a core of mythic

narratives—deeply rooted story patterns that clearly signal to the reader the types of judgments to be made.[8]

In other words, the case study is persuasive on aesthetic grounds, not on the merits of its methodology. How well a case study "draws on . . . deeply rooted story patterns that clearly signal to the reader the types of judgments to be made" persuades readers to believe that a case study has broader applicability. This, Newkirk explains, is how case-study writers get past the inherent methodological problem of appearing to generalize from particulars: "By using these narrative patterns, the account can move beyond the particular or 'idiographic,' and come to embody a set of cultural beliefs." The end result is that "case studies and ethnographic narratives, despite their seeming radicalism . . . , [are] profoundly conservative and conventional."[9]

The desire to create research that is aesthetically pleasing has dogged folklorists working in Appalachia as well. In his excellent analysis of Richard Chase's repackaging of Jack tales for publication, Charles Perdue argues: "The problem is that the 'ideal' tale existed only in Chase's mind, and the tales he collated and published ended up telling us more about Chase and his culture than that of the people from whom he gathered his tales."[10] Research on Appalachian literacy runs the same risk, especially when the researched themselves collude, knowingly or unknowingly, in the transaction. *Other People's Words* provides a case in point.

Aesthetic Persuasion in *Other People's Words*

Purcell-Gates's *Other People's Words* was marketed as one of the first case studies of Urban Appalachians—Appalachian migrants to cities outside the region who maintain a distinct Appalachian identity and connection to "back home." When we read the book jacket text, before we even turn to the first page of the study, we are encouraged to see the data of a mother and son, Jenny and Donny, as emblematic of "urban Appalachians' . . . often severe literacy problems." We are told of Jenny and Donny: "The world they inhabit is an oral one, their heritage one where print had no inherent use and no inherent meaning."[11] It is their Appalachianness, in other words, that is responsible for their low literacy. This assertion, made throughout the book, is typically expressed in dramatic, artistic language, as it is here. The language becomes less ornamented and more academic whenever this broad generalization is complicated.

In the introduction to the book, Purcell-Gates describes herself as a cog-nitivist who "came to see the ways in which literacy and nonliteracy were cultures" and "moved to a view of cognition as culture-bound." She identi-fies her theoretical lens as a "sociocultural theory of learning" in which "all learners are seen as members of a defined culture, and their identity with this culture determines what they will encode about the world and the ways in which they will interpret information." For Purcell-Gates, the "defined culture" of Jenny and Donny is "urban Appalachian"; while she acknowl-edges the more local cultural context of their home, she wishes to know how "Jenny's identity as an urban Appalachian woman and Donny's as a young urban Appalachian man affected their beliefs toward, motivations for, and eventual successes with literacy."[12]

The problem is that these two cultural contexts—the family home and urban/Appalachian culture—are repeatedly conflated throughout *Other People's Words*. We learn, for example: "[Big Donny's older brother and wife] were both literate and their children were successful in school. Their older daughter was training to be a nurse." Jenny's parents are literate, though they read minimally for pleasure and information. Jenny's sister and sister-in-law, who live nearby in the city, read and write well enough to help her decipher bills and forms. We find out that many other family members can write but do not send letters or postcards because "'they all know [Jenny and Donny] can't read [them].'"[13] It seems that, in not being able to read and write at all, Jenny and Big Donny are anomalies in their extended Appalachian family.

It is odd, then, that Purcell-Gates argues so strongly that, "for Donny, print did not signify; it did not code his world; it was not linguistically mean-ingful." The balanced structure is both forceful and aesthetically pleasing here; the triple parallel makes it sound nearly biblical. While the idea that print does not signify seems to be true inside the immediate cultural con-text of Donny's family home, it appears not to be the case in his extended family, where reading and writing play some role. Given the close connec-tion and multiple visits to back home and time spent with these relatives, it would seem that Donny's larger Appalachian cultural context might provide a bit of a corrective to the lack of print in his home. But Purcell-Gates does little to tease out these distinctions, suggesting that it is not the specifics of who Jenny and Big Donny are that lead to Donny's "world without print" but rather their Urban Appalachianness.[14] Purcell-Gates repeatedly refers to Jenny and Donny's *world,* in chapter titles, subheadings, and the text itself. Such a word effectively collapses the immediate family context into the

Urban Appalachian one. We are left with no alternative explanation, such as learning disabilities or individual personality traits, for the nonliteracy of Jenny and Donny's home. Urban Appalachian culture is the only culprit.

Furthermore, Purcell-Gates invokes a number of common tropes about Appalachian culture throughout the text—in some cases to dispute the justice of them—that nonetheless stock the reader's brain with particular images and associations. We are reminded of the stereotypes about Appalachians and Urban Appalachians—to the point of her reproducing three "hillbilly" jokes in their entirety. The first is about Urban Appalachians' close ties to back home; the second is about their promiscuity; the third concerns their lack of hygiene. Once again, Purcell-Gates seems to anticipate the extent to which readers may hold some of these stereotypes; she tells us a few pages later that Jenny "keeps the house immaculate."[15] But which has more narrative and aesthetic power—the jokes or the brief mention of Jenny's clean home?

The context-setting chapter, "Jenny and Donny's World," quotes Obermiller and Maloney that Urban Appalachians "are for the most part of Scots-Irish or Anglo-Saxon heritage."[16] We do not find out whether Jenny and Donny are themselves of this background, but it was standard practice for local-color writers, folklorists, and missionaries in the early part of the twentieth century to see Appalachia as a repository of pure whiteness, despite evidence to the contrary.[17] We are told that "the predominant social organization system of this population is the family-kinship relation," raising the specter of clans and the Klan. While Purcell-Gates goes out of her way a few pages later to tell us that she "never heard either Jenny or Donny make a racist statement," we are also informed that a large Confederate flag hangs over their sofa. We learn of a life that seems destined for hardship; in a particularly literary flourish, Purcell-Gates writes: "Harsh tragedy stalked Jenny's family as it so often seems to afflict other urban Appalachians."[18] There are no identifiable sources of this "tragedy"; Purcell-Gates typically renders actual historical and economic circumstances in agentless terms.[19] Appalachians began to migrate as a result of "the failure of the family farms" and "the closing of the coal mines"; "cultural alienation, poverty, and breakdowns in familial and social networks have contributed to the ills of urban Appalachian families."[20] The cumulative, aesthetic effect is to show us a people who just are the way they are and who, in fact, become defined by these traits. An Urban Appalachian family not stalked by tragedy, who had attained a middle-class existence with solid family and social networks, ceases to seem Urban Appalachian.

We begin reading the main part of Purcell-Gates's study, then, with many of the standard descriptors and story patterns of Appalachians resonating in our minds. At the same time, by identifying Jenny and Donny as exceptions to these rules of Appalachianness, we are to think of them as worthy targets of literacy intervention. This is a standard rhetorical move, dating back to the local-color writers of the period 1880–1910. It allows us to feel sympathetic toward the main characters of our story at the same time that we are invited to condemn the culture they represent. For example, John Fox Jr.'s novels *The Trail of the Lonesome Pine* (1908) and *The Little Shepherd of Kingdom Come* (1903) both feature central characters who are Appalachian exemplars—the daughter of a feuding clan in the former, a tragic orphan taken in by a kind family in the latter—who identify strongly with outsiders who end up providing them with an education.[21] They both symbolize Appalachianness but are not like those other Appalachians, thanks to their interest in outsiders who represent upper-class aspirations and in the literacies of those outsiders. Jenny and Donny are represented to us in a similar way.[22]

Purcell-Gates attempts to represent Appalachian culture positively in many places in the book; every description she offers of a "traditional Appalachian trait" can be seen or spun as positive. These include "independence," "straight-talking," privileging of personal relationships over bureaucratic or "functional" ones, a "sense of propriety which forbids one to 'brag on' oneself," and "pride needed to protect [family] from embarrassment and shame."[23] However, these noble pioneer qualities are also responsible for Jenny's inability to get the schools to pay attention to her child's educational needs and to secure literacy for herself.[24] Purcell-Gates vigorously indicts the educational establishment for its stereotyping and exclusion of Urban Appalachians; she explicitly lays the blame, especially for Donny's nonliteracy, at their feet. But, within her narrative of Jenny's interactions with the school system, we see how her "independence," "straight-talking," "privileging of personal relationships over bureaucratic . . . ones," and "pride" make her an ineffective advocate for Donny; she does not even attempt to have a friend decipher communications that come home from the school. On an efferent level, Purcell-Gates tells us directly that the fault is the school's. But, on an aesthetic level, Jenny's Appalachian traits come in for at least an equal share of the blame.[25]

Many of the impediments that the Jenny character struggles against—particularly her desire for phonics-based learning—are attributed to her Appalachianness. Moffett, in fact, has a whole chapter in *Storm in the Moun-*

tains that tries to link the Kanawha County protestors' preference for strict phonics and traditional grammar instruction with the larger cultural traits and psychology he ascribes to them. Neither he nor Purcell-Gates addresses sufficiently that this desire might stem not from cultural values but from an awareness of the great differences between Appalachian dialects and standard English and the long history of stigmatizing Appalachians on the basis of that difference.[26]

Offering a cultural-trait explanation for nearly every aspect of literacy makes it quite difficult to sort out matters of agency, particularly in Purcell-Gates's case. To what extent is Jenny and Donny's nonliteracy culturally determined, by the cultures of both urban Appalachia and middle-class schooling? How much room is there for individual choice and agency within Appalachian culture when it comes to literacy?[27]

My own entry into research in this field coincided with the peak of wide acceptance of the social-constructivist lens that Purcell-Gates embraces. The "social turn" in literacy studies was intended to bring attention to cultural difference and nuance and provided needed context dependence to purely cognitivist theories of literacy.[28] But an occasional side effect of this embrace of social constructivism—at least by purists—has been the negation of the idea of individual agency. I remember speaking about my work at one conference and saying that I wished to find more ways to ascribe agency to my Appalachian informants when I wrote about their "choices" regarding literacy. Some audience members responded that I was ascribing too much agency to them already by using a word such as *choice*. This creates quite a bind for us as educators; if literacies are culturally determined yet the teaching of literacies is still possible, the only option for those who would seek new literacies is to choose to leave their cultures of origin and join ours. This is exactly what Moffett argues in *Harmonic Learning*, in which he recounts his experiences with the Kanawha County textbook protestors during his research for *Storm in the Mountains:* "The Kanawha County imbroglio taught me that . . . attachments to blood and soil, hearth and ethos, . . . work against intellectual understanding. . . . If social systems are knowledge systems, then to know the most, join the broadest social system."[29] For Moffett, cultural determinism is real, and surrendering cultural attachments is the price of admission to broader literacies.

In her final chapter, "Culture, Language, and Literacy," Purcell-Gates wrestles with this issue, and again we see a distinction along efferent and aesthetic lines. When Purcell-Gates invokes cultural determinism, her language becomes more literary, in both syntax and word choice: "After decades of federally funded programs. . . . We still see millions of illiterate adults and millions more low-literate adults attempting to survive in an increasingly hostile economic environment and raising children in low-literate homes—children who, themselves, will one day perpetuate the dismal cycle." When she writes against such a view, her language and syntax become particularly academic: "I am persuaded by the arguments of the scholar Lisa Delpit, who worries that stances like Gee's suggest Discourse determinism, wherein one is locked into one's social class status by one's Discourse." Despite being persuaded by Delpit, a few pages later she offers a detailed, poetic vision of culture as literate destiny:

> One day in a public library of a small New England town, I watched a young father hold his two-year-old daughter on his lap as he used a computer to search for a book reference. Surrounded by books and by people reading and writing, this child sat entranced. . . . With only this brief encounter, we can predict with a high level of certainty the literacy events and objects surrounding her at home. How lucky she is compared with Donny. . . . When this child begins kindergarten, she will bring with her a rich knowledge of the world of print. She will move easily into literacy.[30]

This vivid example, paired with a hypothetical story of a child from a low-literate home who "will begin kindergarten on the same day," extends for two pages. It is moving, and it sets us up well to accept the primary argument with which Purcell-Gates ends the book: that family literacy programs must abandon "old worn-out 'methods' of teaching reading and writing as decontextualized skills" and instead "move into the homes of children in natural and meaningful ways."[31] For Moffett, the children must leave their homes and come into the schools. For Purcell-Gates, the schools should find a way to move into the homes. Both perspectives, ultimately, represent the learners in these situations as helpless—unable to operate simultaneously in two different worlds, capable of learning only by immersion, not by effort. Neither takes into account the possibility of development within multiple, even contradictory, systems of literacy. But, as Sara Webb-Sunderhaus writes in the closing chapter in this volume, such an ability is a common trait of Appalachians, owing in no small part to the long history of literacy interventions in Appalachia.

Tropes, Tellability, and the Researched

A number of issues combine to undercut Purcell-Gates's intention to "urge the reader to move beyond society's middle-class bias against [Appalachian dialects and culture] to the core of truth contained in Jenny's words." These include her deep commitment to her social-constructivist analytic lens (to the exclusion of the notion that cognitive issues might affect the family's literacy), her conflation of Donny and Jenny's home environment with Urban Appalachian culture, and her deployment of literary language, syntax, and technique in places that reify stereotypes about Appalachian literacy. In addition, Jenny, her research subject, seems at times to collude in the process, as, for example, when she offers comments such as this: "It was a little hard for me to . . . sound my words out . . . 'cause I talk different . . . 'cause I'm you know . . . countrified."[32]

Purcell-Gates offers us many of Jenny's words, rendered in dialect, because she wants her to be able to speak for herself, in her own language. She writes: "Although the interpretation of the data and the resulting implications for education practice and policy are mine, the voices are to a large degree Jenny's and Donny's."[33] Including significant passages of Jenny's voice is one way to achieve the kind of "polyvocality" for which James Clifford argues.[34] But Newkirk suggests another way in which to deal with the need for polyvocality in human subjects research, and it is worth quoting at length:

> The issue is not, as positivistic researchers have argued, the problem of bias or the lack of objectivity. Rather it is one of polyvocality. To what extent should the ethnographer or case-study writer allow discordant voices into the account, voices that complicate the moral judgments readers will make? Or should the reader assume a stance of resistance and fill in the gaps with imagined narratives . . . ? For without some form of resistance, either in the construction of the text or in the act of reading, it is difficult to see how readers can avoid the seductiveness of deeply rooted and deeply satisfying narratives that place us in familiar moral positions.

Newkirk provides a key qualification for the other voices that suffuse a case study or ethnographic text: they should "complicate the moral judgments readers will make."[35] This, perhaps, is why many of the quotes Purcell-Gates offers from Jenny do not really work in the way she hopes. Purcell-Gates is very much aware of the dangers of rendering Jenny's quotes in dialect. She writes: "It is possible my use of them will be interpreted as another example of [mockery and depreciation], . . . [a] usage [that] is the opposite of my intent." But many of the colorful quotes from Jenny permit, rather than complicate, the standard moral judgments of Appalachians as willfully ignorant of anything having to do with literacy, such as this one: "I never took [Donny] to no library! This is the first time I ever set foot in one of these libraries!"[36]

There are moments in *Other People's Words* when Jenny's dialect quotes seem so pitch perfect for an illiterate Appalachian female character that I have to wonder whether Jenny is playing with Purcell-Gates just a bit. Purcell-Gates herself mentions being suspicious of Jenny's claims of non-literacy until she saw further evidence.[37] The psychology of being Othered can lead Others to perform, rather than complicate, the tropes that define their Otherness. It is a way of taking ownership of these tropes and playing with them. There can also be a monetary incentive; these deeply embedded cultural narratives are so gratifying, to use Newkirk's words, that they can be packaged and sold to tourists, as Appalachians have done for decades. Thus, performing these tropes can be a form of resistance to them—a sort of trickster response or a way to fleece the rubes. What looks like acquiescence to stereotypes is actually the opposite.

For example, during one college break, I worked as hostess at Mom 'N' Pop's Country Store and Restaurant. The store marketed "hillbilly dictionaries," full of exaggerated and often archaic dialect. My uniform, a blue gingham blouse with puffed sleeves and a polka-dotted red ribbon tie at the collar, appeared to be a leftover from *Hee-Haw,* the television variety show set in the mythical Kornfield Kounty. The menu was full of intentional misspellings. It was the kind of thing I loathed. So what did I do? I talked to all the customers in the most exaggerated mountain dialect I could muster. I took perverse pleasure in making them think that any version of "mountain girl" as over the top as I was actually existed. It made them seem naive, and, the more I amped up my cartoon character, the more they bought it—literally, sometimes, in the form of tips—and the more stupid I could think they were.

Thus, Appalachians' resistance to the ways in which they have been written about and read by outsiders can take the form of seemingly confirming those representations. This is ultimately not an effective rhetorical strategy to change these tropes, but it is nonetheless a common reaction among the Othered. In "Tropes, Hopes, and Dopes," the folklorist Mark Workman argues that, when tropes about Others deeply penetrate a culture, Others find themselves in an "unresolvable double-bind" in their relationship with those who Other them. He writes: "You're damned if you (attempt to) join and equally damned if you don't—[this] generates the self-hatred of those whose tropic conviction is not as strong as their tropic desire."[38]

Newkirk does not use the word *trope* in his essay, but it seems appropriate when we consider the term not in the strict literary sense as a figure of speech but in the broader way in which it has come to be used in folklore and popular culture studies—as a repeated theme, motif, or story pattern. As an example of "deeply rooted story patterns," Newkirk cites Denny Taylor and Catherine Dorsey-Gaines's *Growing Up Literate,* in which he notes "our tendency" when investigating inner-city schools "to write the drama in terms of victim (minority students) and victimizers (the schools and teachers)"—a tendency to which Purcell-Gates also seems susceptible when writing about Donny's school. Newkirk notes that overtly literary texts, such as *The Women of Brewster Place* (1982), offer a much more complicated vision and complex moral world.[39] One can see the same dynamic at play in the contrast between the literary works of the authors Locklear studies and their interviews. To achieve distinction, literary texts have to contest and contend with standard story patterns. In other words, we tolerate in qualitative research hackneyed themes, characters, story patterns, and motifs that we would never abide in our literary reading.

Why might this be the case? Newkirk argues it is "because of the gratification we get from seeing cultural myths being reenacted."[40] Workman explores how this gratification connects to issues of identity. He argues that "we are all ultimately dopes governed by hopes of being seduced by tropes," that we need folklore because of "its enormous tropic potential," its "capacity to provide us with a sense of 'us' and, thereby, with a sense of 'I' as well."[41] The relationship between Appalachians and academics, particularly those who research and/or teach literacy, may seem at first glance to be a simple one that fits William Hugh Jansen's definition of *exoteric* folklore—we tell ourselves stories about the other to indicate that we are not like them.[42] *Harmonic Learning* provides a straightforward example; in it, James Moffett explains that he chose the word *agnosis* explicitly to contrast with the Gnostic tradition, of which he feels himself to be a part.[43]

But Workman complicates the simplistic distinction between "us" and "[those] who represent everything we are against." He writes that the "essentialist" notion that "identity is affirmed by duplication and undermined by difference"—that we would be better off if the undesirable traits of the Other, such as illiteracy, were eradicated—is ironic because "identity is always a relative phenomenon . . . [and therefore] to obliterate the Other is to obliterate the possibility of the self as well."[44] There is a tension, then, between wanting to both preserve and eradicate cultural difference at the same time.[45] This tension infuses both Moffett's and Purcell-Gates's work. Moffett overtly wants to eradicate cultural difference; he argues this directly in *Harmonic Learning*, but he reinstantiates in *Storm in the Mountains* the trope of Appalachian illiteracy as a core cultural characteristic, virtually impossible to overcome.[46] Purcell-Gates clearly does not want to be accused of such cultural imperialism. Instead, she makes the public schools the villain in her narrative and tries to valorize Urban Appalachian traits as positive. Yet, ultimately, the cultural determinism implied in her analysis suggests that achieving school literacies will necessitate behaviors that are in marked contrast to these Urban Appalachian traits. In very different ways, both authors argue for the alteration of Appalachian difference while their texts themselves work to preserve Appalachian difference. This having it both ways rarely gets noticed by readers, thanks to the tropic power of both texts.

Consider as well the predicament of Appalachian and Appalachian-identified academic literacy researchers, such as the contributors to this volume. The tropic power of Appalachians as illiterate, in a specifically school/academic sense, means not only that becoming an academic literate is "joining the enemy," but also that the very process of academic literacy acquisition will erase our Appalachianness. It also means that our very desire for school/academic literacies means that we were somehow inauthentically Appalachian all along. Self-dislike, if not self-hatred, is a possible result, either of our Appalachianness or our academicness, or both.

Workman writes that this double bind is particularly felt "under the hostile conditions of persecution, in encounters generated by the fear, intolerance, and rejection of difference, [where] the relative viability of our definitions of self are most explicitly put to the test and either reaffirmed, abandoned, or modified."[47] This, perhaps, is why so many of the contributors to this volume have chosen to study Appalachian literacy—to read and reread Moffett and Purcell-Gates and the literate accounts of Appalachians themselves, to plunge ourselves into "the fear, intolerance, and rejection of difference" that can operate on both sides of this relationship and within ourselves.

There is another reason why Appalachians might claim some of the tropes that have been used by outsiders to describe them—to resist, critique, and work to shape aspects of their own local culture or their family culture. Emma Howes's and Gregory E. Griffey's chapters in this volume offer examples of this. One of my dissertation research informants described her family members as far less literate than they actually were. Her comments were embedded in a discussion of her family's lack of support for higher education for girls during her adolescence—a stance that has now markedly changed in that family, in part owing to her critique. This informant's comment also exemplifies what Locklear describes as the process of making "difficult identity decisions" when one participates in research.[48]

For Appalachian-identified people, "difficult identity decisions" can arise any time there is an opportunity to tell the story of one's Appalachianness. Amy Shuman's notion of *tellability* is useful here; she defines it as "who can tell it [the story] to whom."[49] I have a personal repertoire of tellable narratives that I deploy to friends and family members to enact my connection to Appalachia and navigate the difficult identity decisions involved in particular social contexts. To my daughter, I tell "Uncle John and the Molasses Barrel," in which John, racing his brother Doug for the right to sit on the molasses barrel at dinnertime since the family had no chairs for the children, breaks through the lid and ends up covered in molasses. For non-Appalachian friends, there is the story of my mother's first time driving on an interstate highway. Pulled over by the police for driving on the shoulder, she asked the officer, "What's a shoulder?" And for my husband, there's the tale of my granny's "Uncle Jim who was my half-brother"—raised as her grandmother's child even though everyone knew he was the product of her mother's first marriage to a bigamist who had another family on the other side of the mountain.

Each of these stories has a role beyond my feeling Appalachian at the moment I tell them. Ultimately, they are about the type of relationship I am trying to foster between myself and the listener and between the listener and Appalachia. With my daughter, I am trying to make her feel a connection to her Appalachian heritage and the specific characters of my Appalachian family. With friends, I am trying to force them to experience the ways in which the mountains historically dominated Appalachians' perspectives and experience. (I always enjoy the pause of confusion of their faces before they get the story.) With my husband, I share the story I do not often share with others—because it can reinforce the stereotype of mountaineers as oversexed and inbred—to create a private shorthand that links our two very disparate heritages. Whenever we find a man untrustworthy, we say to each other, "Do you think he has another family on the other side of the mountain?"

In her research on Kentucky tobacco farmers, Ann Ferrell identified the tellability factor at work in her research participants as they tried to shape their credibility with their listeners and their listeners' relationships with tobacco farming. She notes that informants are limited to "tellable" narratives particularly when they are "keenly aware" of the public discourses that circulate about them. She catches one of her research participants in such a move when he tells her that he still farms tobacco because of his sense of heritage. But, when she pushes him to say more about "heritage," he answers "income." He goes on to say: "I just tell people 'tradition,' you know, 'cause uh, you know." But really, he tells Ferrell, it is about "income": "I still think tobacco's easier than vegetables. . . . I don't like to pick beans. Be hard on my back." Ferrell comments on how her own impulses might limit participants to tellable narratives. She writes: "I suppose I wanted this farmer to talk about intangible aspects of tradition—perhaps to wax on about his emotional relationship with the crop—and instead he was telling me that tobacco is important because it continues to provide income for his family, and that its economic value is central to his understanding of it as 'a tradition.'"[50] She uses the moment of exposure of the tellable narrative as a chance to question her own assumptions as a researcher and her desire for answers that would give her as a researcher (and writer) the most narrative and aesthetic power.

Ferrell links sticking to a tellable narrative script as, in part, a reaction to being stigmatized. She writes: "Tobacco farmer, as viewed through the screens of the [current] tellable narratives, is now a stigmatized category." As a result, she sees informants repackaging tellable narratives from outside the community: "Farmers have co-opted the narrative of tobacco-as-heritage that was promoted by the industry and the state in the last decades of the twentieth century, putting it to new uses."[51] As Charles Perdue writes about Richard Chase, such a move may end up resulting in research that "tells us more about [our] culture than that of the people from whom [the research is gathered]."[52] Thankfully, Ferrell is a researcher who is remarkably well tuned to the pressures that constrain her research participants and able to spot narratives that, while tellable, are inaccurate or incomplete.

Ferrell advises researchers to collect the kinds of "less conventional" sources of data that can reveal both tellable and untellable narratives.[53] Locklear's work suggests that Appalachian aesthetic products might be one such data source. Perhaps we need to read research as art, to identify its tropic power and constraints, and read art as research, to see what gets told under the guise of fiction.

How to Read Research on Appalachian Literacy

Stories—the tellable ones—have been told and retold about Appalachia since it was first conceived of as a distinct region. We—academics, Appalachians, and those of us who are both—cannot not tell stories about Appalachia. We do it as a reflection of our relationships to Appalachia and to each other.

As readers, then, we need to carefully monitor the effects these stories have on us—even when stories are not explicitly being told. Consider, for example, a quantitative "fact" such as the 1970 census data for literacy in the county from which my family comes. It instructs us to extrapolate literacy rates from high school graduation rates, by which standard the county has a weak showing. Is it possible to read this number without constructing our own characters and story patterns? Do we envision people like Jenny, or do we instead imagine someone like my grandmother, who left school after the seventh grade, as was common at the time, but read Faulkner, wrote poetry, and was actively literate at the time of this census? Our tendency will be to read into the data the story that fosters the sort of relationship we have to Appalachia.

Newkirk encourages us to instead imagine counter-narratives, identify and fill in gaps, and complicate whatever stock characters and traditional story patterns present themselves. As an example, he describes how he imagined the other side of a narrative incident related in Taylor and Dorsey-Gaines's *Growing Up Literate*—not to make assumptions about what actually happened, but to resist the sway of the victims-versus-victimizers narrative pattern that structures the book. This is what he means by "assum[ing] a stance of resistance and filling in the gaps."[54] We ask readers of this volume to do the same. Whatever your relationship to Appalachia now, we hope this book alters and enriches it.

Notes

1. James Moffett, *Storm in the Mountains: A Case Study of Censorship, Conflict, and Consciousness* (Carbondale: Southern Illinois University Press, 1988), 193, 195.

2. Thomas Newkirk, "The Narrative Roots of the Case Study," in *Methods and*

Methodology in Composition Research, ed. Gesa Kirsch and Patricia A. Sullivan (Carbondale: Southern Illinois University Press, 1992), 130–52, 136.

3. Ibid., 149.

4. Peter Mortensen, "Representations of Literacy and Region: Narrating 'Another America,'" in *Pedagogy in the Age of Politics: Writing and Reading (in) the Academy,* ed. Patricia Sullivan and Donna Qualley (Urbana, IL: National Council of Teachers of English, 1994), 100–120.

5. Erica Abrams Locklear, *Negotiating a Perilous Empowerment: Appalachian Women's Literacies* (Athens: Ohio University Press, 2011), 40, 49–50. See also Katherine Kelleher Sohn, *Whistlin' and Crowin' Women of Appalachia* (Carbondale: Southern Illinois University Press, 2006).

6. Victoria Purcell-Gates, *Other People's Words: The Cycle of Low Literacy* (Cambridge, MA: Harvard University Press, 1997).

7. Shirley Brice Heath, *Words at Work and Play: Three Decades in Family and Community Life* (Cambridge: Cambridge University Press, 2012), 1–7. See also Shirley Brice Heath, *Ways with Words* (New York: Cambridge University Press, 1983).

8. Newkirk, "The Narrative Roots of the Case Study," 135. Newkirk is quoting Robert Scholes and Robert Kellogg, *The Nature of Narrative* (New York: Oxford University Press, 1966), 217.

9. Newkirk, "The Narrative Roots of the Case Study," 136.

10. Charles Perdue, "Is Old Jack Really Richard Chase?" *Journal of Folklore Research* 38 (2001): 111–38, 121.

11. Purcell-Gates, *Other People's Words,* book jacket text.

12. Ibid., 7, 4, 8.

13. Ibid., 54, 166, 57, 59.

14. Ibid., 64, 40.

15. Ibid., 25, 30.

16. Ibid., 17. Purcell-Gates is quoting Phillip Obermiller and Michael Maloney, "Looking for Appalachians in Pittsburgh: Seeking Deliverance, Finding the Deer Hunter," in *From Mountain to Metropolis: Appalachian Migrants in the American City,* ed. Kathryn Borman and Phillip Obermiller (New York: Greenwood, 1993), 13–24, 15–16.

17. See, e.g., David Whisnant, *All That Is Native and Fine: The Politics of Culture in an American Region* (Chapel Hill: University of North Carolina Press, 1983).

18. Purcell-Gates, *Other People's Words,* 19, 33, 31, 20.

19. For an extended discussion of this issue, see Sara Webb-Sunderhaus, "Composing Identities: Appalachian Students, Literacy, and Identity in the Composition Classroom" (Ph.D. diss., Ohio State University, 2006), esp. 1–286.

20. Purcell-Gates, *Other People's Words,* 17, 19.

21. Both these novels have had tremendous cultural staying power. *The Little Shepherd of Kingdom Come* was made into three different film versions, in 1920, 1928, and 1961. *The Trail of the Lonesome Pine* was adapted for the screen six different times

between 1913 and 1936, and, as of 2013, a stage adaptation is the official outdoor drama of the state of Virginia.

22. For another example of the trope of the deserving Appalachian, in this case an analysis of how Cora Wilson Stewart identified Appalachians worthy of literacy intervention as she sought support for her Kentucky moonlight schools, see Bryson, chapter 2 in this volume.

23. Ibid., Purcell-Gates, *Other People's Words*, 26, 28, 34, 162, 103, 114.

24. See Allen Batteau, *The Invention of Appalachia* (Tucson: University of Arizona Press, 1990).

25. I use the terms *efferent* and *aesthetic* as they are defined in Louise Rosenblatt, "The Transactional Theory of Reading and Writing," in *Theoretical Models and Processes of Reading* (5th ed.), ed. Robert B. Ruddell et al. (Newark, DE: International Reading Association, 2004), 1363–98. See also Eric Paulson and Sonya Armstrong, "Situating Reader Stance within and beyond the Efferent-Aesthetic Continuum," *Literacy Research and Instruction* 49 (2010): 86–97.

26. For a sophisticated pedagogy that addresses issues of Appalachian dialects in a nuanced and understanding way, see Iddings and Angus, chapter 8 in this volume.

27. For an overview of the shift from seeing stigmatized research subjects as "passive victims" to seeing them as "active challengers," see Bruce Link and Jo Phelan, "Conceptualizing Stigma," *Annual Review of Sociology* 27 (2001): 363–88.

28. James Paul Gee, "The New Literacy Studies: From 'Socially Situated' to the Work of the Social," in *Situated Literacies: Reading and Writing in Context*, ed. David Barton et al. (New York: Routledge, 2000), 177–94.

29. James Moffett, *Harmonic Learning: Keynoting School Reform* (Portsmouth, NH: Boynton/Cook, 1992), 31–32.

30. Purcell-Gates, *Other People's Words*, 191–92, 197.

31. Ibid., 198–200.

32. Ibid., 212, 100.

33. Ibid., 211.

34. James Clifford, "On Ethnographic Authority," *Representations* 1 (1983): 118–46. See also Joseph Tobin and Dana Davidson, "The Ethics of Polyvocal Ethnography: Empowering vs. Textualizing Children and Teachers," *International Journal of Qualitative Studies in Education* 3 (1990): 271–83.

35. Newkirk, "The Narrative Roots of the Case Study," 148–49.

36. Purcell-Gates, *Other People's Words*, 212, 120.

37. Ibid., 15, 51.

38. Mark Workman, "Tropes, Hopes, and Dopes," *Journal of American Folklore* 106 (1993): 171–83, 176.

39. Newkirk, "The Narrative Roots of the Case Study," 147–48.

40. Ibid., 136.

41. Workman, "Tropes, Hopes, and Dopes," 171.

42. William Hugh Jansen, "The Esoteric-Exoteric Factor in Folklore," *Fabula* 2 (1959): 205–11.

43. Moffett, *Harmonic Learning,* 31.

44. Workman, "Tropes, Hopes, and Dopes," 174.

45. This reflects the long-standing tendency by folklorists to both romanticize and pathologize the "folk" they study. See, e.g., Patrick B. Mullen, "Belief and the American Folk," *Journal of American Folklore* 113 (2000): 119–43.

46. Moffett, *Harmonic Learning,* 32, and *Storm in the Mountains,* 187–202.

47. Workman, "Tropes, Hopes, and Dopes," 179.

48. Locklear, *Negotiating a Perilous Empowerment,* 23.

49. Amy Shuman, *Other People's Stories: Entitlement Claims and the Critique of Empathy* (Urbana: University of Illinois Press, 2010), 8.

50. Ann Ferrell, "'It's Really Hard to Tell the True Story of Tobacco': Stigma, Tellability, and Reflexive Scholarship," *Journal of Folklore Research* 49 (2012): 127–52, 136, 140.

51. Ibid., 137, 136.

52. Perdue, "Is Old Jack Really Richard Chase?" 121.

53. Ferrell, "'It's Really Hard to Tell the True Story of Tobacco,'" 145.

54. Newkirk, "The Narrative Roots of the Case Study," 148. Newkirk is referring to Denny Taylor and Catherine Dorsey-Gaines, *Growing Up Literate: Learning from Inner-City Families* (Portsmouth, NH: Heinemann, 1988).

2

Conflicted Rhetorics of Appalachian Identity in the Kentucky Moonlight Schools

Krista Bryson

In response to what she perceived as the state's single greatest need, on September 5, 1911, Cora Wilson Stewart, a native Kentuckian, opened fifty moonlight schools to teach basic literacy to adult students during the evening. The goal of these schools—all of which were located in Rowan County, Kentucky—was to "emancipate from illiteracy all those enslaved in its bondage."[1] Having sent out newly trained moonlight school teachers to recruit adult students only one day before the schools opened, Stewart anticipated an attendance of 150 students for the entire county. Instead, on that first night, over 1,200 adult men and women enrolled in the eight-week-long night classes. Even Stewart, in her estimation of how Kentuckians would seek out literacy, did not predict this turnout. This grand demonstration of her fellow Kentuckians' desire for literacy validated her innovative adult education work and soon gained national attention.

The broad reach of the moonlight schools is evident in the corresponding changes in literacy rates, the development of literacy campaigns modeled after the Kentucky literacy crusade, and the nationwide use of the textbooks Stewart wrote with only Kentucky students in mind.[2] The Kentucky moonlight schools and the Kentucky Education Association were credited by adult literacy educators and even the Bureau of Education of the US Department of the Interior for reducing illiteracy in the area.[3] From

1910 to 1920, the national percentage of illiterates fell by only 1.7 percent, whereas Kentucky's illiteracy rate dropped nearly four percentage points; by 1920, the moonlight schools had been in operation for nine years.[4] Extending beyond the reach of Rowan County were *Country Life Readers,* the textbooks Stewart wrote for the moonlight schools, which were eventually marketed to a broader demography of rural and urban adult learners around the nation.[5]

In addition to the textbooks, in 1922 Stewart published *Moonlight Schools for the Emancipation of Adult Illiterates,* extolling in laymen's terms the program she had developed so that her audience could include experienced and inexperienced teachers as well as anyone who might receive some hope from the book's message.[6] These accomplishments led her to a position of great influence on the discourse of illiteracy in the country. Fifteen years after opening the first moonlight school, she established the National Illiteracy Crusade, was later appointed president of the National Advisory Commission on Illiteracy, and came to be recognized as "the leading spokesperson concerning adult illiteracy in the United States."[7]

Literacy and Rhetorics of Identity

The positive influence of Stewart's work on rural and adult education has been well represented by historians, biographers, and education scholars,[8] but its impact on local and national perceptions of Kentuckians, Appalachians, and rural "illiterates" has been only briefly examined.[9] In this chapter, I argue that Stewart's publications, including the *Country Life Readers, Mother's First Book,* and *Moonlight Schools for the Emancipation of Adult Illiterates,* contribute to an intertwining of myths about literacy and Appalachians. More specifically, these publications offer conflicting national narratives about poverty, literacy, and social reform that simultaneously offer both romanticizing and demonizing/pathologizing portrayals of Appalachians. Together, these myths became the strategically essentializing myth of the illiterate Appalachian, a myth that could serve as a scapegoat for what the rest of the nation saw as the "Appalachian problem."[10] In this chapter, I rely on Harvey Graff's concept of the literacy myth, an analysis of Progressive Era rhetorics of reform, and rural and Appalachian literacy scholars' theories of the relationship between literacy and identity to position Cora Wilson Stewart's moonlight schools texts within broader understandings of the rhetorics of Appalachian literacy and identity.

My mission here is not to defame Stewart or her schools, which contributed greatly to a more liberated population of poor mountain people in Kentucky, but to illustrate how these schools relied on damaging deficit rhetorics of literacy so that today's similar rhetorics can be identified and eliminated. As Erica Abrams Locklear explains: "Despite the problematic nature of some aspects of Stewart's program, and her methods of publicizing that program, when we consider the life-changing impact her crusade had for many mountain residents, it becomes difficult to demonize the totality of her work."[11] Stewart, like many Progressive Era reformers, educators, and literacy crusaders, relied on accepted literacy education pedagogy and an unchallenged history and cultural understanding of Appalachia. However, as Susan Kates has noted, other Progressive Era educators recognized the value education could have in developing students' awareness of their own oppression and moving them to organize themselves. These educators taught not only literacy, as in reading and writing instruction, but also activist rhetorics that incorporated, as Kates put it, "1) an understanding of language usage that is tied to self and an emphasis on the ways language creates world view and epistemology, 2) an insistence on writing and speaking assignments that relate directly to the lives and experiences of specific groups of disenfranchised students, and 3) an emphasis on the social aspects of rhetorical education that make students aware of their duty to others." These kinds of activist rhetorical educations occurred as early as 1884 at Smith College, where Mary Augusta Jordan taught gender and rhetoric classes; at Wilberforce University, where Hallie Quinn Brown, whom Kates describes as "one of the first African American elocutionists in the United States," taught elocution in 1906; and at Brookwood Labor College from 1921 to 1937, where Josephine Colby, Helen Norton, and Louis Budenz taught working-class students writing and speaking.[12]

These activist educational rhetorics provide a stark contrast to the Kentucky moonlight schools. Their program sought to empower poor mountain people of Kentucky through literacy education but without the elements of rhetorical training other programs of the era used: empowering the underprivileged and cultivating respect for language identity and its relationship to power. Stewart created textbooks and even a newspaper that related to her target population in order to spare her students "the humiliation of reading from a child's primer with its lessons on kittens, dolls, and toys." She hoped to engage them with topics that would show them the importance and relevance of literacy to their everyday lives.[13] Her lessons even appealed to students' sense of civic duty and patriotism to inspire them to become literate, but that sense of duty to others was never directed toward the disenfranchised in particular. Instead, it was similar to the type of working-class education Jean Anyon describes in "Social Class and School Knowledge," a pedagogy that produces available, low-wage, obedient workers who are unaware of their own ability to make knowledge.[14]

Over the past forty years, literacy scholars have recognized and named many different myths about literacy. I return to Harvey Graff's comprehensive literacy myth, which he and John Duffy summarize as "the belief, articulated in educational, civic, religious, and other settings, contemporary and historical, that the acquisition of literacy is a necessary precursor to and invariably results in economic development, democratic practice, cognitive enhancement, and upward mobility." This myth confers an identity on the literate as literacy is "invested with immeasurable and indeed almost ineffable qualities, purportedly conferring on practitioners a predilection toward social order, an elevated moral sense, and a metaphorical 'state of grace.'" A key aspect of this literacy myth is fear of its opposite—illiteracy. The myth of the decline of literacy and the numerous national literacy crises raised by it draw on an unfounded fear of increasing illiteracy and its corresponding "end of individual advancement, social progress, and the health of the democracy."[15] The national literacy crisis at the beginning of the twentieth century was particularly pertinent for social reformers in Kentucky, who turned their attention to eradicating illiteracy in the mountains as a means to rectify assumed cultural and economic deficits.[16]

These pervasive beliefs about the mythic power of literacy to fundamentally and positively alter the identity of the literate have become inextricably intertwined with myths about Appalachian identity, ultimately equating Appalachianness with illiteracy. Rural and Appalachian literacy scholars recognize this relationship between (il)literate identity and Appalachian identity.[17] Donehower explains: "Since many negative stereotypes about the rural intellect center on language practices, literacy, in rural areas, serves both as a site of stigmatization and as a set of tools to manage that stigmatization. In Erving Goffman's terms, reading and writing help 'manage' the 'spoiled identity' that results from being stigmatized for one's linguistic and textual practices."[18] I argue that literacy itself is a rhetorical construction and an enactment of identity, capable of simultaneously affirming, denying, and redefining identities, as in the case of Stewart's moonlight school texts.

The Texts of the Kentucky Moonlight Schools

In the writing of the moonlight school texts, Stewart was faced with the dual task of demonstrating her schools' success in significantly reducing adult illiteracy and proving a continuing need for funding. She blamed the region's problems on ignorance resulting from a lack of educational opportunity, a common move used by Progressive education reformers of the time. Appealing to funding sources with romantic claims of her students' racial purity, innate resilience, innocent ignorance, humility, and gratitude, she set up a meritocratic model that placed great responsibility for success or failure on the students. Once the students were given the opportunity to receive an education, any cultural practices that did not fall within the parameters of mainstream middle-class ideals were condemned.

One might question how Stewart could promote such problematic views of her own home state and region since beliefs about the mountain people of Kentucky were easily and commonly transposed to all Appalachians. This can be partially explained through a teasing out of the complex identity work that Appalachians must do. Stewart was an urbane, educated, upper-middle-class Appalachian who could—and did—easily identify as a member of "civilized" Kentucky; she believed she owed it to the people of her state to enlighten and civilize others. The distinction she made between herself and her fellow Kentuckians can be traced back to the myth of "two Kentuckys." Although different local-color writers posit different versions of these two Kentuckys, it was the novelist John Fox Jr.'s version of the literate, intellectual, and wealthy Bluegrass Kentucky and the illiterate, backward, and poor mountain Kentucky that became widely accepted.[19]

The significance of these two Kentuckys becomes more telling in the broader context of the cultural, political, and economic distinctions made between Appalachia and the rest of America. In answer to the nation's post-Reconstruction need to redefine itself, many local-color writings of the 1860s–1890s offered a simple contrastive identity within the mountains of Appalachia.[20] These texts "exploited the folk particularities of people and place," presenting one of two Appalachians. One was the romanticized mountaineer: racially pure, innocent in ignorance, industrious, blindly dedicated to kin, and in tune with nature. The other was the demonized hillbilly: racially impure, willfully and destructively ignorant, lazy, violent, unclean, and incestuous.[21] This construct of Appalachians' "culturalize[d] 'difference'" offered an Other against which the rest of the nation could define itself.[22]

The Appalachian scholar Henry Shapiro argues that this constructed opposition is the result not of a desire to help or to colonize Appalachians but of an attempt to resolve the assumed conflict between the two types of Americans—the civilized and the uncivilized.[23] Within this model, resolving the conflict by civilizing and integrating deviant Appalachians into mainstream society is a source of national pride. Appealing to this desire for a unified, American identity—one based on accepted and mutually beneficial definitions of *civilization*—Stewart claims: "These mountain people now stand at the threshold of a new civilization, eager and hopeful, anxious to enter in and take their part in the work of the world. They need the world's help, its best thought, its modern conveniences, but not more than the world needs them."[24]

The argument that Kentuckians had the potential to be redeemed through the world's "best thought" (i.e., literacy) rests on the claim that they were inherently pure because they descended from "the best ancestry"—British, Scottish, Irish, and Welsh. Stewart described these forebears as "noble," intelligent, "sturdy," "independent and rugged," and desirous of improving their station through education.[25] Although Kentuckians might have been deficient, she reasoned that their lineage ensured their capability to become valuable members of society. The problem was that they lacked literacy.

This appeal to the value of Anglo-Saxon whiteness, which does not wholly or accurately portray the ethnicity and race of the Appalachian people, is particularly apt for the time and region.[26] In her explanation of the value of the mountain people of Kentucky, Stewart draws on romantic notions of mountain culture and racial purity, appealing to the xenophobic and racist sentiments held by much of the nation. She writes: "In a day when racial groups weld themselves together in America and seek to advance the welfare of the country from which they came rather than the welfare of the nation which has received them into its bosom, it is comforting to remember that in these mountains of the southern states America has a reservoir of strength and patriotism in the millions of pure Anglo-Saxon Americans."[27] Emily Satterwhite explains how this nostalgic portrayal of Appalachians not only made them identifiable to the rest of the nation, but also "pegged them as a racially marked tribal people, 'an alien population' that required intervention and uplift," two rhetorical tasks that were necessary for Stewart's Appalachian literacy crusade to succeed.[28]

Stewart ties this rhetoric of Appalachian racial identity to her rhetoric of literate identity, explaining that part of the appeal of the Anglo-Saxons is their "educated ancestry," that is, forebears who read Latin, Greek, and the works of Caesar, Virgil, and Chaucer. Despite being "deprived for years of educational opportunity," Appalachians maintained their innate intelligence.[29] This appeal sharply distinguishes between intelligence and education, thereby priming Stewart's readers to believe that, although Appalachians were capable of learning, they were uneducated. Moreover, the explicit linkage of race, civilization, and literacy in this passage from *Moonlight Schools* is indicative of the appeals to the literacy myth and the Appalachian identity myth that run throughout all Stewart's adult education texts. In this chapter, I identify these myths at work within three interrelated "Appalachian problems" Stewart claims literacy acquisition can solve: violence, cultural deviance, and poverty.

VIOLENCE

One of the more popular myths about Appalachia is that family feuds like those of the infamous Hatfields and McCoys are commonplace. The image of the violent hillbilly has been reproduced countless times since the emergence of popular accounts of nineteenth-century family feuds. None of these portrayals faults economic and social conditions for creating the ideal environment for such violence; instead, the presumed willful ignorance of the hillbilly is blamed. In 1889, T. C. Crawford, a *New York World* reporter, attributed feud violence to the isolation of the Appalachian mountains and the community's corresponding lack of civilization. Even scholarly sources sensationalized Appalachians: in 1901, the *American Journal of Sociology* claimed Appalachians were backward despite their schools and churches, portraying these institutions as primitive and ineffective. Both news media and scholars portrayed these deficiencies as the root of laziness, unemployment, and violence.[30] Such depictions resonate with Graff's literacy myth, which contends that illiteracy is to blame for violence and criminality, erasing the root causes of these problems—economic and social inequality.

Few studies of popular representations of the ignorant, violent hillbilly provide sustained analysis of these characterizations' impact on education and literacy campaigns, particularly Stewart's rationale for educating her fellow Kentuckians.[31] Stewart lived in Rowan County, where the "war" among the Martin, Tolliver, and Logan families resulted in more deaths than the infamous Hatfield-McCoy feud.[32] She is also said to have been the niece of Craig Tolliver and was likely influenced by this familial connection.[33] Further demonstrating her interest in Appalachian feuds, in 1904 she sold an article titled "The Breathitt County Vendetta" to *Wide World Magazine,* recounting in detail the events of a feud between the Hargis and Marcum families, and portraying them as warring with the "ferocity of savages."[34]

Stewart later used nationwide awareness and condemnation of these feuds to garner financial and policy support for the moonlight schools; as in her earlier popular accounts, she blames Appalachians' violence and criminality on illiteracy. She claims her schools will save her fellow Kentuckians from the illiteracy that kept them in "darkness and isolation," ushering them into "a new civilization."[35] What she mentions but does not further discuss is that the savage feudists she writes about were not all uneducated; instead, many were among the region's economic and political elite. Dwight Billings and Katherine Blee explain that in Clay County, located south of Stewart's own Rowan County, feuds occurred "between two families of highly educated, wealthy elites and their supporters." The supposed ignorance and poverty of the violent hillbilly are also often portrayed as a result of Appalachia's complete social and economic insularity, another myth that Billings and Blee negate. Since the Civil War, Appalachia has been part of larger regional and national market networks; the majority of its economy relies on the exportation of natural resources like coal and timber.[36] While the falsity of her claims may not have been evident to her, Stewart drew on mistaken understandings of these feuds to gain local, regional, and national support for the moonlight schools.

Appealing to the myth of the civilizing effect of literacy, Stewart contends that the people of Rowan County lacked community spirit, a flaw she argues would be remedied by literacy attainment. Beside a photograph of a man and woman standing side by side, she includes the caption: "They were schoolmates and that is a tie that binds." Here, she positions the community created by schooling and education as one far superior to that created by town, county, or region. The photograph alone does not suggest that the school has formed a community where none exists; it only presents education as another means of forming connections with other individuals, albeit a significant one. Stewart's interpretation of the following letter from a moonlight school trustee, however, pushes this claim even further, suggesting that Appalachians were formerly lacking in "community spirit" altogether:

I have lived in this district for fifty-five years, and I never saw any such interest as we have here now. The school used to just drag along and nobody seemed interested. We never had a gathering at the school-house and nobody ever thought of visiting the school. We had not had a night school but three weeks until we got together right. We papered the house, put in new windows, purchased new stovepipe, made new steps, contributed money, and bought the winter's fuel.

Now we have a live Sunday school, a singing school, prayer meeting once each week, and preaching twice a month. People of all denominations in the district meet and worship together in perfect unity and harmony, aged people come regularly, and even people from the adjoining county are beginning to come over to our little school-house.[37]

Stewart interprets this letter as evidence of "an awakened, if not trained leadership, a whetted desire for cooperative activity where individualism and stagnation had prevailed," appealing to the myth of the rugged, independent, and complacently isolated mountaineer. The letter allows her to contend that her claims about the transformative power of literacy are correct. As she writes: "Friction and factional feeling melted away in districts where they had existed, and a new spirit of harmony and brotherhood came to take their place. Men and women who had hitherto been divided by contention and strife now worked side by side in concord." Here, she expands the letter writer's claims of the community-building effects of schooling and its surrounding activities, such as building construction and church participation, to include arguments that her literacy crusade eradicated strained social relations. Without explicitly citing the regional feuds as one impetus for literacy education in the region, she draws on language that suggests that these divided communities found a common purpose through the actual work of creating and maintaining schools. She further implies that, prior to the creation of the schools, the factions formerly had nothing to draw them together. Stewart knew her audience well. After her 1913 appeal to Kentucky governor James B. McCreary for the founding of a state commission investigating illiteracy, he responded in a proclamation against illiteracy, claiming that anyone who wanted to "lessen crime," among many other social ills, would support his initiative.[38]

Stewart's interpretations of the photograph and letter omit historically recognized sites of Appalachian community formation, including kinship networks, religious denominations, workplaces, and cultural activities. Her account furthers the stereotype of the uncivilized, cultureless, individualistic Appalachian, an account that contradicts her frequent valorizations of the Appalachian people in the readers, for example: "The best people on earth live in Rowan County."[39] Although Stewart admitted that that claim was a strategic appeal to the students' sense of pride, throughout *Moonlight Schools* she directs this romantic sentiment toward school supporters and other teachers. When examined alongside other apparent inconsistencies, this complexity and contradiction point to the influence of her conflicted identity on her seemingly opposing rhetorical goals and strategies. She never spoke of her students as *Appalachian*, perhaps because *Appalachian* was not the common identity category that it is now and the term would not allow her to easily distinguish herself from her students.[40] However, she could make distinctions between herself—a well-off, educated woman from the Kentucky Bluegrass—and the poor mountain people of her home state.

CULTURAL DEVIANCE

In *Moonlight Schools* and the literacy textbooks she wrote specifically for Appalachian Kentuckians, Stewart positions Appalachians as culturally deviant. Despite these books' different audiences and purposes, she uses similar rhetorical strategies, often condemning the primitiveness and irresponsibility of specific practices and the people who use them. Her readers, including the *Country Life Readers* and *Mother's First Book,* critique these practices by emphasizing knowledge that students could supposedly relate to and benefit from in their everyday lives. Subjects include the duties of citizenship, basic hygiene, nutrition, housekeeping, and farming methods. Some of these lessons are instructional; one particular lesson focuses on improving Kentuckians' current agricultural practices by explaining methods for selecting, judging, and testing seed corn. However, as with many Progressive Era literacy campaigns, numerous lessons attempt to shame students into taking up practices that are culturally specific and not necessarily more beneficial. In this way, the readers promote and normalize cultural standards that may be at odds with students' ways of life and, thus, their very identities.

One of the most unifying aspects of any culture is language. Illiteracy is commonly cited as the cause or defining characteristic of Appalachians' cultural designation as the deviant and inferior Other, as Iddings and Angus (chapter 8 in this volume) explore; further, nonstandard dialects and accents are often used to mark particular identities as ignorant or deviant. In her account of the lessons taught in the moonlight schools, Stewart emphasizes "English drills" as among "the most popular drills, as well as the most needed." The drills she describes, however, are not typical grammar drills. Instead, they are accent-reduction drills that teach students to pronounce the *g* of the ———*ing* at the ends of verbs and correct their "mispronunciations"—for example, *seed* (for *saw*), *crick* (for *creek*), *kiver* (for *cover*), *git* (for *get*), *hit* (for *it*), *hyeard* (for *heard*), *tuk* (for *took*), *haint* (for *aren't*), and *skeerred* (for *scared*). She characterizes these deviations from "proper" English as "bad English" and "monstrosities of pronunciation" resulting from a complete lack of "language conscience"—ignoring the possibility that these pronunciations are one aspect of Appalachians' rhetorically constructed identity.[41] These accent-reduction lessons cement the idea that Appalachian English has grammatical deficiencies indicative of Appalachian illiteracy.

Stewart highlights her efforts at linguistic reform in her memoir, noting that her efforts came "long before" the inaugural "National Better Speech Week."[42] Her work was among the first attempting to eradicate the Appalachian dialect, setting a precedent for future language instruction in the region. Specific linguistic features like those emphasized in her language classes became associated with Appalachia and illiterate speech, a stigma that to this day no amount of linguistic theory has been able to erase from the national imaginary.[43] Speakers of Appalachian English are very aware of this stigma, and in response some alter their accents and grammar to conform to Standard American English.[44] This desire for conformity is quite evident in Stewart's account of the "popularity" of the "English" drills in the moonlight schools; all the drills were elective, so these students clearly felt that accent reduction and grammatical speaking were important to the process of becoming literate.

Alternatively, some speakers, in a rejection of the stigma associated with their language, may emphasize or even exaggerate their Appalachian accent and dialectal features for rhetorical effect. There is no evidence of such behavior in Stewart's accounts of her students, but Appalachian literacy scholars have noted instances of such rhetorical language use. Kim Donehower (chapter 1 in this volume), for example, shares how she deliberately intensified her accent when she worked at a restaurant that traded in Appalachian stereotypes. Katrina Powell's work on letters written by families living in the Shenandoah National Park in the 1930s demonstrates that this community of Appalachians used literacy and language to resist the identities constructed for them. In particular, the letter writers adopted the bureaucratic language of government officials to make written requests while simultaneously retaining certain linguistic and discursive features used in their communities. By doing so, they established an ethos that asserted the value of their culture within the structures of government bureaucracy.[45] This demonstration of genre knowledge, paired with deviations from that genre, challenges the association between illiteracy and vernacular language, thus contesting the stigma associated with Appalachian language. Certainly, Stewart's efforts to mainstream moonlight school students' accents and dialects could be seen as a similar kind of rhetorical move that allows students to function in multiple discourse communities. The lessons were not framed that way, however. Instead, they were framed as corrections to "bad English"—unsurprising for the time, but still damaging to Appalachian identity.[46]

Stewart's discussions of housekeeping and hygienic practices offer further examples of damaging corrective approaches to cultural difference. In Kentucky's mountain communities, housekeeping and hygienic practices were undeniably different from those of the mainstream, and the two are linked in Stewart's readers because they are dependent on one another. For example, in communities without clean water or indoor plumbing, certain hygienic practices and housekeeping chores were onerous or even impossible, resulting in household conditions that contributed to illness.[47] Lessons advocating certain hygienic and housekeeping practices in the moonlight school readers were, thus, a warranted tactic to prevent disease and numerous other health problems. The rhetorics used in these lessons, however, draw on the literacy myth and cultural shaming. These hygienic conditions were not found in every area of the county, and Stewart's crusade, like many Progressive Era campaigns, relied on stereotypical portrayals of the uncleanliness of Appalachian people to illustrate the need for reform.

To illustrate the benefits of adhering to mainstream housekeeping standards, *A Mother's First Book* includes a testimonial from a female homemaker who recently learned to read and write. The newly literate writer draws together a valuing of literacy, mainstream housekeeping practices, and a sense of self-worth, making an exceptional claim about how well her family has assimilated to the new culture presented by the moonlight schools:

> These are happy days for me. I feel as if I have a new lease on life. I have learned to write my own letters and to read those that come to me. You should see the pride I take in my work. We have put running water into our house and we are now about the cleanest people you ever saw. John will be home from college soon and Mary is coming

from Kentucky for a visit. We plan to show those older children of ours one of the neatest homes in the world.[48]

This letter proclaims the benefits of literacy without ever making explicit how becoming literate affected the way this family keeps their home. After giving a general statement of how she feels about her "new lease on life," the writer provides evidence of the recent developments in her happiness. She can read and write, she has indoor plumbing, and she takes pride in her work. Her family is clean, and her home is neat. Never explaining how education is related to these significant lifestyle changes, the letter implies causality between literacy and mainstream cultural values and sets up these values as unquestionably positive—a dangerous conflation of ethics and social standards.

Establishing the worth of new practices and values necessitates a condemnation of the former housekeeping practices of now-literate families. Those condemnations may be implicit, like that in the homemaker's letter, or explicit, such as in the following passage that students were to read:

"This place is dirty and ugly.
The house needs paint.
The yard is full of weeds.
A lazy, shiftless family lives here."
"Yes, but how do you know that?"
"I know it from the house.
Lazy, shiftless people live in dirty, ugly homes."
Lazy, shiftless people live in dirty, ugly homes.[49]

This literacy lesson is much more explicit in its judgments about the physical state of a home, reflecting modern, middle-class values, and overlooking other likely causes of disrepair. Although not all towns in Rowan County were coal-mining towns, coal, fire clay, iron ore, and timber were major industrial products in the county.[50] These extractive industries were pervasive in the daily lives of their workers, and the state of houses in these towns often reflected the funding and practices of the industries. The Appalachian scholar Ronald Eller notes that coal operators did not give much consideration to the layout of the towns or the material comforts of the houses. The low wages and restricted free time of many families also contributed to the condition of their homes. Even if the families had money and time for maintenance and repair, the local conditions were often insurmountable. The ever-present dust, mud, and mine waste—not only in the physical space of the towns, but also in the clothes and on the bodies of the families—made homes impossible to keep clean.[51]

Yet Stewart's readers do not point to these and other socioeconomic explanations for homes that did not meet mainstream standards. Instead, the character of the family living in the home completely dictates whether the house is clean or dirty, nice or ugly, as emphasized through the repetition of the final line connecting the failings of the home to the failings of the homeowners. The effectiveness of this characterization relies in part on its moral undertones. As a mainly Protestant population, Kentuckians might have been more responsive to lessons that were reminiscent of those they were already familiar with through the Bible. This small literacy lesson calls on the biblical maxim "cleanliness is next to godliness" and appeals to the myth that literacy and morality go hand-in-hand.

While health problems could and often did arise from poor housekeeping and hygienic practices in the region at that time, the readers' approach to remedying them is an exercise in cultural shaming. Rather than indicting an economic system that forced many impoverished families to choose between buying food and buying toothpaste, the readers approach the problem as a personal one that could be solved if each person had a proper understanding of hygiene. Here, mainstream culture operates under the guise of literacy education to dictate what values and standards of living are acceptable for people in Appalachia while also victim blaming and diverting attention from the causes of the housekeeping and hygiene differences. Ultimately, this lesson shames individuals into valuing and enacting mainstream knowledge, encouraging them to rely not on "their own experiential knowledge and the accumulated wisdom of family and friends" but on printed materials like textbooks.[52]

Much like the lessons on household upkeep and hygiene, agricultural passages from the *Country Life Readers* imply that, to be successful, farmers must rely on mainstream knowledge gained from print literacy instead of their own lived experience. This rhetoric seems to have similar goals as that of other agrarian progress narratives like those of the agricultural journal the *Progressive Farmer*, which Cynthia Ryan identifies as part of a neoliberal regime that encourages capitalistic enterprise at the expense of the well-being and livelihood of the individual farmer.[53] The following passage, like others in the *Country Life Readers*, employs the shaming of the home-centered lessons, almost scolding farmers for not seeking outside knowledge to improve their farms' yields:

> "Some Big Farmers"
> You say that you don't know any of these? Haven't you read about any of them? What do you read about if you do not read about the big farmers in your farm books and farm papers?
> You don't read anything! Well, one might have known that by looking at your farm. What a farmer reads shows in his farm.[54]

Again, like the letter from the homemaker and the lesson on the dirty home, this lesson claims that literacy or other basic values can be read or seen in the material conditions of people's lives: "What a farmer reads shows in his farm." It is in this type of enthymematic statement about the unquestionable power of education that the literacy myth lies in wait for readers, encouraging them to read Appalachia and use Appalachian landscapes as evidence of illiteracy.

Interestingly, in her memoir of the schools' founding, Stewart never fully elaborates on the poverty of the region, but she does acknowledge the financial difficulty of her students in order to explain just how valuable a literacy education is to Kentuckians. She portrays literacy as an asset for which they were willing to sacrifice basic necessities: "It is a thing which has caused many a slender mountain maid and many a frail lad to assume the work of a man when by so doing they could earn a little money to provide for a few weeks of school. It is the same desire that caused many a mountaineer to give his last few acres of land, his labor and his last dollar."[55] While she valorizes her students' willingness to sacrifice their homes and livelihoods for their educations, she also bemoans their lack of attention to contemporary methods of housekeeping and farming.

POVERTY

For Stewart, the moonlight school supporters, and her students, perhaps the most motivating outcome of literacy was its supposed role in economic progress. Although improved economic viability is not guaranteed to all who are considered literate, Stewart appeals to this literacy myth by using her students' lives as examples of literacy's economic benefits. She provides the following example: "One man, foreign born, who had been working at a lumber camp at the meager wage of $1.50 per day entered the Moonlight School and specialized in mathematics—that part of it pertaining to his business, and at the close of six weeks' session, was promoted at a salary double that which he had received before."[56] Here, Stewart relies on her intended audience to fill in the unstated connections she makes: first, the student specializing in mathematics received a raise because he became literate or more literate in an area that would benefit his employers; second, any moonlight school student could achieve a comparable salary increase as a result of education. The use of this statistic as evidence belies the fact that these opportunities for advancement were scarce, as were jobs in general.

The implied causal link between the student's literacy education and his improved economic condition ignores the undeniable economic problems that made a livable wage unattainable for most in the region. It also places full responsibility for poverty on the individual. Seemingly benign statements like Stewart's are often the most destructive because they are particularly useful when rationalizing victim blaming. Graff provides apt evidence that attaining literacy does not guarantee higher earnings. Despite the fact that the majority of unskilled and semiskilled workers in nineteenth-century Hamilton, Ontario, were literate (75 percent of the unskilled and 93 percent of the semiskilled), they were still unable to advance in their occupation, and not one occupation group consisted primarily of either literates or illiterates. Graff concludes it is not illiteracy that limits an individual's economic advancement but "ethnic and class ascription."[57] However, accounting for the true causes of this systematic economic difference would force not only schools but also the country as a whole to accept responsibility for inequity, instead of blaming individuals' lack of literacy or other moral failings. A rhetoric that acknowledged inequity would also fall distinctly and troublingly outside the national narrative of equal opportunity and individualism that was and is so prevalent in America.

Legacies of the Moonlight School Texts

By writing the moonlight school texts, Stewart ensured for her schools and commissions the attention and funding that contributed to one of the most successful literacy crusades in US history. Despite the many positive portrayals of Kentuckians in her texts, she lays the responsibility for rectifying their economic inequities at their feet, completely sidestepping the systemic factors that contributed to the problem of Appalachian exploitation. She explicitly rejected holding government institutions and private corporations accountable; in a letter addressed to "the teachers of Kentucky" that was distributed through the state press, she wrote that "there is no time to waste in crying 'shame' or in fixing the blame" for the high illiteracy rate in Kentucky. Even as she called attention to the material obstacles to her students' attendance—including difficult and dangerous travel, exhaustion from the strenuous work of their jobs, and parental responsibilities—she held individuals responsible for how they moved forward once they were given the opportunity to become literate.[58] In other words, with her embrace of emancipatory literacy came the belief that individuals are responsible for overcoming all obstacles—even those that may be insurmountable.

This disconnect in rhetoric can be explained in numerous ways. Stewart had the complex task of demonstrating how Appalachian deficits could be overcome through literacy acquisition while neither wholly blaming Appalachians or public institutions for their literacy failures. Both goals were filtered through her terministic screen—that of a well-educated, upper-middle-class Appalachian woman versed in the rhetoric of benevolence work, education reform, and the Appalachian deficit model. Balancing these tenuous goals and her own personal background required a delicate weaving together of the literacy myth and select, divergent myths about Appalachia.

Despite the literacy crusade's success, the pairing of the literacy myth and myths about Appalachia was—and is—a dangerous one. The danger here is twofold. One danger is that those with the power to affect Appalachians' lives via public policy will use these myths to validate "an occupation and exploitation of the landscape's natural resources, and paternalistic control over and utilization of the people's human resources."[59] The other is that Appalachians themselves will internalize these stigmatizing myths to their own detriment. When a marginalized population is taught to unquestioningly attribute its own problems to a lack of opportunity, it becomes a personal failure when opportunity arises and the problems are still not solved.

Because such stigmatizing discourse is used in the benevolent rhetorics of a literacy crusade, we might be tempted to excuse it or overlook its effects. Certainly, blaming only Stewart for the perpetuation of the illiterate Appalachian stereotype seems unfair. It is necessary to recognize that her conflicted rhetoric highlights the complexity of Appalachian identity; she was Appalachian, yet her education and socioeconomic status did not fall within the Appalachian stereotype. She may have identified as both Appalachian and non-Appalachian, able neither to embrace an Appalachian identity nor to let it go. Instead, as so many with stigmatized group identities have done, she may have tried to "normify" her own conduct while attempting "to clean up the conduct of others in the group" through literacy education.[60]

For Appalachians, the desire to end such stigmatization of Appalachian identity is often concurrent with the desire not to be stigmatized themselves. This desire is understandable but unfortunate, because it ultimately results in damaging benevolent rhetorics like Stewart's. To encourage a critical, benevolent rhetoric that does not reify stereotypes of Appalachian and literate identities, I advocate approaching literacy as a rhetorical construction and an enactment of identity. Conceptualizing literacy in this way can potentially allow us to see the ways in which well-intentioned, highly successful literacy crusades such as Stewart's can cause long-lasting damage to the identity of the population targeted for reform.

Notes

I would like to thank Sara Webb-Sunderhaus and Kim Donehower for their patience and generosity in working on this collection. They have made and continue to make invaluable contributions to the people of Appalachia.

1. Cora Wilson Stewart, *Moonlight Schools for the Emancipation of Adult Illiterates* (New York: Dutton, 1922), 9. See also Willie Nelms, *Cora Wilson Stewart: Crusader against Illiteracy* (Jefferson, NC: McFarland, 1997), 35. Throughout this chapter I use Stewart's implied definition of *illiteracy*—the inability to read and write. At the time of her publications, the intricacies of the term *illiterate* were not debated; it indicated only the inability to read and write. It did not acknowledge the varying degrees of ability to read and write or different racial, cultural, and class definitions of what constituted valid oral or written discourse.

2. The 1913 Bureau of Education bulletin *Illiteracy in the United States and Experiment for Its Elimination* was key in spreading the word about Stewart's moonlight schools outside Kentucky. See Peter L. Mortensen, "Representations of Literacy and Region: Narrating 'Another America,'" in *Pedagogy in the Age of Politics: Writing and Reading (in) the Academy*, ed. Patricia A. Sullivan and Donna J. Qualley (Urbana, IL: National Council of Teachers of English, 1994), 100–121, 117.

3. Yvonne Honeycutt Baldwin, *Cora Wilson Stewart and Kentucky's Moonlight Schools: Fighting for Literacy in America* (Lexington: University Press of Kentucky, 2006); Nelms, *Cora Wilson Stewart*, 41.

4. "120 Years of Literacy," *National Assessment of Adult Literacy*, November 2012, https://nces.ed.gov/naal/lit_history.asp; Baldwin, *Cora Wilson Stewart*, 88.

5. Baldwin, *Cora Wilson Stewart*, 88.

6. Stewart, *Moonlight Schools*, viii.

7. Nelms, *Cora Wilson Stewart*, 41. See also Baldwin, *Cora Wilson Stewart*.

8. In 1914, Stewart's speech to the Kentucky legislature on the schools and their effect on illiteracy led to an "unprecedented" unanimous vote establishing the Kentucky Illiteracy Commission. Nelms, *Cora Wilson Stewart*, 47.

9. See Jane Greer, "Women's Words, Women's Work: Rural Literacy and Labor," in *Reclaiming the Rural: Essays on Literacy, Rhetoric, and Pedagogy*, ed. Kim Donehower, Charlotte Hogg, and Eileen E. Schell (Carbondale: Southern Illinois University Press, 2012), 90–106; and Erica Abrams Locklear, *Negotiating a Perilous Empowerment: Appalachian Women's Literacies* (Athens: Ohio University Press, 2011).

10. Henry D. Shapiro, *Appalachia on Our Mind: The Southern Mountains and Mountaineers in the American Consciousness, 1870–1920* (Chapel Hill: University of North Carolina Press, 1978).

11. Locklear, *Negotiating a Perilous Empowerment*, 34.

12. Susan Kates, *Activist Rhetorics and American Higher Education, 1885–1937* (Carbondale: Southern Illinois University Press, 2001), 13–14 (see also 6–8).

13. Stewart, *Moonlight Schools*, 23–24.

14. Jean Anyon, "Social Class and School Knowledge," *Curriculum Inquiry* 11, no. 1 (Spring 1981): 3–42.

15. Harvey Graff and John Duffy, "Literacy Myths," in *Encyclopedia of Language and Education*, vol. 2, *Literacy*, ed. Brian Street and Nancy Hornberger (New York: Springer, 2008), 457–68, 41, 44–46. Graff and Duffy claim that evidence of a literacy crisis is mostly anecdotal and rarely supported by empirical evidence. Ibid., 45.

16. Mortensen, "Representations of Literacy and Region," 110.

17. See Kim Donehower, Charlotte Hogg, and Eileen E. Schell, *Rural Literacies* (Carbondale: Southern Illinois University Press, 2007); Mortensen, "Representations of Literacy and Region"; Katrina M. Powell, *The Anguish of Displacement: The Politics of Literacy in the Letters of Mountain Families in Shenandoah National Park* (Charlottesville: University of Virginia Press, 2007); and Webb-Sunderhaus, chapter 9 in this volume.

18. Donehower, Hogg, and Schell, *Rural Literacies*, 57.

19. See Fox's novels *The Kentuckians* (1898), *The Little Shepherd of Kingdom Come* (1903), and *The Trail of the Lonesome Pine* (1908).

20. For examples of local-color writing that defined the Appalachian Other, see Will Wallace Harney, "A Strange Land and a Peculiar People," *Lippincott's*, October 1873, 429–38; and Charles Egbert Craddock (Mary Noailles Murfree), *In the Tennessee Mountains* (Boston: Houghton Mifflin, 1884). For recent scholarly discussions, see Shapiro, *Appalachia on Our Mind*, 5; and David C. Hsuing, *Two Worlds in the Tennessee Mountains: Exploring the Origins of Appalachian Stereotypes* (Lexington: University Press of Kentucky, 1997), 104.

21. Allen Batteau, *The Invention of Appalachia* (Tucson: University of Arizona Press, 1990), 39.

22. Emily Satterwhite, *Dear Appalachia: Readers, Identity, and Popular Fiction since 1878* (Lexington: University Press of Kentucky, 2011), 12.

23. Shapiro, *Appalachia on Our Mind*, xvi, 28.

24. Stewart, *Moonlight Schools*, 5.

25. Ibid., 1–3.

26. This romantic notion of race in Appalachia remains less subject to scholarly and popular critique because it appears to be a positive characterization with noble intentions and is a strategic invention used to secure economic and other types of advantages for a population that was racialized on first immigrating to the United States (see David R. Roediger, *The Wages of Whiteness: Race and the Making of the American Working Class* [New York: Verso, 2003]). For an explanation of a similar politics of culture that existed in the Hindman and Pine Mountain Settlement Schools, see David E. Whisnant, *All That Is Native and Fine: The Politics of Culture in an American Region* (Chapel Hill: University of North Carolina Press, 1983).

27. Stewart, *Moonlight Schools*, 5.

28. Satterwhite, *Dear Appalachia*, 66.

29. Stewart, *Moonlight Schools*, 2.

30. Altina Waller, *Feud: Hatfields, McCoys, and Social Change in Appalachia, 1860–1900* (Chapel Hill: University of North Carolina Press, 1988), 7.

31. Greer ("Women's Words, Women's Work") and Locklear (*Negotiating a Perilous Empowerment*) consider Stewart's rhetorical strategies and their effects but only briefly mention that Stewart used the notoriety of the county from the infamous Martin-Tolliver-Logan feud to garner support for her campaign.

32. Baldwin, *Cora Wilson Stewart*; Nelms, *Cora Wilson Stewart*; Lowell H. Harris and James C. Klotter, *A New History of Kentucky* (Lexington: University Press of Kentucky, 1997).

33. John Pearce, ed., *Days of Darkness: The Feuds of Eastern Kentucky* (Lexington: University Press of Kentucky, 1994), 112.

34. Cora Wilson Stewart, "The Breathitt County Vendetta," *Wide World Magazine* 13 (June 1904): 157–65, 158. See also Edward T. Moran (Cora Wilson Stewart), "The Rowan County War: The Inner History of a Famous Kentucky Feud," *Wide World Magazine* 9 (July 1902): 321–30; and Nelms, *Cora Wilson Stewart*, 8.

35. Baldwin, *Cora Wilson Stewart*, 15 (quoting Cora Wilson Stewart to Senator Allen, October 17, 1929); Stewart, *Moonlight Schools*, 5.

36. Dwight E. Billings and Katherine Blee, *The Road to Poverty: The Making of Wealth and Hardship in Appalachia* (New York: Cambridge University Press, 2000), 24.

37. Stewart, *Moonlight Schools*, 44–45.

38. Ibid., 45–46, 57–67.

39. Quoted in ibid., 22.

40. Although representations of mountain people, hillbillies, and other stereotypes were prevalent in the late nineteenth century, William G. Frost, the president of Berea College in Kentucky from 1892 to 1920, was the first to define the Southern Appalachians as a geographic and cultural region. Then John C. Campbell's *The Southern Highlander*

and His Homeland (New York: Sage, 1921) became the "landmark study and definition of the region" (David Walls, "On the Naming of Appalachia," in *An Appalachian Symposium: Essays Written in Honor of Cratis D. Williams,* ed. J. W. Williamson [Boone, NC: Appalachian State University Press, 1977], 56–76, 67), and the federal survey "Economic and Social Problems and Conditions of the Southern Appalachians" (Washington, DC: US Government Printing Office for the Bureau of Agricultural Economics, the Bureau of Home Economics, and the Forest Service, 1935) further cemented this definition of Appalachia as a geographic region with particular cultural, political, and economic features.

41. Stewart, *Moonlight Schools,* 26–27.

42. Ibid., 27.

43. It was not until 1967 that linguists began to argue that such linguistic differences are not bad grammar or mispronunciations but valid regional dialects that are as rule based as any standard dialect. Now the work of scholars like Kirk Hazen (e.g., "Defining Appalachian English," in *Linguistic Diversity in the South: Changing Codes, Practices, and Ideology,* ed. Margaret Bender [Athens: University of Georgia Press, 2004], 50–65) has elevated these dialects to languages or Englishes that contribute to Appalachian culture. See William A. Stewart, *Language and Communication Problems in Southern Appalachia* (Washington, DC: Center for Applied Linguistics, 1967), 1–43.

44. Kirk Hazen and Sarah Hamilton, "A Dialect Turned Inside Out: Migration and the Appalachian Diaspora," *Journal of English Linguistics* 36 (2008): 100–128, 123.

45. Powell, *The Anguish of Displacement,* 7, 81–103.

46. Stewart, *Moonlight Schools,* 27.

47. Professor W. R. Thomas noted that, in mining communities, "there may be no electric lighting plant, sewer, or water system" and that "where the small developments are numerous and the mines are close together, the crowding which ensues leads to very unsatisfactory living conditions." W. R. Thomas, *Life among the Hills and Mountains of Kentucky* (Louisville, KY: Standard Printing Co., 1926), 9.

48. Quoted in Baldwin, *Cora Wilson Stewart,* 170.

49. Cora Wilson Stewart, *Country Life Readers: First Book* (Atlanta: B. F. Johnson, 1915), 25.

50. Thomas, *Life among the Hills and Mountains,* 200–201.

51. Ronald D Eller, *Miners, Millhands, and Mountaineers: Industrialization of the Appalachian South, 1880–1930* (Knoxville: University of Tennessee Press, 1995), 182–85.

52. Quoted in Greer, "Women's Words, Women's Work," 94.

53. Cynthia Ryan, "'Get More from Your Life on the Land': Negotiating Rhetorics of Progress and Tradition in a Neoliberal Environment," in Donehower, Hogg, and Schell, eds., *Reclaiming the Rural,* 52–71, 61.

54. Cora Wilson Stewart, *Country Life Readers: Second Book* (Whitefish, MT: Kessinger, 1916), 50.

55. Stewart, *Moonlight Schools,* 3.

56. Ibid., 38.

57. Harvey J. Graff, *The Literacy Myth: Cultural Integration and Social Structure in the Nineteenth Century* (New Brunswick, NJ: Transaction, 1991), 198.

58. Stewart, *Moonlight Schools*, 83 (quote), 16.

59. Douglas Reichert Powell, *Critical Regionalism: Connecting Politics and Culture in the American Landscape* (Chapel Hill: University of North Carolina Press, 2007), 115.

60. Erving Goffman, *Stigma: Notes on the Management of Spoiled Identity* (New York: Simon & Schuster, 1986), 108.

3

Appalachian Identities and the Difficulties of Archival Literacy Research

Emma M. Howes

Perhaps the best advice I received about beginning archival research in composition and rhetoric (or any discipline, for that matter) was to get to know your archivists as their vast knowledge of their collections far surpasses that of any online searches. With this advice in mind, my dissertation research on company-sponsored literacies in the lives of Appalachian women working in the textile mills of North and South Carolina from 1880 to 1920 has included dozens of emails to archives across the Eastern Seaboard. For the most part, I have used a basic template to address these archives, introducing myself as a graduate researcher affiliated with the University of Massachusetts, describing my project and the kinds of texts I hope to find in the collections, and referencing a few texts I have found on my own that seem promising at each institution. These requests are typically met with a fairly predictable response, with archivists suggesting items within their collections as well as other archives to check out: polite, simple, often somewhat unmemorable in the first few correspondences. In fact, I had begun to feel as though I had mastered this art of archive-speak until my search for the literacy artifacts of Appalachian mill women introduced me to Leon.

The request began as they all do; my recent work with the Young Women's Christian Association Collection at Smith College had led me to examine mills in Greenville, South Carolina, which were often larger than

North Carolina mills and located within the Appalachian region itself. In addition, many of the mills in South Carolina instituted formal welfare work to socialize workers from rural areas to middle-class values and lifestyles. The owners provided classes in literacy, cooking, housekeeping, and sewing, among other subjects, to create a more efficient and productive workforce.[1] Welfare work, which drew on nineteenth-century ideologies of paternalism and benevolence, covered a wide range of educational and social programs targeting industrial workers. According to Andrea Tone, these programs were economic and social investments made by industry owners to thwart government intervention into the living and working conditions of factory workers. In addition, as Lori Ginzberg states: "Charitable enterprises provided some cushion for the poor in the form of material goods, temporary shelter, small subsidies, and the care of children even as the benevolent urged the poor to conform to the tenets that would ostensibly raise them from their current condition."[2] For these reasons, welfare work both was radical in its charitable contributions to industrial communities and contributed to the conditions that made industrial exploitation possible.

I hoped to investigate how literacy campaigns played into these conditions. On the basis of my research at Smith, I hoped that the belief in the value of welfare work expressed by South Carolina mill owners such as Thomas Parker, coupled with a higher percentage of workers from the mountains employed by the state's mills, would increase my chances of finding documents produced by Appalachian women workers, the Holy Grail that eluded me. With this in mind, I began a new email campaign, looking first for textile museums that might provide information on welfare work and literacy practices of female workers. My search led me to the Greenville Textile Heritage Society, a group whose Web site seemed like a promising lead. I promptly wrote my email and sent it off.

A few days later, I received a response from Leon Neal, a retired aerospace research engineer born in 1938 in the mill village of Caroleen, North Carolina, and raised there. My email had been forwarded to him; he is a local historian with a vested interest in the mills owing to his family's roots as workers in the industry. Until this point in my research, I had little contact with living people who had occupied the spaces I studied; the archives provided me with voices from the mills, but they were disembodied and often belonged to administrators or welfare workers. Leon's direct connection was exciting as I knew I needed insider sources to help fill out the long-lost experiences of workers from the late nineteenth century and the early twentieth.[3] As icing on the cake, Leon's family was from Rutherford County, North Carolina, along the edge of the state's Appalachian region as defined by the Appalachian Regional Commission. It was Leon's grandmothers that my project sought to study.

Leon proclaimed in his email:

> I am extremely PROUD of my cotton mill village heritage and as a "lay historian" I spend quite a bit of time on activities we hope will help to preserve a "more balanced" historical view of life in Southern cotton mill villages. (Note: I know that the vast majority of written materials about this life is biased to the point of being false primarily because it was written by outsiders who did not really understand the cotton mill workers, their lives, and their work—i.e. labor workers, academics, Yankee visitors who knew nothing of what they saw, and others[.] The mill workers themselves were too busy living and working to spend time writing about their lives.) So you can see that I am "prejudiced." I cannot imagine a more "Camelot" place for a boy to grow up than my cotton mill village.

He positioned himself as a writer of insider mill history, expressing from the start concerns about the way in which southern mill workers were historically written about as passive because they worked long hours in bad conditions but often resisted unionization. He continued, giving me his list of suggested reading, prefacing it by saying: "To even begin to try to understand the textile workers you have chosen to study—female or male—you should begin by trying to understand who these people were—how they thought—what was their heritage—and how did they 'feel.' If you do not understand the people then any attempt to understand what they wrote is bound to produce errors."[4]

For a moment I was taken aback. I agreed with Leon's sentiments but was surprised to be clumped into a group of researchers—academic carpetbaggers, of sorts—who came into the region as outsiders and produced biased histories that "tend[ed] to 'look down on' the Southern cotton mill workers."[5] While Leon was terribly kind in responding and in his generous suggestions for books, he was also very protective of a people, a time, and a place—his people, time, and place—traditionally portrayed in a negative light by researchers from outside the mill community.

The institutionalized outsider view of mill workers referenced by Leon is exemplified in the writings of Lillian Long, who served as a YWCA secretary in charge of textile mill operations in the early twentieth century. Organizations like the YWCA offered their services in the tradition of benevolence, a practice of middle- and upper-class white women framed in the late nineteenth century as "a responsibility to control the poor and 'vagrant.'"[6] This work was gendered, raced, and classed, institutionalized by organizations like the YWCA as an outlet for young women with college educations.[7] The YWCA in particular also associated benevolent work with the Christian duty of young women to help those less fortunate and spread Christian gospel. Long and others supported the well-cited ideologies that industrialization would provide a "cure" for the "mountain problem," defined as rural white poverty and the "frontier ways" of women, men, and children from the Southern Appalachians.[8] In this way, southern industrialization and the welfare work that supported the socialization of workers were viewed as moral and spiritual movements, positioning mills as "divine institution[s] . . . established that people might find themselves and be found."[9] Without outside intervention, the mill worker was merely a social and economic problem; it was only through cultivation that the "Anglo-Saxon stock" of the perceived population could be fully realized.[10] Conjuring the identity of the mountaineer in documents about southern mills invoked the literary figure made popular in nineteenth-century local-color and travel writing and created an ideological atmosphere justifying the exploitation of a people and a place.[11]

It was no wonder that Leon was concerned about my work. While more recent scholarship on mills has attempted to create more balanced views of mill life and workers, researchers still have a tendency to bring their own biases into their work, an accusation that echoes methodological writings on feminist theory.[12] I took a couple of hours to respond to Leon's email, my stomach reflecting my nervousness as I went over in my head what to say to align myself as an ally. I imagined my grandfather's resistance to northern liberal academics; born in Gaston County, North Carolina, and raised in Salem, Virginia, he would just as easily have expressed the same disillusionment and, in fact, did so every time Ted Kennedy came on the television. Leon had read my email, which used formal language and identified me as an academic from Massachusetts, positioning me within a group of whom he was weary: "outsiders who did not really understand the cotton mill workers, their lives, and their work." In addition, almost all the sources I had thus far collected were research he understood as "biased to the point of being false." While I knew that most texts I encountered were highly political, I had found little to counter them. I was growing excited. Had I finally found an in to a community I had not yet been able to fully access because of my geographic position? And had he just called me, a native of Richmond, Virginia, a Yankee?

Leon represented the first time I was faced with the direct accountability of researching a group of people; a man born and raised in a company town whose fond memories of his life there complicated many traditional academic readings of the space. My understanding of feminist methodology had prepared me to always consider the way in which I represented the bodies in my studies, contextualizing and historicizing them within the social spaces they inhabited, and seeking agency and resistance within the spaces of oppression.[13] But it would take a lot for me to use the term *Camelot* to describe a company town, my Marxist training kicking in, screaming "false consciousness." Whether Leon's motivation was the protection of his community or a reflection of his childhood memories, it felt as if there was a gorge between the two of us, and I had to find the middle ground.

Leon's claims were not made in isolation. Articles such as "Ah, Sweet Paternalism" point out the luxuries of the company town of Wheelwright, a model mining town in the Kentucky mountains that provided extraordinary amenities to workers and is frequently painted with the heavy colors of nostalgia in the memories those who lived under the care of the company.[14] Wheelwright was a unique place in the amount of resources it offered to workers, falling on a broad spectrum of welfare work that made it difficult to generalize about company town life in the South.[15] How do we, as researchers, navigate the space between the shining accounts that appear of company town life and the reality of worker exploitation that we have often been so well trained to uncover and condemn? Where is the space for the happy mill worker, relieved to move from the constant manual labor of farming in the mountains? And what do we do with the highly exploited laborer, the child laborer, and the harsh working and living conditions only a few miles away?

The extraordinary diversity of experiences within the mills makes it necessary to consider that, while many workers were exploited, many also benefited from the resources offered by mill welfare work, especially in model company towns. In this chapter, I reflect on the challenge of representing lives that are not easy to categorize, experiences that are "both/and" more than they are "either/or." Leon's "Camelot" village was very real for him and likely many others, though he occupied a different subject position there than the women I study would have. His comments highlight the complexity of representing working-class experiences as well as doing research on close-knit communities, characterizations of which by outside writers often offering an image that was hurtful and politically motivated. The challenge of writing ethically and critically of the past was one with which I had been brought face-to-face, and the face that was staring me down was ready to hold its ground.

The Literate, the Illiterate, and Everything in Between

As I sat in my library carrel, Leon's email also brought to mind questions manifesting my biggest fear: the fact that few literacy artifacts from the mills remain that were produced by female operatives during the early days of industrialization. Fairly low literacy rates have generally been attributed to southern textile mill towns, rates defined through deficits in ways similar to (and in some cases directly related to) the way in which rates for the Appalachian region generally are defined. But scholars of literacy history remind us that portraits of illiteracy were often perpetuated to emphasize ideological creations of difference, especially in the nineteenth century.[16] For example, Peter Mortensen's recovery work on literacy rates during the early twentieth century suggests that numbers in the mountains of Kentucky and Virginia were roughly comparable to those throughout the southern states in the 1900 census (18–23 percent in select counties compared to 16.44 percent in the South and 7.7 percent nationally). In contrast, rates within the region were considered much higher in the imaginations of many middle-class Americans; even the Southern Education Board estimated the illiteracy rate of Appalachia to reach an inflated 50–65 percent during the same time period.[17]

While similar statistics are not immediately available for mill communities—and likely varied greatly between them—these numbers allow us to consider the way in which conceptualizations of particular groups as literate or not by outsiders (and those within the community) are not entirely based in experience. Instead, they are heavily tainted by the formation of a hierarchical social space. As white Appalachians and mill workers were framed by public opinion around the turn of the century as Anglo-Saxons who therefore had the *potential* to be productive members of society, they were simultaneously Othered as premodern and superstitious, needing the modernization of settlement schools, industrial labor, and welfare work to transition from primitive frontier ways to more appropriate town lifestyles.

Schooled literacy campaigns were seen as a critical part of this socialization process. Literacy classes, reading rooms, libraries, and other educational efforts encouraged workers and their families to see the world through the eyes of the consumer class, teaching girls and women to can as well as to cook with foods bought from the company store.[18] The inaccuracies Leon cited in the literature on mill town life, including some portraits of (il)literacy and ignorance, raised money within organizations like the YWCA to support mill welfare work. But, as Krista Bryson and Erica Abrams Locklear point out in their analyses of Cora Wilson Stewart's portraits of illiteracy in the Kentucky mountains, while those portraits raised money for educational efforts to support literacy learning in the region, they also perpetuated stereotypes and simplified the experiences of those living there.[19]

Uncovering ways in which literacies that were sponsored by the mills and those that workers brought with them circulated within company towns allows us to further understand how literacies affect conceptions of identity and work as a resource for people in spaces of transition. While there is no doubt that there were nonliterate as well as literate people in mill towns, if we understand literacy as a resource for textual navigation and manipulation and are guided by questions within the New Literacy Studies "to understand how language functions in society," we open historical exploration to a broader range of literacies and literacy events.[20] Preliminary research illustrates traces of literacy events connected to homes in some company towns, including the presence of handwritten notes to supervisors and written family records in Bibles as well as references to mail order catalogs and magazines.[21] In addition, the records of Lillian Long and others indicate that literacy learning and exposure to texts were at least nominally a large aspect of work by organizations such as the YWCA in mills including Monaghan, near Greenville, South Carolina.[22] Thus, we see that texts were in fact circulating within the living spaces of women, men, and children in southern mills, including written notes, family records, and mass-circulating catalogs; what remain to be examined are the ways in which workers interacted with these texts, consuming and producing artifacts that stood to either reinscribe or rewrite social conditions for women and their families.

Although the material reality of working-class white women in mill villages between 1880 and 1920 varied from mill to mill, it was likely one of near-constant labor for many women as those engaged in paid labor in the mills were faced with not only eleven-hour workdays but also housework.[23] While estimates inevitably differed from household to household—and likely from day to day—the Women's Bureau in 1926 suggested that women in the mills spent an additional unpaid three hours a day doing housework.[24] In a short essay published by the Affiliated Schools for Workers in 1936, a northern operative reports of her southern counterparts that married women performed housework before and after work without such "conveniences" as a kitchen sink.[25] It is clear that women operatives likely had little time to produce (or consume) large numbers of texts. And, of the texts they did produce, few archives were interested in preserving the artifacts of working-class women and men until the 1970s—almost a century after the start of the South's industrial boom in 1880—making them unlikely to be found in academic archives and all the more difficult to track down.

With so little textual evidence remaining, how can we study women whose voices have not survived history in a manner accessible to archival research? Further, what kind of study can one form from the crossfire of the highly ideological texts that do exist? Leon's initial email highlights clashes that have haunted mill labor history in the South and the formation of the Southern Appalachian region as a whole: the tensions between the southern rural white worker and the northern (white) academic or industrialist, the insider and the outsider, the producer and the consumer. Since the mill boom of 1880, labor historians have bounced between claims that the mills were the salvation of the poor rural white and claims that their oppressive working conditions and exploitation trapped workers in a cycle of poverty.[26]

Ironically, both advocates and critics of the southern mills position mill workers as objects—empty vessels entering the industry devoid of their own culture (or at least devoid of a culture worth mentioning)—and in need of civilizing. They are the fatalities of industrialization whose voices and progressions are erased in history's narratives. But, as Cathy McHugh points out in her study of the Alamance Mills in North Carolina: "The southern cotton mill village was neither a world wholly created by the mill managers nor was it solely a community created by the cotton mill operatives."[27] Among research that is often one-sided, how do we find this middle ground as researchers, particularly as so many of our sources are, to use Leon's phrase, "biased to the point of being false"? Historical restoration work in literacy studies has previously turned to the writings of marginalized populations to give them voice, allowing them to (re)construct their own stories through their own literacy events.[28] As these kinds of texts are currently unavailable to unveil the voices of mill women, how might we navigate the ideological divide of the texts that do remain?

Expanding Notions of Literacy and Identity: A Materialist Feminist Lens

To address the intricacies of representation introduced by Leon's emails, I propose the use of a materialist feminist lens to allow historiographers of literacies to honor the lived complexity of ideologically defined identities like that of the Southern Appalachian mill worker and address the limited sources available to reconstruct the lives of working-class women, men, and children. It is a premise of materialist feminism (and Marxist thought) that "meeting human needs is the baseline for history" and that "human needs have an individual, corporeal dimension [in that they aim to keep the body alive] and a social one in that meeting them is always a historical, collective practice."[29] If we consider literacies to be a resource for meeting social and material needs, then studying how they are produced and distributed through literacy sponsorship raises questions about who benefits from education campaigns and what is at stake in this distribution. Further, in highlighting literacy sponsorship as an exchange, we can explore the gray areas in which literacy learning improves lives at the same time that it can disrupt them.[30]

A materialist feminist lens also encourages us to further uncover the uneven impact of industrialization on women who labor both within and outside the home, highlighting how all lives are affected by capitalist economics. As welfare work targeted Appalachian women in mill communities and strove to perform the duty of socializing them to town life, literacy campaigns spoke to larger Progressive social movements that believed the increase in cultural capital from formal schooling would create better workers and better citizens in the industrializing United States.[31] By exploring literacy in relation to mill women, we can honor the rich mill village heritage of Leon's memories while contextualizing it in capitalist development.

We can see this shift to explore mill village and working-class culture in historical studies and labor history in the work of Jacqueline Dowd Hall, David Carlton, and many others studying southern mills beginning in the 1980s. Drawing data primarily from a large number of oral histories collected as the Southern Oral History Project at the University of North Carolina at Chapel Hill as well as from other labor archives, these researchers uncovered the presence of a working-class culture within mills as well as "day-to-day resistance" to mill policies. Carlton points out, however, that some of this work "reduce[s] the mill to an irrelevance, except for its role as aggressor and repressor," shifting the pendulum as researchers continue to work through how to rewrite industrial relations.[32] These studies make clear the difficulty in finding an academic middle ground, though they certainly provide a strong base for future research in their thorough treatment of life in the mill village. Closer study of the allocation of literacy within mill villages may bring us toward this middle ground, examining how literacy learning brought positive opportunities as well as normalizing ideological positions, complicating further the binaries that continue to haunt historical representations of these spaces and those living and working within them.

When we expand our notions of literacies to incorporate the New Literacy Studies theories, new aspects of life in mill villages are opened for exploration. This is possible when literacy becomes a resource—a tool for achieving particular goals—as opposed to a skill that one does or does not possess.[33] Questions of literacy are seldom forwarded in the studies and oral histories referenced above past the number of years of schooling women received and whether they could *read* and/or *write*, terms difficult to tease out. In this way, we have very limited access to the textual lives of women workers, but careful examinations of their stories may present literacy events to explicate ways in which texts affected their lives. Literacy and literacy campaigns within southern mill villages have remained mostly unexamined since the turn within literacy studies in the 1980s to focus on the ideological basis of literacies.[34] The work of Shirley Brice Heath is an exception, presenting a powerful ethnographic study examining home and schooled literacy practices in a Carolina Piedmont mill town after the closing of the mill itself.[35] Heath identifies multiple literacies based on race, gender, and class within the Piedmont communities she studies, including the highly contextual, community-oriented nature of the literacies in the neighborhood of Trackton, which is made up of working-class African Americans. If we look past census data, years of schooling, or self-perceptions of (il)literacy and utilize Heath's expanded notions of literacy to include reading and interpreting price tags at the local store and identifying food labels, we may be surprised by the richness of women's textual lives within company towns.[36] Although Heath does not explicitly use a materialist feminist lens, her work offers a jumping-off point for studying literacy within the lives of previously passed-over populations. When we reexamine oral histories or archived documents for the presence of literacy events, we must remember that such events have a wide array of manifestations, including communal reading and writing and extracurricular literate practices such as record keeping and private writing.[37]

In addition, a materialist feminist lens offers a rich vocabulary with which to discuss the distribution of resources that Brandt identifies as literacy sponsorship.[38] It allows us to foreground how literacies meet human needs—physical, social, and affectual. If we understand distribution to be intentional, we can better understand *why* particular sponsors target particular groups and what they hope to gain through these relationships.[39] In this way, we can use resources surrounding the historical context of a given place and time to better understand how literacies were conceptualized and distributed.[40] Materialist feminism also allows us to take our understanding of women's pivotal role in the development and implementation of capitalist economics—performing the "invisible work" of reproducing labor power as well as "public work" in mills and other factories—and apply it to the significance of targeting women in welfare work as mill administration hoped that by changing households they could change groups of people.

Most significantly, materialist feminism allows us to consider the ways in which literacy sustained and forwarded the lives of women and their families during a time of tremendous economic and social change. We must reconceptualize women in company towns beyond passive consumers of the culture distributed by administration and welfare workers; they were also producers of a unique culture that included former ways of living and new opportunities and resources. The text boom of the late nineteenth century and the early twentieth illustrates the complexities of women's identities in the budding consumer capitalist society as the rise of mass-circulated texts aimed at selling household goods targeted women as household consumers.[41] But room also existed for women to be producers as they learned to read and write nontraditional texts, including the walls of their homes and, in the case of mill villages,[42] their yards, exhibiting manifestations of social class, or habitus.[43] Framing women as both consumers and producers of text (and culture) emphasizes the dialectic of knowledge production and the formation of the social world. This provides insight into the ways in which women exerted agency within spaces most often associated with oppression and exploitation.

One example is Ida Moore's Federal Writers Project interview with Kate Brumby, published in 1939. Brumby was a former mill worker whose family migrated from the Appalachian region of Virginia (Rockbridge County) and the foothills of North Carolina (Catawba County). When she was interviewed, she was in her home in an unnamed North Carolina mill village. She self-identified to Moore as "illiterate" early on, exemplifying a site where a materialist feminist lens can allow us to examine the lives of mill workers while seeking complexity in our representations. The handful of visual and alphabetic texts referenced in Brumby's company home make it apparent that texts circulated throughout the space, combining representations of popular culture icons such as Dick Powell with religious texts, including *Christian Psalms and Hymns,* a book belonging to Brumby's literate father.[44] We also find a Larkin mail-order catalog, *Comfort Magazine,* and a book of Sunday school lessons. The picture of Powell contrasts with Brumby's expressed belief that "picture shows" are the "Devil's territory," a belief likely bolstered by her religion. In this way, Brumby's home suggests the layering of multiple literacies that coexist in and cocreate her worldview.[45]

Moore's depiction records a number of literacy events, providing valuable information about how texts circulated within some mill homes. At first glance, the texts, including calendar pages, Christian scriptures, and popular mail-order catalogs, paint Brumby as a consumer of media, religion, and commodities. A Sunday school lesson ends the interview, stating that peace comes from the Lord, not knowledge, wine, or material wealth. Moore's positioning of this revelation leaves us with an image of Brumby and her community as content and uncritical of their lives in the shadow of the mill and its cronies. But a materialist feminist lens that focuses on the ways in which literacy meets the needs of mill workers shifts emphasis to the complexity of Brumby's interactions with texts. This grants her agency in creating space within a space that has been created for her.[46]

The presence of the Larkin catalog and *Comfort Magazine* offers another rich moment to analyze. Both were popular national circulars aimed at influencing the consumption patterns of rural populations. Larkin encouraged bulk consumption of home goods by offering incentives to groups or individuals who purchased larger quantities of its products.[47] We see hints of this as Brumby's neighbor, Rosa, introduces Larkin into the home with the expressed goal of getting enough orders from the community to get herself a rug.[48] In its early years, *Comfort* also provided free or discounted items in exchange for subscriptions, rewarding customers for contributing to the database of consumers created by the magazine's founder.[49] Increased consumption was encouraged by publishers, who clearly understood their social role in modernizing rural homes by the introduction of appliances and gadgets.[50] The appliances women like Brumby and Rosa acquired through these catalogs were instrumental in cutting down the time they spent on housework. Thus, the rise of consumer culture in the early twentieth century commoditized needs, tying the population to wage labor at the same time that it introduced new technologies that made many aspects of life easier, especially for women and within the domestic space.

The literacy events surrounding the circulation of these two texts are community events that occur when a particular text brings members of a group together for the purpose of textual production and/or consumption. Rosa, for example, assists the illiterate Brumby and her adult son in navigating the Larkin catalog, while Brumby's daughter, Jessie, reads to her from *Comfort*.[51] Community literacy events are associated with the Appalachian region, especially working-class communities, and are frequently gendered female.[52] Thus, they provide a glimpse at how communities in which not all members are fully literate circulate texts, learning from each other how to navigate the catalog to meet individual and group needs. As community members move through the pages of the text, they gain access to particular social spaces that define middle-class habitus they may choose to purchase and display.[53] Although Brumby may not *read* alphabetic text in the Larkin catalog, she and her son navigate the pages to find items with the help of Rosa; multiple members of the community participate in the event of reading the text and writing down orders for the commodities advertised within the pages of the mailer. The catalog therefore serves as a reading primer for Brumby. Surrounded by her community and family, the former mill worker gains access to text as well as consumer capitalism, encouraged to resee her surroundings in the colors of the catalog's rugs. The expansion of the print industry and the accumulation of workers within company towns created new needs for appliances, store-bought foods, clothing, and other material items that working families no longer had the time or the energy to make at home.

The presence of *Comfort Magazine* allows us to expand the notion of literacy as a tool for meeting needs past the material and into the realm of affect. The stated purpose of the circular was to "simplify life" by providing goods to a readership of primarily rural women. In addition to striving to save women time through modern appliances and gadgets, the magazine was known for weaving its advertisements into stories emphasizing the characters' comfort and ease. For example, in a story from 1932, a man hurts himself slipping on ice, only to discover his wife just bought an insurance plan that will pay for his doctor's bills. The story appears next to an ad for an insurance agency.[54] Using a materialist feminist lens, we can read this placement alongside the publication's purpose as connecting literacy, consumption, and affectual needs, which Rosemary Hennessy suggests are outlawed in a capitalist economy. Within the structure of capitalism, worker energy is sold as labor power instead of being invested in developing human potential and responding to the affectual needs of individuals. Hennessy's analysis suggests that the constructions of desire in advertising during the late nineteenth century and the early twentieth responded to the outlawing of affective needs when industrial methods of production and the commodification of needs became hallmarks of American capitalism.[55] The rerouting of energy resulting from new forms of labor left a deficit in the ability of workers to realize their human potential, subsequently filled by consumer capitalism through commodity consumption. In this way, we might imagine how the "sentimental tales of struggles between characters who were all good or all evil" might provide a level of comfort for readers, especially as the magazine furnished access to products that quelled its readers' anxieties.[56]

The role of the mill itself is not entirely clear in the interview with Brumby, and the piece's later time period suggests that it took place by the early 1920s, after the end of most welfare programs.[57] Thus, while we may not be able to draw immediate conclusions from this interview in relation to the mill-sponsored literacies of early welfare work, we can begin to construct an image of mill women as both consumers and producers, benefiting from mill village resources even as their surplus labor resulted in the largely unshared profits of mill administration. Tracing how literacies circulated within mill villages through communal textual encounters with catalogs and calendar pages complicates the ways in which life in company towns has traditionally been conceived. It rewrites the common creation of the villages as shut off from outside influence even as this influence may have been limited. In addition, we should consider not only women's roles within industrial and consumer capitalism but also how access to literacies both bolstered aspects of their oppression (consider the Sunday school lesson that ends the interview) and allowed them to access technologies to meet their material and affectual needs. The distribution (or lack thereof) of literacy has long been understood as a potential source of the reinscription of social inequality, but the grassroots circulation of texts in Brumby's home encourages us to look deeper into the experiences of the (il)literate to find the experiences that resist this violence.[58] The resistance illustrated in the excess of textual presence in Brumby's home and daily experiences speaks to Leon's resistance, which asserted the mill village experience as one that was almost utopic, in great contrast to most academic and historical records.

To Revisit a Place, a Time, and a People

It has been quite some time since Leon's first email. Since then I have met him and his wife in North Carolina, where he gave me not only innumerable references on mill history, both material and textual, but also several recommendations for BBQ along the way. After extensive questioning, I think I finally convinced him that I was, in fact, not entirely a Yankee and that my interest in dialogue was genuine. My inbox has ever since been visited by his messages checking up on my progress. He has in many ways turned into a mill fairy godfather, a voice of nostalgia bringing its own biases that counter my own. To my delight, Leon enthusiastically accepted my request to include quotes from his emails in this chapter, eager to join in the conversation around the (re)construction of textile mill town and Appalachian literacies. He has been reading and writing mill history for decades, publishing his essays in textile heritage newsletters that rewrite history from the grassroots level. The resources he has accumulated throughout his lifetime equate to several volumes on the subject, and, though most of his offerings speak to a time period long after the one I study, I feel incredibly fortunate to have access to them and to Leon himself. His eagerness, however, makes the silences in my own archival findings speak even louder, as the women of the early mills are only peripherally represented in the resources kept formally in institutional archives and informally by historians like Leon. While this is not to say that these resources do not exist somewhere, it begs the question of feminist work to reconstruct missing histories as we seek avenues through which populations with fewer resources than Leon has can speak.

As this volume illustrates, there is growing interest in work to reread and reconstruct historical and contemporary Appalachian literacies as scholars try to better understand how language circulates and functions in the everyday lives of women, men, and children who have traditionally been positioned against the march of industrial and consumer capitalism. This move adds to the complex formation of socially ascribed difference in the post–Civil War United States: that of the white Others, the mountaineers, the hillbillies, the white trash, the grannies, the clay eaters, the southern highlanders, the lint heads, not to mention the populations of African American, Jewish, Native American, and other Appalachians often erased entirely by historical accounts of the region.[59] Materialist feminism offers tools for understanding the ways in which literacies were distributed to these populations even as textual evidence of how literacies were used may prove limited. As much of my current archival work has unearthed documents primarily relating to attitudes toward teaching literacy to workers from the perspectives of mill administrators and welfare workers, my understanding of literacy campaigns as the selective distribution of a resource allows me not only to think about how this resource may have affected the experiences of women like Brumby but also to assess how literacy sponsorship figured into industrial methods of production to create better workers and better citizens.

Given the social and labor history of the Southern Appalachians and Piedmont mills, where literacy has been framed in terms of deficit, it is important to seek the ways in which sponsorship campaigns are both exploitative and liberatory. Thus, campaigns likely increased some opportunities even as they may have failed to significantly change the economic and social conditions of the lives of some literacy learners. There is a particular sense of urgency in uncovering the stories of women thus situated, seeking ways in which they utilized literacies as resources for speaking back to these representations and the oppressions they came into contact with, creating their own sense of identity and culture that no doubt was in conversation with larger social portraits. Even as textual resources to accomplish these goals may be few and far between, historicizing and contextualizing literacy sponsorship in ways that complicate literacy distribution as inseparable from capitalist development create a fuller view of what it means for literacy to be seen as a resource, for better and for worse. In other words, as literacy distribution is in conversation with the distribution of other resources and forms of capital, it is an act that should be critiqued as it is welcomed. We must ask what sponsors intend to gain, as Brandt suggests, at the same time that we recognize the potential literacies have to empower learners.

Mill villages in the Piedmont and Southern Appalachian regions were similar to other company towns throughout Appalachia: though they provided some material comforts, resources were accessed at a cost. The New Literacy Studies have recognized for decades that literacies and how they circulate are *never* apolitical. In more recent work on literacy sponsorship, researchers are asked to seek the ways in which participants in literacy transmission interact with larger institutional forces, questioning the exchange of capital when literacy sponsors enter communities. In recognizing the transmission of literacy as an exchange within capitalist economies, we complicate literacy sponsorship to include gains and losses of literacy sponsors and literacy learners, whose relationship with reading, writing, and the worldviews that accompany taking on new literacies is ultimately complex. Particularly when the voices we seek are difficult to locate, by examining the texts available using a materialist feminist lens we can begin to unearth bits and pieces of the relationships that have developed historically between women and literacy sponsors in an effort to historicize and contextualize literacies in the lives of working women.

Notes

I thank the Sallie Bingham Center at Duke University for its sponsorship through the Mary Lilly Research Grant and the American Association of University Women for its support through the American Fellowship program. In addition, I thank the archivists and assistants at Smith College's Sophia Smith Collection, the University of North Carolina's Southern History Collection and North Carolina Collection, Duke University's Rubenstein Library and Sallie Bingham Center, Leon Neal, the Greenville Textile Heritage and Monaghan Mills Historical Societies, the Textile Heritage Center at Cooleemee, and the South Carolina Room at the Hughes Main Library in Greenville.

1. Jacqueline Dowd Hall, Robert Korstad, and James Leloudis, "Cotton Mill People: Work, Community, and Protest in the Textile South, 1880–1940," *American Historical Review* 91 (1986): 245–86; Thomas Parker, "The South Carolina Cotton Mill Village: A Manufacturer's View," *South Atlantic Quarterly* 9 (1910): 349–57.

2. Andrea Tone, *The Business of Benevolence: Industrial Paternalism in Progressive America* (Ithaca, NY: Cornell University Press, 1997); Lori D. Ginzberg, *Women and the Work of Benevolence: Morality, Politics, and Class in the Nineteenth-Century United States* (New Haven, CT: Yale University Press, 1990), 216.

3. Nancy Naples breaks down the insider/outsider binary that often makes invisible the complexities of human interactions by suggesting that neither researchers nor participants ever wholly hold one position or the other within communities. See Nancy Naples, "The Outsider Phenomenon," in *Feminist Perspectives on Social Research,* ed. Sharlene Nagy Hesse-Biber and Michelle L. Yaiser (New York: Oxford University Press, 2004), 373–81, 373, 376. However, I still use the insider/outsider reference to indicate that my geographic and cultural position is different from those of the women I study. My own identity as a southern white woman attending graduate school in a northern state stands to complicate the simplicity of this binary as I have roots in North Carolina textile counties, although my immediate family no longer lives there.

4. Leon Neal, email message to author, February 13, 2012.

5. Ibid.

6. Ginzberg, *Women and the Work of Benevolence,* 5.

7. Mrs. A. P. Potter, *The College Girl's Mission* (Chicago: International Committee

of Young Women's Christian Associations, ca. 1892–1901), 5, YWCA Papers, Sophia Smith Collection, Smith College, Northampton, MA.

8. *Suggestions for Southern Cotton Mill Policies* (New York: National Board of the YWCA of the USA, 1908), 7–8, YWCA Papers.

9. John W. Speake quoted in Lois MacDonald, *Southern Mill Hills: A Study of Social and Economic Forces in Certain Textile Mill Villages* (New York: Astoria, 1928), 17.

10. Wilma Dunaway rightly situates the focus of studies of the Appalachian region on white populations as "the ultimate act of academic and journalistic racism." Wilma Dunaway, *Women, Work, and Family in the Antebellum Mountain South* (New York: Cambridge University Press, 2008), 3. This racism is also, I suggest, reflected in the historic construction of the region's populations as Anglo-Saxon. The rhetorical and material constructions of whiteness allow us to consider the ways in which the southern mill industry and its primarily white workers were ideologically positioned in the region during the late nineteenth century and the early twentieth, when white hegemony struggled to regain power after the Civil War and Reconstruction. For additional scholarship on whiteness, Anglo-Saxon identity, and Appalachia, see Henry Shapiro, *Appalachia on Our Mind: The Southern Mountaineers in the American Consciousness, 1870–1920* (Chapel Hill: University of North Carolina Press, 1978); and Allan Batteau, *The Invention of Appalachia* (Tucson: University of Arizona Press, 1990). Allen Tullos's *Habits of Industry: White Culture and Transformation of the Carolina Piedmont* (Chapel Hill: University of North Carolina Press, 1989) more directly addresses the southern mill industry.

11. Alan Banks, "Class Formation in the Southeastern Kentucky Coalfields, 1890–1920," in *Appalachia in the Making: The Mountain South in the Nineteenth Century*, ed. Mary Beth Pudup, Dwight B. Billings, and Altina L. Waller (Chapel Hill: University of North Carolina Press, 1995), 321–46, 322.

12. For a brief review of more balanced accounts of mill life and workers, see David Carlton, "Paternalism and Southern Textile Labor," in *Race, Class, and Community in Southern Labor History*, ed. Gary Finks and Merl E. Reed (Tuscaloosa: University of Alabama Press, 1994), 17–26; and Neal, email message to author, February 13, 2012. For feminist perspectives on researchers' biases, see Gayatri Chakravorty Spivak, "Can the Subaltern Speak?" in *The Post-Colonial Studies Reader*, ed. Bill Ashcroft, Gareth Griffiths, and Helen Tiffin (New York: Routledge, 2006), 271–311; and Katherine Kelleher Sohn, *Whistlin' and Crowin' Women of Appalachia: Literacy Practices since College* (Carbondale: Southern Illinois University Press, 2006).

13. Chandra Mohanty, "'Under Western Eyes' Revisited: Feminist Solidarity through Anticapitalist Struggles," in *Feminism without Borders: Decolonizing Theory, Practicing Solidarity* (Durham, NC: Duke University Press, 2003), 221–51.

14. Valerie Honeycutt Spears, "Ah, Sweet Paternalism!" *Appalachian Journal* 34, no. 1 (2006): 4–5.

15. Harriet Herring, *Welfare Work in Mill Villages: The Story of Extra-Mill Activities in North Carolina* (Chapel Hill: University of North Carolina Press, 1929).

16. Peter Mortensen, "Representations of Literacy and Region: Narrating 'Another America,'" in *Pedagogy in the Age of Politics: Writing and Reading (in) the Academy*, ed. Patricia Sullivan and Donna Qualley (Urbana, IL: National Council of Teachers of English, 1994), 100–120, 106, 112; Katrina Powell, *The Anguish of Displacement: The Politics of Literacy in Letters of Mountain Families in Shenandoah National Park* (Charlottesville: University of Virginia Press, 2007), 12.

17. Mortensen, "Representations of Literacy and Region," 106, 108. It is immediately necessary to remember that what counts as literate activity has varied greatly over many centuries, making it necessary to contextualize census and other forms of data as well as recognize that the definition of *literacy* can include some reading, some writing, or very little at all, depending on the purpose of the tally being taken. In her study of working-class literacies in North Carolina, Shirley Brice Heath reminds us that literate practices can be thought of as including functional literacy events, such as reading price tags in a store, and can be communal. See Shirley Brice Heath, *Ways with Words: Language, Life and Work in Communities and Classrooms* (New York: Cambridge University Press, 1983). See also Anita Puckett, "'Let the Girls Do the Spelling and Dan Will Do the Shooting,'" *Anthropological Quarterly* 65, no. 3 (July 1992): 137–47; and Sohn, *Whistlin' and Crowin' Women of Appalachia*.

18. Hall, Korstad, and Leloudis, "Cotton Mill People."

19. Bryson, chapter 2 in this volume; Erica Abrams Locklear, *Negotiating a Perilous Empowerment: Appalachian Women's Literacies* (Athens: Ohio University Press, 2011), 32.

20. Deborah Brandt, *Literacy in American Lives* (New York: Cambridge University Press, 2001); Rosemary Hennessy, *Profit and Pleasure* (New York: Routledge, 2000), 98–99; Powell, *The Anguish of Displacement*, 7.

21. "Notes," Cannon Mills Records, David M. Rubenstein Rare Book and Manuscript Library, Duke University; Evans Family Bible, Cannon Mills Records; Ida Moore, "A Day at Kate Brumby's House," in *These Are Our Lives: As Told by the People and Written by Members of the Federal Writers' Project of the Works Progress Administration in North Carolina, Tennessee, and Georgia* (Chapel Hill: University of North Carolina Press, 1939), 129–59.

22. Monaghan Scrapbook, YWCA Papers. Monaghan Mills was considered a model textile village, putting it on a par with towns like Wheelwright, Kentucky. It offers an excellent site to study the way in which literacy was thought to affect industrial workers through the well-documented views of Thomas Parker, the mill's owner and a supporter of classes for mill workers for better business, and Lillian Long, who supervised welfare programs through the YWCA. On the other hand, we must remember that Monaghan's status created a unique space with regard to the amount of time and money invested in programs for employees. Elizabeth Pearce Bilderback, "Women Welfare Workers in the South Carolina Textile Mills, 1890–1935" (master's thesis, University of South Carolina, 1993), 29.

23. I focus primarily on white women working in the mills from the Appalachian

region, but it is necessary to keep in mind that, until the mid-twentieth-century civil rights movement, African American women were also present, though often consigned to janitorial positions. Evidence based on reports from "colored" mills published in the journal *Durable-Durham Doings* during the year 1919 suggests that mills employing African Americans did exist in North Carolina (and, thus, elsewhere in the region). See Ardonia Norwood, "Durham Mill No. 2 (Colored): The Geo. D. Girls," *Durable-Durham Doings: Published Monthly by the Employees of the Durham Hosiery Mills* 1, no. 6 (July 15, 1919): 3.

24. Linda Jean Frankel, "Women, Paternalism, and Protest in a South Carolina Textile Community: Henderson, NC, 1900–1960" (Ph.D. diss., Harvard University, 1986), 104.

25. "Southern Mill Hands," in *I Am a Woman Worker: A Scrapbook of Autobiographies,* ed. Andria Taylor Hourwich and Gladys L. Palmer (New York: Affiliated Schools for Workers, 1936), 38.

26. MacDonald, *Southern Mill Hills,* 17; John Campbell, "The Mountain People and the Cotton Textile Industry of the South" (ca. 1908–1912), John C. Campbell and Olive D. Campbell Papers, Southern Historical Collection, University of North Carolina at Chapel Hill.

27. Cathy McHugh, *Mill Family: The Labor System in the Southern Cotton Textile Industry* (New York: Oxford University Press, 1998), 100.

28. For a few examples, see Jacqueline Jones Royster, *Traces of a Stream: Literacy and Social Change among African-American Women* (Pittsburgh: University of Pittsburgh Press, 2000); Kim Donehower, Charlotte Hogg, and Eileen Schell, *Rural Literacies* (Carbondale: Southern Illinois University Press, 2007); and Amy Goodburn, "Literacy Practices at the Genoa Indian School," *Great Plains Quarterly* 19, no. 1 (2000): 35–52.

29. Hennessy, *Profit and Pleasure,* 210.

30. Locklear, *Negotiating a Perilous Empowerment.*

31. Jenny Cook-Gumperz, "Literacy and Schooling: An Unchanging Equation?" in *The Social Construction of Literacy* (2nd ed.), ed. Jenny Cook-Gumperz (New York: Cambridge University Press, 2006), 19–49.

32. Carlton, "Paternalism and Southern Textile Labor," 21–22.

33. Brandt, *Literacy in American Lives,* 5.

34. For an interesting analysis of purchase records from homes in textile-mill and other working-class communities, see David Paul Nord, "Working-Class Readers, Family, Community, and Reading in Late Nineteenth-Century America," in *Communities of Journalism: A History of American Newspapers and Their Readers* (Urbana: University of Illinois Press, 2001), 225–45. However, Nord focuses not on texts themselves but on the amount of income spent buying magazines, newspapers, and books according to cost-of-living surveys from the period 1890–1891.

35. Although her work does not address company-sponsored literacy practices, Heath is notable as a scholar working in company towns and with former mill workers.

36. Heath, *Ways with Words,* 105, 191.

37. Moore, "A Day at Kate Brumby's House," 154.

38. Deborah Brandt, "Sponsors of Literacy," *College Composition and Communication* 49, no. 2 (1998): 165–85.

39. Brandt, *Literacy in American Lives,* 19–20; Donehower, Hogg, and Schell, *Rural Literacies,* 50.

40. See Jessica Enoch and Scott Wible, "Archival Encounters: Dealing with Absence," *Archival Encounters,* Webinar 4, Rhetoric Society of America, April 22, 2013.

41. Brandt, *Literacy in American Lives;* Helen Damon-Moore and Carl F. Kaestle, "Gender, Advertising, and Mass-Circulation Magazines," in *Literacy in the United States: Readers and Reading since 1880,* by Carl F. Kaestle, Helen Damon-Moore, Lawrence C. Stedman, Katherine Tinsley, and William Vance Trollinger Jr. (New Haven: Yale University Press, 1991), 245–71; Hennessy, *Profit and Pleasure.*

42. Competitions were held regularly in some villages for the best yards, gardens, and even babies to encourage hygiene, ownership of one's space, and a venue for mill administration and welfare workers to subtly encourage workers to conform to particular standards of living (see Harriet Herring, "Welfare Work in North Carolina," *Mill News,* February 18, 1909, Cone Mills Corp. Records, no. 5247, Southern Historical Collection, Wilson Library, University of North Carolina at Chapel Hill).

43. For a similar analysis of working-class homes, see Margaret Finders, *Just Girls: Hidden Literacies and Life in Junior High* (New York: Teachers College Press, 1997), 92–98.

44. *Christian Psalms and Hymns: To Aid in Public and Private Devotion, Selected and Arranged by Jasper Hazen* (Albany, NY: For the Association, 1849).

45. Moore, "A Day at Kate Brumby's House," 130–32, 148–50, 153, 158–59.

46. Ibid., 158–59.

47. "A Brief History of the Larkin Company," *The Larkin Collection,* n.d., http://www.monroefordham.org/Projects/Larkin/history.htm.

48. Moore, "A Day at Kate Brumby's House," 154. While the explicit relationship between the rug and Brumby's order is not clear, it is likely either that the women were members of a "Larkin Club," which was part of the company's layaway program, or that the rug was one of the premiums offered by the company as part of its branding. See "A Brief History of the Larkin Company."

49. Dorothy Steward Sayward, *Comfort Magazine, 1888–1942: A History and Critical Study* (Orono: University of Maine Press, 1960), 29.

50. Thomas Schlereth, "Country Stores, County Fairs, and Mail-Order Catalogues: Consumption in Rural America," in *Consuming Visions: Accumulation and Display of Goods in America, 1880–1920,* ed. Simon Bronner (New York: Norton, 1989), 339–75, 365–67, 372–73.

51. Moore, "A Day at Kate Brumby's House," 158.

52. See Puckett, "'Let the Girls Do the Spelling'"; Heath, *Ways with Words;* and Finders, *Just Girls.*

53. For a fuller analysis of a similar event (home interiors parties), see Finders, *Just Girls*, 92–98.

54. Sayward, *Comfort Magazine*, 26–27, 31–34.

55. Hennessy, *Profit and Pleasure*, 84, 208, 215–17.

56. *Comfort* got its start during the late nineteenth century as a venue for the sale of Oxien, an all-around medicine that relieved a large variety of symptoms, such as dyspepsia, nerves, lung problems, and rheumatism. Sayward, *Comfort Magazine*, 7, 12, 24.

57. Hall, Korstad, and Leloudis, "Cotton Mill People," 265–66.

58. Brandt, *Literacy in American Lives*. See also Elspeth Stuckey, *The Violence of Literacy* (Portsmouth, NH: Boynton/Cook, 1991).

59. Dunaway, *Women, Work, and Family*, 3.

4

The Transition to College for First-Generation Students from Extractive Industry Appalachia

Todd Snyder

Staring down at the empty Scantron bubble sheet, gripping my No. 2 pencil, I began to wonder what the hell I had gotten myself into. I don't remember the specific question, but I think it had something to do with photosynthesis. "Pick C, and go to the next one," I mumbled underneath my breath. Unfortunately, I didn't know the answer to the next question either. I wasn't sure how far picking C would get me, but, at that point, I was willing to take my chances. I had guessed my way through the math portion of the test, and now I was doing the same with science reasoning. By the time I made it to the last page, I caught myself daydreaming—thinking back to the "college talk" that occurred with my parents back in August.

My parents were clueless. I was clueless. We didn't know whether I was supposed to take the ACT or the SAT or both. Somebody had told my mother that applicants who did not earn a score of 18 on the ACT would be rejected by college admissions without further consideration. The thought of my intellectual worth, my opportunity to attend college, being quantified into a numerical value on a one-size-fits-all test was frightening. We, of course, didn't know whether the rumor was true or what specific measures needed to be taken to ensure my success. We were clueless but determined to figure it out. My parents suggested that I go speak with my high school guidance counselor. They had envisioned a future for me that none of us could fully understand.

Before I could make it through my prepared list of questions, the counselor, leaning back in his chair, interrupted me:

COUNSELOR: Todd, have you ever thought about vocational education?

17-YEAR-OLD ME: Uh, no. Not really.

COUNSELOR: Since it doesn't sound like you are 100 percent sure of what you want to do, you might want to think about vocational training. For instance, you could get a two-year welding certificate and be out in the workforce instead of racking up student loan debt or wasting your time changing majors. Just think, two years, and you are out there making money. Todd, some of these guys make a good living.

17-YEAR-OLD ME: Uh, I'm not really interested in stuff like that.

COUNSELOR: It's just a suggestion. Your dad has a good reputation as a worker. I bet your dad could probably get you on at the mines. Get you a good job up there with a two-year welding certificate. You could be out there making money. . . . You could settle down, buy you a home . . . have a real good life.

I share this memory not to suggest that my guidance counselor was a bad person or that he wasn't doing his job properly. There are thousands of Appalachian kids who have benefited from vocational training; they live happy and productive lives as welders and mechanics. I share this memory because my counselor's advice made me feel circumscribed. He had mistaken me for a welder, a coal miner—and it hurt. His advice made me feel trapped within a particular occupational history, as if I weren't college material. To him, I was the opposite of Shakespeare's young Henry V, not a prince falling short of his great potential, but a coal miner's son overreaching his academic abilities.

I finished the final section of the ACT early. It seemed like everyone else was still working. Maybe "Pick C, and go to the next one" had led me astray. Maybe the counselor was right. Maybe I shouldn't have been offended by his suggesting that I work with my hands. Standardized testing had long tried to convince me that I wasn't too adept at working with my mind. Part of me secretly hoped that I had just flunked the ACT and that my decision would be made. The other part of me didn't want to let my parents down and wasn't ready to pick up a dinner bucket and head to the mines.

College and Coal Country

For most first-generation college students from rural Appalachia, the process of preparing for and transitioning into college life is fraught with anxiety and indecision. The socioeconomic realities fostered by rural Appalachian extractive industry economies create an environment that is disadvantageous to success in the sink-or-swim world of higher education. Staying afloat, both academically and financially, can be quite difficult. These are students from poor coal-mining towns—areas marked by physical, cultural, and economic isolation. They are students considered to be at risk when the material circumstances of their lives are connected to academic retention. Missing from contemporary research on Appalachian college students is the cultural nuance that accurately demonstrates the social pressures these students face: the college talks Appalachian teenagers have with their parents, the guidance they receive from counselors, and the ways in which these conversations are affected by socioeconomic realities. We need to pay serious attention to the impact working-class extractive industry economies have on the educational attitudes and ambitions of Appalachian learners. The collegiate roadblocks these students overcome are not as visible as the mountains that surround their hometown communities. They are far more complex than figuring out the magic score they need on the ACT to get into college.

My educational journey is still something of a blur. I went from being a first-generation college student in September 2000 to teaching first-generation college students, as a graduate assistant, in September 2004. Seven years later, people started calling me Dr. Snyder, and I am still in the process of trying to figure out how it all came to be. Today, I teach at a private college in upstate New York, at a school I could never have afforded to attend, a school where my ACT score would likely have resulted in a rejection letter.

For me, college was a transformative experience. This is not to say that such a transformation is easy or painless. Looking back on my educational journey, I've come to understand many of my college literacy struggles as by-products of the extractive industry culture that defined my small-town Appalachian upbringing. I grew up in Webster County, West Virginia, a small coal-mining community located slightly east of the geographic center of the only state completely engulfed by the Appalachian Mountains. My being from Webster County directly affected the way I viewed and prepared for my college education; my surroundings served as both motivation and deterrent. The ways in which people from my hometown community addressed issues concerning college education, be they text-based literacy practices or sociocultural attitudes concerning postsecondary education, shaped my college literacy.

Coming to recognize my college anxieties, fears, and educational unpreparedness as symptomatic of the extractive industry economy that dictated the collective consciousness of my hometown was perhaps the most liberating of all my collegiate intellectual discoveries. Now that I am on the other side of the fence, so to speak, I feel a scholarly, and perhaps moral, obligation to share my experiences, and the experiences of other college students from my neck of the woods, with those concerned with issues of educational inequality. My aim in this chapter is to connect the Marxist notion that suggests our attitudes and ambitions are a reflection of the social structures surrounding our thinking to conversations about first-generation college students from rural Appalachia and the struggles they face when attempting to move from coal country to college.

Extractive Industry Appalachia: Economic Isolation and Cyclic Poverty

Pinpointing the role of the extractive industries in shaping the educational attitudes and aspirations of rural Appalachian college students is no easy task. Scholars have long debated the extent to which these industries have affected cultural norms in the region. Some have placed the blame for Appalachian socioeconomic inequality squarely at their feet. For example, in *Uneven Ground,* Ronald Eller works to connect post–World War II Appalachia's cultural woes to corporate greed.[1] Others, such as Crandall Shifflett in *Coal Towns,* have argued that, when compared to the pre–Industrial Revolution/ subsistence-farming days, life in Appalachia actually improved as a result of the extractive industries.[2] David Hsuing, in *Two Worlds in the Tennessee Mountains,* and Michael Montgomery, in "The Idea of Appalachian Isolation," suggest that Appalachian isolation has been exaggerated and misunderstood by scholars from a variety of disciplines.[3] In casting my oar into this Burkian parlor, I must humbly acknowledge my biased perspective. Mine was a childhood directly affected by the realities of extractive industry isolation.

No major interstates or highways pass through Webster County; the nearest airport is a good two-hour drive away, and there is one stoplight in the entire county. Children of Webster County do not grow up around major public libraries or college campuses. We do not frequent museums, movie theaters, or shopping malls. We live up hollers with our cousins, parents, and grandparents. We are born here, and we grow up believing here is where we belong. Our thinking in this regard is connected to the history and formation of our community—a history that is impossible to separate from that of the extractive industries.

Although the Appalachian Mountains are geographically to blame for the region's physical isolation, the extractive industries are largely responsible for both the formation and the preservation of the small communities that make up rural Appalachia. Until the late nineteenth century, much of Appalachia remained uninhabited, largely owing to the region's mountainous terrain. This would change when the entrepreneurial spirit of the Industrial Revolution brought extractive industry officials to the region at a record pace. Procuring the land and buying up mineral rights, early captains of Appalachian industry shaped the socioeconomic realities of life in the region. Before long, much of Appalachia, as it is today, was owned by outside corporations.

In the late nineteenth century, when coal, timber, and railroad companies fully began to recognize Appalachia's untapped natural resources, measures were taken to ensure a cheap and readily accessible workforce, a process eloquently described in Helen Matthews Lewis and Edward Knipe's "The Colonialism Model": "To house and serve these workers and their families, the mining companies, lumbering interests, and railroads built encampments for the newcomers. These *camps* or *colliery towns* [were] complete with company owned houses, stores, theatres, clinics, hospitals, and schools."[4]

This was an era in which extractive industries controlled every facet of life in small-town Appalachia, when workers were paid in company script that had to be spent at the company store. From an economic standpoint, the subjugation and domination of the Appalachian people were achieved and maintained through "corporate ownership of the majority of the land, effectively blocking other industries from entering the region in an attempt to maintain this part of Appalachia as a mono-economy." Over the years, "numerous scholars have referred to Central Appalachia as an 'internal colony' or 'internal periphery' created to provide cheap resources to fuel the rest of the country," with Appalachia's physical isolation benefiting outside interests who sought to "ensure a cheap—and captive—workforce."[5] Although extractive industry officials positioned themselves as liberators bringing civilization to untamed corners of rural Appalachia, their presence has done little to advance the culture. Alan DeYoung reminds us that, despite promises of upward mobility, "many Appalachian counties and communities remain among those described by [Tom] Gjelten as isolated and depressed, and by [Bender et al.] as mining-based, persistently impoverished, and/or retirement-income-dependent."[6] One need not be an expert on Appalachia to be aware that its isolation, poverty, and dependency on the extractive industries has led to a history of inadequate health-care resources and educational institutions. The extractive industries promised prosperity but gave us cyclic poverty.

The second major educational roadblock that small-town Appalachian college students face is connected to the cultural rhetoric(s) found within rural extractive industry communities. Because small-town Appalachian economic structures were deliberately established for a noneducated workforce, it should come as no surprise that education levels are low in these areas. Furthermore, poverty levels are high because extractive industry officials have established a monoeconomy that offers little more than dangerous, low-paying work. As a result, many of these communities lack college literacies—the ability to "do things with texts" to gain admission to, and succeed in, the "social space" of higher education.[7]

My hometown certainly fits the Appalachian mold in regard to education and poverty. Statistically, we can be read as the children of uneducated, working-class parents. According to US Census Bureau data collected between 2007 and 2011, only 67.9 percent of Webster County adults over the age of twenty-five have obtained a high school diploma or GED, a figure 17.5 percent lower than the national average. Only 8.6 percent of county residents have obtained a bachelor's degree or higher, a figure that is 19.6 percent lower than the national average. Only 3.5 percent of county residents have graduate or professional degrees. The median annual household income is $25,990, which is $26,772 lower than the national average. And 24.3 percent of county residents live below the poverty level, a figure 10 percent higher than the national average.[8] As children of Webster County, we are easily given to fatalistic thinking. We recognize those who have and those who do not. Our teachers know the college kids from the poor kids; they know the welders from the scholars. Our fatalism is in part due to our home's most obvious sociocultural characteristic—a long-standing economic dependence on the extractive industries. We've been taught that coal is who we are.

Extractive Industry Appalachia: Rhetoric, Ideology, and College Literacy

Webster County is a community of coal miners, loggers—of *workers*. All the men in my family have worked in the extractive industries in some fashion. My father began in the mines two days after his high school graduation. He was from an era when very few, if any, Webster County parents encouraged their children to attend college. His decision to turn down a walk-on opportunity on the football team at a small Division III college was the biggest regret of his adult life. After high school, he was forced to reconcile with the fact that coal mining would be his trade, as was the case for his father and his father's father. Before I was even born, he was determined to make damn well sure that his children had the opportunity to go to college. He was going to do everything in his power to see that they didn't end up in the mines.

This story is not uncommon in small-town Appalachia—parents who dream college dreams for their children out of a sense of regret; first-generation college students who aim to alter the trajectory of their family histories via postsecondary education. The problem is that even small-town Appalachian parents who do care deeply about their children's educational futures often lack the educational backgrounds and financial means to adequately prepare their children for academic life. Good intentions in the absence of cultural capital often result in poor planning and improper academic advising. Often, the surrounding community does not provide access to, and sometimes discourages, higher education, especially when it is deeply indoctrinated by the small-town ideology promoted by the extractive industries.

Still today, extractive industry officials work tirelessly to control both the economic and the ideological realities of life in small-town Appalachia. It would be a mistake to assume that parents, even those who want to see their children achieve their college dreams, are immune to their rhetoric. For instance, in "Community Economic Identity," Shannon Elizabeth Bell and Richard York demonstrate how extractive industry public relations campaigns, such as the "Friends of Coal" campaign (a so-called grassroots effort funded by the West Virginia Coal Association in 2002), employ the appropriation of "cultural icons that exploit the hegemonic masculinity of the region" and thus aim to "maintain their power through ideological manipulation." Through "elaborate framing efforts to maintain and amplify coal's status as the economic identity of West Virginia," the "Friends of Coal" campaign seeks to connect the coal industry's identity to "representations of cultural or regional identity that resonate with individuals of a particular area or community."[9] For some time, scholars such as Anita Puckett have demonstrated how young Appalachian men and women come to see the workforce in a gendered, generational, and sometimes fatalistic fashion because they are born into economies where a college education is not a prerequisite to landing a good job.[10] The college literacies found in these communities almost always reflect a pro–extractive industry agenda because industry officials have the economic means to promote gender values that are advantageous to their cause. The "Friends of Coal" campaign is a perfect example of such a promotion.

During its inception, the "Friends of Coal" campaign brought together local college football coaching legends Don Nehlen (West Virginia University) and Bob Pruitt (Marshall University) for newspaper, magazine, and television advertisements promoting a pro-coal agenda. This was also a campaign that brought together West Virginia's only two bowl subdivision schools for a series of football games played under the moniker of the "Friends of Coal Bowl." As Bell and York accurately point out, this move was "particularly relevant [to West Virginia football fans] because, until 2006, the two [football programs] had played only once since 1923."[11] When the news broke about the newly invented in-state rivalry, I couldn't have been more excited. I was a student at Marshall University when the Friends of Coal Bowl began; I even attended a few of the games held at my campus. Like most of my peers, I bought Friends of Coal Bowl merchandise and applauded when pro-coal ads were shown on the jumbo screen during time-outs and commercial breaks. This was a clever rhetorical approach, one that was designed to cater to and reinforce already established notions of Appalachian masculinity. It was a message that resonated well with former local high school football stars like my father, men born and raised in a region where sports and coal mining mark the masculine identity performances of *real* Appalachian men. As it progressed, the "Friends of Coal" campaign added more celebrities who demographic research suggested would resonate with working-class West Virginians (e.g., NASCAR driver Derek Kiser and professional fisherman Jerry Starks).

The "Friends of Coal" campaign eventually found its way into West Virginia public schools via a coal education program named CEDAR in which "teachers in the counties of Boone, Logan, Wyoming, Mingo, and McDow-ell (some of the top coal-producing counties in West Virginia) are offered grant money to create and implement classroom study units on coal using the CEDAR materials, and the three teachers in each grade level (K–12) with the best *performance* have the opportunity to win cash prizes."[12] According to CEDAR's official Web site, the mission of the program "is to facilitate the increase of knowledge and understanding of the many benefits the coal industry provides in daily lives by providing financial resources and coal education materials to implement its study in the school curriculum."[13] Programs such as CEDAR serve as evidence of the economic power and ideological influence the extractive industries have in many Appalachian communities. The self-doubt and indecision Appalachian students experience in regard to the academy is often the by-product of a socioeconomic and educational landscape that was not built to ensure access to a college education.

The Ethnographic Case Study

Twelve years removed from my first crack at the ACT, I find myself on the other end of the classroom—an assistant professor of rhetoric and composition, an academic adviser to incoming college freshmen, an Ivory Tower gatekeeper. This has changed the way I think about college preparation and the sociocultural factors that affect how students run this race, so to speak. The overwhelming majority of my upstate New York students arrive on campus socially and academically prepared to succeed. Their confidence and level of familiarity with the do's and don'ts of life in the academy continually remind me that some students are at a cultural disadvantage when it comes to college preparation.

My first serious attempt as a scholar at moving beyond a statistical understanding of the college literacies of students from extractive industry Appalachia came in the form of a case study. Because I wanted to compare my educational experiences with those of other individuals from my hometown, I chose to interview two first-generation college students from Webster County before and during their first semesters in college. The study featured a two-part methodology. First, both participants were interviewed in person on separate days and almost one week before they were to leave for college. During the initial interview, both participants were asked a series of open-ended questions about their high school experiences, college-going decisions, and concerns about college life.

The second part of the study featured e-response journals. During the fall semester of each participant's freshman year, I distributed four sets of questions via email. I asked the participants to think of their responses as journal entries documenting their freshman experience. The question sets came at three, six, and nine weeks into the semester, with a final set emailed one week after final exams. Each e-journal contained three questions (twelve total). Participants wrote their answers in a Microsoft Word document and emailed them back to me. I had no further contact with them about their answers. My goal was to allow their rhetoric to serve as evidence of their educational worldviews.

Marshall and Tina: College Kids from Extractive Industry Appalachia

Marshall, who came from my hometown of Cowen, was eighteen years old at the time of the study.[14] His father, a high school dropout, is a truck driver for a local coal-mining company. His mother graduated from Webster County High School and has worked various jobs in the community. His older brother, currently employed at the same coal mine as his father, is a graduate of this same high school. Organized school sports are a huge part of Marshall's life. During his senior year in high school, he lettered in football, basketball, and baseball. It was during his days on the playing field that Marshall decided he was going to become a high school coach. To reach this goal, he would have to first become a teacher, a dream that led to his becoming the first member of his family to pursue a college degree. His institution of choice was a four-year college with an enrollment just over seven thousand students, nestled in a small Appalachian town with a population of fewer than twenty thousand residents. The school is located 108 miles from his home in Cowen.

Tina, from Webster Springs, was also eighteen years old at the time of the study. Her father, a local Methodist preacher, is a graduate of Webster County High School, as is her mother, a worker at a local nursing home. Unlike Marshall, Tina was not involved in high school athletics or social clubs. Instead, she pegs herself as more of an "outsider." I found this self-description fascinating because my first impression of her was that she, like Marshall, was much more of an extrovert than an introvert. To me, Tina appeared to be the more academically prepared of the two participants. She was ranked eighth in her graduating high school class and was a member of the National Honor Society. She describes herself as a "heavy reader" and suggests that religion plays a significant role in her life. Her career goal is to become an elementary school teacher. Though she is uncertain of which grade she would like to teach, she knows she would like to work with younger children. Her institution of choice was a small West Virginia liberal arts college affiliated with the United Methodist Church. The school is located in a town of just over five thousand residents and has an enrollment of just over twelve hundred students. It is eighty-four miles from Tina's home in Webster Springs.

At the end of the five-month study, coding Marshall's and Tina's responses proved easier than I had initially anticipated. I uncovered two dominant cultural rhetorics that I believe are directly tied to each participant's rural Appalachian upbringing.[15] First, both participants demonstrated what I call *pioneer rhetoric*. This rhetorical self-positioning indicates that they feel as if they are entering uncharted academic territory. They see their professors and peers as native to an academic world to which they do not belong. They see their parents and their communities/schools as unable or unwilling to prepare them for such a journey.

Second, both participants employed what I call *home rhetoric, or the Appalachian pull*. This rhetoric suggests that they feel a social or familial obligation to return to their hometown communities both during and after the completion of their college journey. Marshall's and Tina's responses serve as evidence of a constant pressure to be connected to their communities. For these participants, going away to college feels like a self-imposed exile from the place of their familial histories. These rhetorics are symptomatic of life in extractive industry Appalachia and have clearly affected the college literacies of both participants.

Pioneer Rhetoric: Academia as Lonely Frontier

Marshall and I began the initial face-to-face interview by discussing the college admissions process. When asked about the most difficult aspect of applying to college, Marshall replied: "My parents didn't know how to help with financial aid and the whole money situation. . . . [O]ur conversations usually ended with a fight." He also stressed the role his girlfriend and her family played in helping prepare his financial aid materials: "My girlfriend [Amy] and I did everything on our own. My parents didn't really have a clue about financial aid or anything like that. She [Amy] has a brother at [West

Virginia University], so she kind of knew the drill. . . . [W]ithout Amy I wouldn't have went to college." Throughout the interview, Marshall chose to depict his parents as helpless spectators to the college admissions process. At one point he bluntly stated: "I can't really talk to Mom about the financial side of things. I usually talk to Amy's mom."

When first-generation college students cannot turn to their parents for answers, they often look to friends or extended family for explanations. This educational roadblock becomes problematic when combined with the fact that Marshall is from a community that, from a historical perspective, contains very few college-educated individuals. Webster County's extractive industry economy, of which his father and brother are working members, has played a large part in limiting the number of college graduates who reside in the region. More often than not, when Webster County graduates do obtain a college degree, they are forced to find work elsewhere.

Research shows that few first-generation college students have "concrete or substantial plans to enter college before actually taking steps to bring it [sic] to fruition."[16] In keeping with this unfortunate tradition, Marshall's financial aid problems appeared to be the result of poor planning. As was the case for me, Marshall did not seriously begin thinking about college until late in his high school career. In fact, he seemed more than willing to give his girlfriend's family credit for his last-minute college acceptance. At no point during the interview did he suggest that school officials or family members played a positive role in the college enrollment process. Unfortunately, he gave little indication as to whether his parents actually encouraged his college aspirations. Instead, he made references only to financial aid disputes and money quarrels.

The last-minute approach to college preparation is one that is, in many ways, a by-product of Webster County's sociocultural framework. I had never stepped foot on a college campus until I was a high school senior; I didn't even know what a college campus looked like. I'm guessing the same was true for Marshall. When you grow up in coal country, top-notch college preparation is not an expectation or a reality. For instance, in Milwaukee, local public school systems "agree[d] to pay an Arizona consulting firm almost $400,000 for a program called TargetTeach"—a service offered by a firm that specializes in raising standardized test scores.[17] For a variety of socioeconomic and cultural reasons, TargetTeach hasn't found its way to Webster County.

Like Marshall, Tina struggled to get her admissions materials together before the deadlines. When asked about the biggest difficulty of preparing for college, she replied: "Financial aid was the biggest thing. Finding money was the scariest thing. It was so stressful. I kept thinking how I am going to do this. I think my parents were wondering the same thing."

Although Tina's college talk with her parents did not appear to be as hostile as Marshall's, it was clear that money was an issue. Our conversations regarding tuition, room and board fees, and other college expenses reminded me that college preparation is about more than having parents who know whether you need to take the ACT or the SAT. In Appalachia, uneducated parents are often lower or lower middle class. Considering rising tuition rates and our current economic climate, it should be no surprise that many Appalachian parents discourage their children from taking on such a financial burden. Many of these students go to public high schools that promote coal education programs, schools with guidance counselors who are quick to remind students of the financial burden of a college education and educators who are quick to remind students that their fathers can "probably get [them] on at the mines."

During my initial face-to-face interview with her, it became apparent to me that Tina was very proud of her status as a first-generation college student. When asked about her family's education history, she replied: "I do not have any family members that have gone to college. My foster father went to seminary school, but nobody has gone to college. I'm really proud that I am the first to go. I know that when I step on campus I am going to be wondering how I made it to this place."

Tina's response reminded me of Sarah, a nontraditional/first-generation college student featured in Katherine Kelleher Sohn's ethnographic study *Whistlin' and Crowin' Women of Appalachia*. In Sohn's study, Sarah is quoted as having noted: "The key person in my development, especially with regard to education, is my mother, Naomi, whose dream of graduating from college was realized when I walked across the stage in 1993."[18] Like Sarah, Tina often insinuated that her parents are living vicariously through her educational journey. Tina's response also reminded me of the pride I felt as a beginning college student. Although I was nowhere nearly as prepared for college as she was, I remember feeling like I was about to do something special. The fact that I was being given an opportunity to do something that no one in my family had ever done before was an academic motivator. This sense of pride helped turn the indecisive seventeen-year-old who secretly hoped that he flunked his ACT test into the college student who sat in the front row of every one of his classes. During my career as a college professor, I have seen plenty of entitled and apathetic students who could use a little dose of Tina's ambition. The nihilistic notion that the college degree is the new high school diploma has yet to make its way to Webster County. Growing up in extractive industry Appalachia can act as a motivator for students who see a college degree as an advancement of their family's occupational and educational history.

Many of Marshall's and Tina's comments during the semester support research suggesting that "first-generation students are more likely to be handicapped in accessing and understanding information and attitudes relevant to making beneficial decisions about such things as the kinds of academic and social choices to make while in attendance."[19] Early on, it became clear that the social aspect of college life was difficult for both Marshall and Tina:

> QUESTION: What has been the most difficult aspect of college life thus far?
> MARSHALL: The first thing that surprised me wasn't anything to do within classes but it was the huge variety of people that there are. There are people here that you only think you would see on TV.
> TINA: The social aspect of college life is much more difficult than the actual work. The portion of homework that I receive daily isn't any different than high school. It's living around different kinds of situations that makes things difficult from time to time. There is this one girl. It bothers me just seeing her. She has three piercings in her lip. She is one of those people who wear black lipstick and hang out in front of dorm buildings smoking all night. I know she is probably a decent person, but I can't help but feeling strange living around her. Sometimes I just want to scream or call my parents and have them pick me up [*kidding*].

These responses suggest that both Marshall and Tina have experienced a version of culture shock that is common among students from rural Appalachian backgrounds. Marshall's suggestion that he is living among the kind of people featured on television deserves serious consideration. This statement likely suggests that he has had little to no contact with individuals from any ethnic, racial, and cultural background other than his own. His comments also indicate that he may hold a stereotypical view of these individuals based on his limited exposure to diverse cultures. Because almost every member of his family is from small-town Appalachia, Marshall's parents and family members may not be able to offer him advice as to how to interact with individuals from different cultural or ethnic backgrounds. His parents are from a small coal-mining town with little to no racial or ethnic diversity: according to US Census Bureau data collected between 2007 and 2011, 98.5 percent of Webster County citizens identify themselves as white; a scant 0.5 percent of residents reported speaking a language other than English in their homes.[20] Thus, it is possible that Marshall sees these individuals as Other to his normative hometown atmosphere. His comments also suggest that his only contact with diverse cultures has come from television. This leads me to believe that he views himself as a fish out of water.

Tina's reaction to her pierced dorm mate suggests a similar cultural mind-set. Like Marshall, Tina seems taken aback by the cultural climate of her small liberal arts campus. Her uneasiness is connected to the visual performance of identity by her fellow dormitory resident. She is willing to accept the fact that her pierced classmate is "probably a decent person," but she is quite honest about her uneasiness. She, like Marshall, appears to be having a difficult time seeing herself as a member of the college community. Her classmates do not perform their identities in the same way that Webster County residents do. Therefore, she "can't help but feeling strange living around" this particular student. Her joke about calling her parents also reminds us of the old adage that suggests there is a lot of truth told in jest.

More often than not, Marshall and Tina described college life as much different than they had anticipated:

QUESTION: What was your initial impression of your college campus?
MARSHALL: I couldn't believe the amount of alcohol and drugs that are available just by mentioning it to someone. People really have too much free time. I think it gets them into trouble. I really wasn't ready for that side of things. I guess you have to be careful who you hang around with.
TINA: At first it seemed like there were just too many people. It felt like I was never going to get to know everyone. I felt like I was lost in the shuffle.

Once again, Marshall's and Tina's responses reflect a clear social anxiety. For Marshall, college life has seemingly brought about temptations and social dangers that he had not anticipated. One could argue that this lack of familiarity is also a result of sociocultural isolation. On the basis of these comments, we can infer that Marshall was genuinely surprised by the accessibility of alcohol and drugs on college campuses. Perhaps his family members are unaware of how these temptations would manifest themselves. It appears that Marshall is learning how to avoid potentially dangerous situations on his own.

These responses also demonstrate how Marshall and Tina sometimes Other themselves when talking about their respective institutions and university peers. As a fellow first-generation college student from Webster County, I understand the fear of being "lost in the shuffle." I also understand Marshall's sudden realization that college life brings about new levels of social pressure. As an undergraduate, I often felt as if I were a visitor rather than a true inhabitant of the academy. Although feelings of being "lost in the shuffle" are common among college freshman, these emotions are especially strong for first-generation college students from rural environments. When students from isolated backgrounds do not have family members or parental figures who have attended college, this transition process can make them feel as if they are educational pioneers entering a new and confusing world.

Hometown Rhetoric: The Appalachian Pull

During our initial face-to-face interview, Marshall displayed an almost textbook version of what the scholars Erica Chenoweth and Renee Galliher call *historicism,* that is, when Appalachian first-generation college students see themselves as part of a local history and choose educational paths that allow them to remain part of that history.[21] Describing why he wanted to become a high school teacher, Marshall said: "My dad played ball at Webster, my brother played ball at Webster, my cousins played ball. You know, I just think it would be really cool to come back [from college] and coach here. It would be cool if I could coach my kids here one of these days." Although he recognizes that he is breaking a family tradition by pursuing a college degree, it is clear that Marshall sees himself as a part of a history within Webster County. His goal is to leave Webster only long enough to obtain a college degree, then return home to find a great job. He recognizes that his family has roots in the county, and his responses suggest that he is reluctant to start anew in another county, state, or region. He calms this fear of leaving the protective isolation of his hometown by assuring himself that college will last only "four years" and that he will one day be able to return.

To describe why she chose to pursue a career in education, Tina said: "There are tons of teachers [at Webster County Elementary School] about to retire. There should be so many openings by the time I get out. I think it would be amazing. Teaching in the same school I went to." Tina sees her profession not only as one that might potentially be in demand in Webster County but also as an occupation of significance within her regional history. Like Marshall, she wants to return to her local school with an elevated status. She hopes to one day replace the teachers who influenced her as a student, just as Marshall hopes to take the place of the coaches who inspired him on the field. A college education is, for both Marshall and Tina, an opportunity to take part in this changing of the guard.

I can relate to Marshall's and Tina's career motives. When I was in college, I felt a strong desire to return to my hometown community and become a big fish in a small Appalachian pond. I consciously wanted to live the rest of my life in Webster County but feared that coal mining, the Snyder trade, might be the only realistic option for me. Webster County was where I belonged, I thought. I wasn't sure as to how the college-educated version of me would fit within the economic realities of the community. This was a fear I struggled with well into my college education. After earning my degree, who was I going to be? What was I going to become? Historicism is about more than Appalachian college students having a strong sense of connection to their hometown communities. It is also about imagination. Historicism shapes our ability to imagine our future selves.

While I was surprised by Marshall's willingness to acknowledge his lack of family support during the admissions process, I was not surprised by his reluctance to admit that proximity played a huge part in his choice of educational institution. On the surface, Marshall "didn't care about [his college] being far from Cowen." In fact, he repeatedly said that location had very little to do with this choice. However, later in the interview, he openly stated that he "didn't want to go to a big school." He also said that his institutional choice was ideal because "it wasn't too big and it was close to home." In "Factors Influencing College Aspirations of Rural West Virginia High School Students," Chenoweth and Galliher define *localism* as a trait recognizable in students who consciously plan on living their entire lives in their hometown regions.[22] I would argue that localism should also be attributed to students who choose occupations that fit or mirror life within their normative hometown expectations—life within extractive industry Appalachia. Localism is about more than where people plan to live. It is about how they plan to live their lives and how their choices are a reflection of the material circumstances of their upbringing.

Tina, more so than Marshall, was willing to embrace the fact that she didn't want to attend a college that was located far away from Webster County. She described her college as the ideal choice because she "wanted small classes where [her] professors could interact with [her] personally" and because "it was close to home." Later in the interview, she openly stated that she had "a big fear of being away from home." When asked to describe this fear, she said: "I am worried about living around people I do not know. I love the idea of living in a new place, but I like my parents and friends around me. I admire people who can just pick up and move, but that is not me." Both Marshall and Tina constantly used the exact phrase *close to home* when discussing their choice of institution. From these responses one can infer that home plays a huge part in this process.

Neither Marshall nor Tina had spent an entire weekend at college. First-generation college students often express, as Barbara Bradbury and Peter C. Mather put it, "a need to be both geographically and emotionally close to family members." These behaviors remind us of the pull of localism for rural Appalachian students: Bradbury and Mather refer to this concept as *the pull of home.*[23] I would argue that this pull is much stronger for Appalachian students than for non-Appalachian students. Marshall's and Tina's need to return home each and every weekend reminds us that many first-generation college students from Appalachia consciously plan to return to their hometown communities after college. These students view their time in the academy as a necessary sacrifice until the day they return to where they belong, just as many extractive industry workers come to view work as the necessary sacrifice of life. This attitude is especially troubling when considering the economic limitations of these communities:

QUESTION: How have your parents, family, and friends reacted to your first semester as a college student?

MARSHALL: My mom and dad are still not going good with it. They want me home. My mom calls wondering about me two or three times a day. It has also been difficult with Amy. She is still a junior [in high school]. Sometimes I talk with them on the phone for about two or three hours every evening. This sucks when I have stuff to do. Sometimes I feel like I am being pulled both ways.

TINA: My parents really miss me; they aren't really going crazy or anything like that. I leave on Thursdays at about 8:30 and come back on Mondays at about 1:00 or 2:00 in the evening. So I really get to see them about five days a week. It's good because I can still go to church with them and I really don't have to miss out on their lives.

Marshall's and Tina's comments make me wonder how many Appalachian families have inadvertently sabotaged the college careers of their children by encouraging them to come home each weekend to attend family functions and community activities. Both Marshall and Tina are clearly pulled in different directions. On the one hand, they are faced with a brand of culture shock that causes them to question whether they truly belong on their respective campuses. At the same time, they are faced with the constant pull of their families and hometown communities.

Social pressures to return home are potentially damaging to students who are often ill prepared for the rigors of academic life. The hours spent on the phone with his family are a distraction to Marshall. The same can be said for Tina's constant visits home, and she has scheduled her classes so that she can spend the least amount of time possible on campus. In fact, her final comment in her journal is quite telling: "I really don't have to miss out on their lives." She seems to feel that she is missing out on the lives of her loved ones because of her academic commitments. Both she and Marshall are from a culture that, because of its extractive industry roots, is anything but nomadic.

Perhaps all college students, regardless of their sociocultural/educational backgrounds, experience some version of homesickness that resembles the Appalachian pull. Age, maturity, and proximity of college to home all play a part in a beginning college student's comfort level in the academy. Also, many Appalachian students consciously choose to return to their hometown communities after college because of love of family and home or because of job opportunities; this is especially the case for those from more urban settings. However, it would be remiss to ignore the connection between such attitudes and the cyclic poverty often found in rural extractive industry towns like the ones Marshall and Tina come from.

College Diplomas and Coal Country

After the completion of this study, I asked Marshall and Tina to consider how their first semester in college changed the way they now view the academy. Tina's response was one that I will not soon forget: "College isn't a fairy tale. Go into it with a realistic mind-set." Reflecting back on my own educational unpreparedness, I realize that I had to overcome much more than ACT test anxiety when applying to colleges. It wasn't that I grew up in a house bereft of literacy or that my parents didn't stress the importance of education. My college literacy was shaped by the material realities of my hometown community. The blame for my standardized-testing struggles should not be placed on my parents or even my teachers; I was lucky to have parents and teachers who cared about my educational future. Transitioning into college life was difficult for me because I was a part of a sociocultural economic system that handicapped my ability to prepare for and excel in academics. The economic climate that I grew up in was almost completely dependent on the extractive industries, and the attitudes and aspirations of the men in my community were a reflection of this reality. My community didn't feature private schools or charter schools; students from my community went to *the* school, the only one in town. Our parents didn't enroll us in pricey test prep courses such as those offered by the *Princeton Review*. Nor did they encourage us to attend out-of-state colleges. Until graduate school, I had never met anyone who had attended an Ivy League institution. My college literacy, or lack thereof, was a reflection of the cultural norms promoted in my community. My college ambitions, or lack thereof, were a product of my desire to push against an occupational norm. My insecurities were a product of my lack of confidence in successfully doing so.

A rereading of my ACT experience demonstrates that my parents were highly involved in my college preparation; they were the driving force behind my college ambitions. Such a narrative complicates the common notion that first-generation college students are likely to drop out of school owing to a lack of parental support. I would argue that many first-generation college students decide to pursue a postsecondary education because their parents have struggled as a result of their own lack of educational opportunities. Both parents and students alike are often motivated to change their family histories. We should explore these motivations.

Somehow, along the way, I lost track of what it felt like to view college as an abstraction, to feel as if I were playing a game rigged in somebody else's favor. Somewhere between my college talk, my guidance counselor meeting, and my eleven years as a college/graduate student, I overcame those feelings of insecurity.

"Your dad could probably get you on at the mines."

Tina is correct. "College isn't a fairy tale." But it absolutely transformed my life.

Notes

1. Ronald Eller, *Uneven Ground: Appalachia since 1945* (Lexington: University Press of Kentucky, 2008).

2. Crandall Shifflett, *Coal Towns: Life, Work, and Culture in Contemporary Towns of Southern Appalachia* (Knoxville: University of Tennessee Press, 1995).

3. David Hsuing, *Two Worlds in the Tennessee Mountains: Exploring the Origins of Appalachian Stereotypes* (Lexington: University Press of Kentucky, 1997); Michael Montgomery, "The Idea of Appalachian Isolation," *Appalachian Heritage* 28, no. 2 (2000): 20–31.

4. Helen Matthews Lewis and Edward Knipe, "The Colonialism Model: The Appalachian Case," in *Colonialism in Modern America: The Appalachian Case,* ed. Helen Matthews Lewis, Linda Johnson, and Don Askins (Boone, NC: Appalachian Consortium Press, 1978), 9–31, 11.

5. Shannon Elizabeth Bell and Richard York, "Community Economic Identity: The Coal Industry and Ideology Construction in West Virginia," *Rural Sociology* 75 (2010): 111–43, 119.

6. Alan DeYoung, "Constructing and Staffing the Cultural Bridge: The School as Change Agent in Rural Appalachia," *Anthropology and Education Quarterly* 26 (1995): 168–92, 172. See also Tom Gjelten, *A Typology of Rural School Settings* (Washington, DC: US Department of Education, 1982); and Lloyd D. Bender, Bernal L. Green, Thomas F. Hady, John A. Kuehn, Marlys K. Nelson, Leon B. Perkinson, and Peggy J. Ross, "The Diverse Social and Economic Structure of Nonmetropolitan America," Rural Development Research Report 49 (Washington, DC: Economic Research Service, USDA, 1985).

7. For the definition of *literacy* on which this is based, see Webb-Sunderhaus and Donehower, introduction to this volume.

8. US Census Bureau, "Webster County, West Virginia," *State and County Quick Facts,* December 6, 2012, update, http://quickfacts.census.gov/qfd/states/54/54101.html.

9. Bell and York, "Community and Economic Identity," 111, 126, 130.

10. Anita Puckett, "'Let the Girls Do the Spelling and Dan Will Do the Shooting': Literacy, the Division of Labor, and Identity in a Rural Appalachian Community," *Anthropology Quarterly* 65 (1992): 137–47.

11. Bell and York, "Community and Economic Identity," 130.

12. Ibid., 136–37.

13. Coal Education Development and Resource of Southern West Virginia, "About Us," *CEDAR West Virginia: Building Awareness of West Virginia's Coal Industry,* n.d., http://www.cedarswv.com.

14. All names have been changed.

15. For a more detailed analysis of the cultural rhetorics that shape Appalachian students' relationships with education, see my *The Rhetoric of Appalachian Identity* (Jefferson, NC: McFarland, 2014).

16. Patrick F. Schultz, "Upon Entering College: First Semester Experiences of First-Generation, Rural Students from Agricultural Families," *Rural Educator* 26, no. 1 (2004): 48–51, 50.

17. Peter Sacks, "Do No Harm: Stopping the Damage to America's Public Schools," in *Education Matters: Exploring Issues in Education,* ed. Morgan Gresham and Crystal McCage (New York: Pearson Custom, 2009), 32–49, 57.

18. Katherine Kelleher Sohn, *Whistlin' and Crowin' Women of Appalachia: Literacy Practices since College* (Carbondale: Southern Illinois University Press, 2006), 120.

19. Ernest Pascarella, Christopher Pierson, Patrick Terenzini, and Gregory Wolniak, "First-Generation College Students," *Journal of Higher Education* 75 (2004): 249–84, 252.

20. US Census Bureau, "Webster County, West Virginia."

21. Erica Chenoweth and Renee Galliher, "Factors Influencing College Aspirations of Rural West Virginia High School Students," *Journal of Research in Rural Education* 19 (2004): 25–49.

22. Ibid.

23. Barbara L. Bradbury and Peter C. Mather, "The Integration of First-Year, First-Generation College Students from Ohio Appalachia," *NASPA Journal* 46 (2009): 388–411, 388.

5

How Reading and Writing Saved a Gay Preacher in Central Appalachia

Gregory E. Griffey

On October 17, 2004—my twenty-fourth birthday—a small community of Missionary Baptists in Central Appalachia branded me literate. Standing in the packed-out, one-room, stem-family church of my childhood in the mountains of southwestern Virginia, an all-male group of Baptist preachers and deacons questioned me on the details of my biblical literacy. From the Genesis account of creation, to the birth, life, death, and resurrection of Jesus, to the Revelation of Saint John—I was asked to give an account of my ability to read and preach the Bible. Then a final question came: "Do you believe the King James Version of the Bible is the only version inspired by God for English-speaking peoples?" Answering in the affirmative, and with no formal seminary education, I was ordained to preach the Bible just as my maternal grandfather and paternal great-grandfather had been before I was born. They are now dead, and their graves lie on two different hillsides, one of which rests just outside the door of the church in which I was ordained, yet their presence and legacies as Spirit-filled preachers continue to live in the narratives of our family and our faith. As I stood literate before God and that congregation of mountain believers, I knew I had big shoes to fill.

Both my maternal grandfather and my paternal great-grandfather were indigenous preachers in southern West Virginia and southwestern Virginia, respectively. My maternal grandfather was Missionary Baptist, and my paternal great-grandfather was Free Pentecostal Holiness, both traditions having deep roots in the Central Appalachian region.[1] Their respective religious traditions led them to disagree over theological issues. While the Missionary Baptists tended to be more Calvinist in their theology, viewing personal salvation as a sovereign act of God that could not be undone, those identifying with the Pentecostal Holiness tradition understood personal salvation in more Arminian terms, believing that it occurs when human beings choose it and work to keep it.[2] The Pentecostal Holiness of my Appalachian community also believed that the outward manifestation of one's personal salvation would be witnessed by the community through gifts of the Holy Ghost, characterized by exuberant expressions that usually included vocal shouts, speaking in tongues (glossolalia), and communally agreed-on signs of spiritual strength and unwavering religious conviction. Excluding speaking in tongues, the Missionary Baptists also understood certain exuberant expressions and emotional outbursts as signs of a person's openness to what they might call *the moving of the Spirit*. Yet they believed that the outward manifestation of one's salvation would be witnessed not by exuberant expressions but by day-to-day living that gave witness to the truth of the biblical text.

While these and other differences served as distinctions between the religious beliefs of my paternal great-grandfather and my maternal grandfather, both preachers exercised devotion to the practices of reading, teaching, and preaching the Bible. Both gave time to routine Bible study, taught the Bible to their families and religious congregations, and committed large portions of the King James Bible to memory. Neither had any formal theological or seminary education, and they agreed that such education was neither needed nor to be desired for a preacher called by God. My paternal great-grandfather died when I was a child, making my memories of him more limited than those of my maternal grandfather, who died when I was an adolescent. Since my memories of my paternal great-grandfather are few, this chapter will reflect briefly on the literacy practices and values of my maternal grandfather, whose life, faith, and biblical literacy remain more accessible to my memory. First, I explore how my grandfather practiced and valued literacy both as a West Virginia coal miner and as a mountain preacher, noting the functions of literacy within both identities. Building on my grandfather's story, I then show how reading and writing within the familial mountain culture of my grandfather functioned as coping mechanisms for me, as a mountain preacher and as a young adult gradually identifying as a gay man. Finally, I examine ways in which the literacy practices and values of my Appalachian religious heritage have been hybridized by my more recent academic study in seminary.

Throughout, this chapter brings biographical narrative into conversation with literacy scholarship, complicating common presumptions about literacy, gender, and Appalachian mountain religion. It joins growing efforts in literacy studies to "treat literacy 'in context'" and to resist "the position which views literacy as merely a matter of generic skills, as a unitary process, one where 'readers' and 'writers' are generalized subjects without any social location and . . . more or less efficient processors of text."[3] If, as Brian Street argues, literacy research "has a task to do in making visible the complexity of local, everyday, community literacy practices and challenging dominate stereotypes and myopia,"[4] then this chapter does, I hope, just this by rereading Appalachia through the literacy practices and values of a gay mountain preacher and his grandfather, complicating common notions of Appalachian mountain religion as characterized primarily by its orality.

My Grandfather Preacher: A Sponsor of Literacy

The literacy scholar Deborah Brandt has become well known for her conceptualization of literacy in terms of both individual and economic development. She coined the phrase *sponsors of literacy* to describe "any agents, local or distant, concrete or abstract, who enable, support, teach, model, as well as recruit, regulate, suppress, or withhold literacy—and gain advantage by it in some way."[5] Sponsors of literacy may represent various causes or literacy constituencies, including religious, educational, government, cultural or even familial. "Although the interests of the sponsor and the sponsored do not have to converge (and in fact, many conflict)," she writes, "sponsors nevertheless set the terms for access to literacy and wield powerful incentives for compliance and loyalty."[6] Whether explicitly or implicitly, literacy sponsors hold significant influence over literacy practices and values for both individuals and communities.

According to Brandt's conceptualization of literacy sponsorship, my maternal grandfather functioned as an influential sponsor of literacy for our family, a literacy emissary of sorts, representing somewhat incompatible and competing ways of valuing and practicing literacy. To this day, my mother recalls his efforts to suppress or regulate literacy in the family, whether by eschewing formal education in general (especially college education) or through verbal disapproval directed at her adolescent love of reading. "Always got your nose in a book," he would say. "Girls leave home to get an education, get into trouble, and never come home again." Both my grandfather and my mother knew what Sara Webb-Sunderhaus found in her study of literacy in Appalachian families: namely, that literacy can become "a dangerous force," one that can drive painful distance between family members.[7] My mother's adolescent love of reading conflicted with my grandfather's stance on academic literacy. At the same time, in the words of Brandt, my grandfather wielded "powerful incentives for compliance and loyalty." These incentives certainly seemed compelling to my mother, who still recalls her adolescent and young adult desire for favor in the eyes of her father. Despite her love of reading, she never went to college. In the words of Erica Abrams Locklear: "Gaining new technical, social, and cultural literacies, especially ones that might not be shared by those in the learner's home community, almost always comes at a price."[8] It was a price my mother was not always willing to pay.

My grandfather spent most of the middle decades of the twentieth century in dark coal mines and on steep logging trails in West Virginia. Those familiar with the history and culture of West Virginia coal and logging towns might not think it surprising that he placed little value on the practices of reading and writing. At most, reading was *adaptation,* a metaphoric term used by the linguistic anthropologist Sylvia Scribner to describe literacy as "the level of [functional] proficiency necessary for effective performance in a range of settings and customary activities."[9] My grandfather's customary activities as a coal miner and working-class laborer demanded small value for the acts of reading and writing, other than for purposes necessitated by a working-class life. When reading was necessary, he called on his wife, who possessed relatively advanced conventional reading skills. This gendered division of literacy labor is discussed later in this chapter.

Even though his literacy skills might be considered severely lacking by conventional standards—and even though he eschewed formal education and feared that my mother's love of reading would take her away from home and get her "into trouble"—my grandfather did not, however, devalue reading altogether. According to his own testimony about an indispensable chapter in our family narrative, he received a divine literacy imperative when he "surrendered" to God's call to preach. As a coal miner and working-class laborer, reading might have held minimal value for him; but, as a preacher, reading became a divine essential. During church meetings, my grandmother would give affirmative witness through head nods and tears as my grand-father proudly and routinely recounted the day when he, though never for-mally educated, read aloud his very first verse from the King James Version of the Bible. According to my grandfather, a preacher was called to preach the biblical text—"the inerrant and infallible Word of God." His identity as a preacher made biblical literacy a divine essential and forever complicated his status as a sponsor of literacy in our family.

Kim Donehower has observed how literacy can be an explicit factor in struggles for identity and identification. "One's stance on how to practice and value reading and writing," she states, "becomes a way to identify or to dis-identify with particular traditions or groups."[10] For my grandfather, the ability to read was more essential to his ministerial identity than it was inessential to his life before his days in ministry. In fact, according to his own testimony, his ability to read was an answer to a preacher's prayer and a sign authenticating his call. As he told it, he made a bargain with God: if God wanted him to preach, then God would have to give him the ability to read. God answered his prayer on the night he read aloud his very first verse from the Bible, an ability that was not learned and earned but instan-taneous, given through a miraculous gift of grace. The miracle of literacy was part and parcel of sanctified evidence of God's call. It helped cement his identity as a preacher obeying God's call and served to disidentify him as a disobedient Christian or even a charlatan preacher.

Having an identity intimately tied to an ability to read while at the same time eschewing formal education made my grandfather what Sara Webb-Sunderhaus has called a sponsor of *a competing meaning of literacy.* In her study "A Family Affair," Webb-Sunderhaus adopts Brandt's conceptualiza-tion of literacy sponsorship to explore how immediate and extended family members serve as literacy sponsors in the lives of students enrolled at two open-admission universities in Central Appalachia. Noting how literacy beliefs and practices are closely tied to the performance of identity for the students in her study, she shows how a single family member can function as both an encouraging and an inhibiting sponsor of literacy. "Seemingly contradictory messages about literacy could come from the same person," she writes, "such that the same person could be both a sponsor and an inhibitor—or perhaps more accurately, a sponsor of a competing meaning of literacy."[11] In other words, a family member who suppresses literacy—like my grandfather—might also be one who enables it.

On the one hand, my grandfather suppressed and regulated literacy, eschewing formal education, and scolding my mother for having her "nose in a book." On the other hand, he enabled and even prized literacy as a central and authenticating component of his own identity as a preacher. But it was his own sponsor of literacy—namely, the church—that encouraged and cultivated his own biblical literacy practices and values. As Webb-Sunderhaus notes in her study: "Institutional beliefs about, and rewards for, certain types of literacy help foster or sponsor certain beliefs and performance."[12] It was the institution of the church that encouraged certain beliefs about and rewards for the literacy of my grandfather. Ecclesiastical teaching about the role of the preacher included an expectation that he hold knowledge about the biblical text. A preacher's identity elicited accompanying beliefs and practices about biblical literacy, and the church was a major disseminator of that literacy in our community. The reward for biblical literacy was a revered place in mountain life. Biblical literacy gave the preacher authority and meant that he was accorded respect and esteem among the community, both inside and outside the church. When family, church, or community members wanted to know something about the Bible, they would frequently call on my grandfather. Whether he held the right answers to their inquiries is another matter; what is important here is that he was esteemed in our rural community because of God's call, in large part authenticated by his biblical literacy.

My grandfather took seriously his ability to read the Bible, evidenced by routine Bible study and extensive biblical quotations in spontaneous sermons and prayers. While his preaching was certainly oral (he never wrote sermon outlines or manuscripts), the centrality of biblical literacy in his theology and ministerial identity complicates commonly accepted notions of mountain preachers and their religion as characterized primarily by their orality. Emotional worship, passionate preaching, and Spirit-filled praying were certainly defining characteristics of my grandfather's old-time-religion style. He prayed for a move of the Spirit as he preached extemporaneously. And, for sure, folks often received his oral statements about the Bible without reading the Bible for themselves. Yet, at the same time, perhaps because he was Baptist, he placed lesser emphasis on emotion and spontaneity than did his Holiness counterparts. He was sometimes critical of emotion and so-called hand-me-down religion. He was much more likely to appeal to chapter and verse in the Bible than a new word from the Spirit when making theological claims or settling theological arguments. While mountain religion can to some degree be characterized by its orality, as some scholars have done,[13] for my grandfather (and in my own experience as a mountain preacher) the centrality of the biblical text and its written word cannot be underestimated.

Literacy as Salvation: How Reading and Writing Saved Me

While my grandfather might have served as a suppressive sponsor of literacy for my mother, he functioned as an enabling literacy sponsor for me as a male preacher. Because of his reading and interpretation of Titus 1:6, which instructs the ordained to be the "husband of one wife," he (unlike his Pentecostal Holiness neighbors) would have objected to a granddaughter or any woman in the family announcing that she had been called to preach. His objection arose not just from his ability to read and interpret the Bible but also from his emphasis on its authority when determining appropriate ecclesiastical expectations for men and women, an emphasis that was encouraged and cultivated by the prevailing teachings of his religious community. Though at the time of my ordination I was the husband of no one, it was expected that I would one day fulfill the admonition of Titus 1:6, becoming the husband of one wife. This expectation would never fully come to pass. Nevertheless, both my identification as a preacher and my gender contributed to the ways in which my grandfather served as an enabling sponsor of literacy for me.

Like my grandfather's, my call to preach was a call to preach the biblical text. Therefore, the ability to read was a divine essential for me—a central aspect of my ministerial identity—just as it was for him. As evidenced by the event of my ordination, biblical literacy played an important role in my community identification as a preacher. My ability to quote portions of the King James Version of the Bible from memory—including chapter and verse numbers—was a key manifestation to my mountain community that I was a devoted man of God. Yet there are also differences between the literacy values of my grandfather and my own. While my grandfather's ability to read was given through a miraculous gift, my ability to read and write was learned and earned. My grandfather eschewed formal education, but I graduated high school and had already begun an associate degree at a local community college by the time I was ordained. My mother—perhaps hoping I would get the education she never pursued—served as an encouraging sponsor of literacy for me by insisting that I attend college and by making sure that the house was quiet and comfortable while I was home studying.[14]

Unlike my grandfather's, my literacy practices and values extended beyond the religious realm. Although the ability to read remains an essential part of my identity as a preacher, literacy was never solely tied to that part of my identity. I engage in acts of reading and writing in order to expand my knowledge of an array of worldly affairs and for the enjoyment that reading and writing afford.

Even in the context of the church, literacy served me in ways it did not serve my grandfather. Most notable perhaps is the way in which biblical literacy exempted me from participation in culturally normative masculine activities and ultimately offered a way to cope with a budding gay identity. As a growing boy in the mountains, I held little interest in hunting, fishing, repairing car engines, or collecting tools—the kinds of activities that, as Todd Snyder describes, "mark the masculine identity performances of *real* Appalachian men."[15] I preferred playing the piano, helping my mother in the kitchen, and planting flowers. By the time I became a freshman in college, I had developed a growing love for reading and writing, practices not commonly associated with men in my familial culture. If men had an interest in reading and writing for the mere enjoyment such activities might afford, I never heard them speak of it publicly, especially in the presence of other men. No one seemed surprised if a woman—like my mother, for example—enjoyed reading novels or writing poetry. But a man who found enjoyment in such practices might be called a *sissy*, especially if he preferred such things to the more traditional masculine activities. Even reading and writing for high school homework lessons generally were not practices that men prioritized above more normative masculine activities.

There were times when I envied my female peers because, even if formal education for women was frowned on, women were nonetheless expected to have greater interest and capacity than men when it came to reading and writing. Anita Puckett demonstrated this in her intriguing study "'Let the Girls Do the Spelling and Dan Will Do the Shooting.'" Documenting how literacy practices are gendered in the rural eastern Kentucky community of Ash Creek, she showed how, culturally, "literate practices are God-given attributes of women's 'nature,'" providing "context in which a woman can negotiate her social, religious, and cultural identity." From reading the Bible, to filling out money orders, to writing letters and announcements for special occasions, through the tasks of reading and writing women in Ash Creek "obtain some recognizable and valued result and assist in shaping a woman's community identity." Puckett found that men's identities, however, "are not linked to these literate practices, creating minimal or non-literate behavior." In Ash Creek, "many residents, especially men," were "non-readers or read labels or announcements ideographically." And the women who can read "walk a literate tightrope, called upon to assert an identity that affirms 'good' reading and writing skills but constrained by cultural norms and social practices in the directions and forms their writing can successfully assume to maintain social propriety and their family name."[16]

One exception Puckett found with regard to men's literacy in Ash Creek was male preachers: "Preachers are expected to read, although often not as fluently as many women, and set examples of reading practices for them." As with my grandfather and me, male preachers in Ash Creek were not only allowed but also expected to be literate, serving as literacy sponsors for others in the community. According to Puckett, this entire gendering of literacy practices and values "encompasses a set of practices touching the center of Ash Creek cultural and personal identity."[17] In other words, the ways in which women and men—and, for the purposes of this chapter especially, male preachers—practice, value, and even shun various types of literacy are integral to the ways in which Appalachian communities and individuals might wrestle with gendered identities and identifications.

Gary Farley and the Appalachian religion scholar Bill Leonard also include gendered expectations in their discussion of male preachers in the mountains:

> The more effective, or "successful," of this type of preacher usually is distinguished by a certain charisma—gifts of spiritual insight, homiletical flourish, and pastoral concern. His skills also may include the ability to perform the "manly" tasks of the mountain culture, such as hunting, fishing, various sports, woodcraft, agricultural knowledge, and strenuous manual labor. Abilities in music and story telling also are prized. The preacher is expected to be a person of deep integrity, loyalty, good counsel, and courage. His hands must be hard, their grip firm; his "fly must be closed" (no sexual immorality); and, as some will say, there must be "no lace on his pants."[18]

While Farley and Leonard's observation to some degree resonates with my own experience as a mountain preacher, things appear more complex when cultural literacy practices are considered. Indeed, mountain folk might expect their preacher to have "no lace on his pants," but they also might overlook his lack of participation in traditional masculine activities if he were instead reading the Bible in preparation for a Sunday worship service or writing an outline for a Bible study lesson. For example, when my father would invite me along on a hunting trip, my identification as a preacher gave me cultural permission to respectfully decline his offer by reminding him of my religious obligations of reading the Bible and preparing for Sunday worship. If mountain preachers are expected to perform the manly tasks of mountain culture, the acts of reading the Bible and writing sermon outlines paradoxically offered a way for me to *escape* those tasks.

Reading the Bible, however, not only gave me a way out of traditional masculine activities. It also afforded me godly reverence and esteem among other men. Reading the Bible might have been functional in that it was a way to know God and the way of salvation, but it was also attractive because it represented true godliness. Because of the attractiveness of biblical literacy in mountain culture, my biblical literacy made me attractive to other men, an attraction for which I longed. It paradoxically gave me a way out of culturally normative masculine activities as well as an esteemed position within the male domain. In essence, literacy in this religious context publically affirmed my masculinity while exempting me from traditional masculine practices. To borrow from Sylvia Scribner, reading and writing as a mountain preacher were "states of grace" for me because they endowed me with "special virtue" in the male world. Biblical literacy offered me a way to cope with the conflicting identities and identifications of *preacher, sissy,* and *gay.* In Scribner's words it was, quite literally, "literacy as salvation."[19]

My experience also resonates with Scribner's description of literacy as power, "a means for poor and politically powerless groups to claim their place in the world."[20] This was certainly the case for me as I began slowly coming to terms with an unabated physical attraction to men. The church held zero tolerance for known or expected homosexuality. Preachers routinely used the so-called clobber passages or texts of terror to assure us that homosexuals were reprobate sinners, on the road to an eternal, fiery hell.[21] In my early days as a preacher, I too was sure to condemn homosexuality with references to the biblical text, lest anyone hold the slightest degree of suspicion about my own sexual preferences. If I could not hide my lack of interest in normative masculine activities, I could surely hide my physical attraction to men—and quoting the biblical text within the context of a ministerial identity was one way to do it. Biblical literacy was literacy as power, a scandalous way for me to claim my place in the church, my family, and my community. It was a subversive means to claim my place in a culture that made little space for sissies and even less space for known homosexuality. Scribner's words could well have been my personal mantra: "Not to be literate is a state of victimization."[22]

Functioning to some degree as a coping mechanism, literacy saved me for a number of years in Central Appalachia. With time, however, I longed to practice reading and writing in ways that felt more authentic to me within the context of my community. Even as my subversive use of reading and writing served as a salvific force for me as a young preacher slowly coming to terms with a gay identity, with time it also began to feel inauthentic because I was using literacy in ways that I knew were at odds with the ways my community understood it. For example, I was reading the Bible and writing sermons (community-approved literacy practices), but I was also reading books and websites that were affirming of homosexuality and gay identities (literacy practices that would have been considered at odds with a preacher's identity). I knew that reading the Bible and writing sermons informed by these new literacy practices would most certainly not be an approved use of literacy in my community. But, the more I read, the more I learned that there were religious communities in the world where I could practice and value literacy in ways that were congruent with both my ministerial and my gay identities. Learning this, I gradually began coming out as a gay man and reaching out to the kinds of communities I had once only read about online or in the books I had kept hidden from my religious community.

Today I live as an openly gay man. I legally married my husband in Washington, DC, in 2012, and we celebrated our marriage with friends in a Christian blessing ceremony in Central Appalachia that same year. I no longer use my role as preacher to escape the manly tasks of mountain culture. Neither do I hide behind pulpits, spouting sanctimonious condemnation of the very sexual nature that I possess. At the same time, my more authentic uses of literacy have come with great costs. I am no longer welcomed in the pulpit of my childhood church or any mountain church where I once preached. I have also experienced what I had long feared: the same mountain community that taught me how to read and love the biblical text quickly used the biblical text to warn me of the error of my ways and ultimately to disqualify me as a preacher. Biblical literacy in part legitimized my call to preach in mountain religious life, and the Bible has been used as textual authority to disqualify my status as a preacher.

To return to an idea of Webb-Sunderhaus's, being disqualified as a preacher on the basis of the same biblical text from which I preach is a harsh reminder of how literacy can become a "dangerous force," driving painful distance between family members and longtime friends. The first time I used writing publically in a way that felt authentic to me was when I wrote a letter to the editor of our local newspaper, the *Bristol Herald Courier*, following the release of the gay-themed mainstream movie *Brokeback Mountain* (2005). In the letter I stated that born-again Christians live and wrestle with same-sex attractions. At the time, I was serving in a ministry leadership role with a local Baptist congregation. I was ultimately disqualified from that role and asked to leave the congregation because my public use of writing was deemed contrary to the teachings found in the biblical text. But, while that and other acts on the part of my religious cohorts illustrate the dangers and distances driven by literacy, perhaps nothing compares to the literacy act of my mother, who confronted me one night with Bible in hand, her voice quivering with accusation and eyes marked with tears as she read aloud to me of false prophets from 2 Peter 2:22: "But it is happened unto them according to the true proverb, the dog is turned to his own vomit again; and the sow that was washed to her wallowing in the mire" (KJV). Indeed, authentic uses of literacy cost me a cherished place in mountain life even as they helped me claim my place in the world. Unfortunately for my mother, her father's fears have now materialized in the life of his grandson: I left home, got a seminary education, and, in my mother's eyes, got myself "into trouble."

Appropriating Literacy: Community Practices and the Academy

In a study of literacy choices in the small Appalachian town of Haines Gap, North Carolina, Kim Donehower uses Deborah Brandt's conceptualization of literacy sponsorship to explore how both secular and religious literacy sponsors from outside the Appalachian region have challenged Appalachian identities and identifications. Historically, as outside sponsors came to the mountains to educate residents of Haines Gap, local denizens who accepted these sponsors had to assimilate, reject, or appropriate the literacy practices of their sponsors in light of their own literacy practices and values. "Learning with a sponsor," Donehower writes, "involves coming to terms with the alternate worldview that sponsor offers to those who wish to study literacy. It also means coming to terms with that sponsor's view of one's own literacy and one's community."[23] Her study resonates with my own experience as an Appalachian preacher seeking recognition as a legitimate clergyperson in religious life outside Appalachia. No longer welcomed in the churches where I once preached, I began seeking official clergy recognition with the Alliance of Baptists and the United Church of Christ. Both communions have made public statements favoring the ordination of lesbians and gays. Both communions also require that clergy have formal seminary education, defined as the traditional master of divinity or its equivalent. Because I was born and bred in Appalachian mountain religion, these communions could for me be considered what Donehower considers outside sponsors of literacy, holding an "alternate worldview" from that of my Central Appalachian faith community. Formal seminary training had never before been a prerequisite for me to preach the Word of God. In fact, my Appalachian church community placed me in the pulpit even before I was ordained. To become recognized clergy with either of these communions meant that I had to come to terms with their views of my own literacy and their views of the literacy values of my Appalachian religious heritage.

My literacy journey has become what Donehower refers to as *appropriation*—modifying and hybridizing both my indigenous Appalachian literacy practices and values with the more recent literacy practices and values I have taken up through seminary and more mainline forms of Protestantism. In part because of my biblical literacy, I earned the Appalachian identifications of *preacher* and *man of God* even years before my ordination. But it was not until the day of my ordination that I was afforded another title: *Reverend.* Holding on to my Appalachian religious heritage, I still distinguish the word *Reverend* in front of my name as a mark of calling, signifying that I have been called of God and ordained in an Appalachian faith community that at one time witnessed and affirmed that calling. The abbreviation *M.Div.* following my name, however, is a mark of formal education, not of calling. Each designation marks a particular literacy practice and value. Both of them together offer a visual representation of how I appropriate my Appalachian religious literacy heritage with the literacy practices and values I have embraced through more formal academic study. My call to ministry comes from God, as witnessed and affirmed by the people of God. It is independent of formal education. However, in the same way that biblical literacy is a central and authenticating element of a preacher's identity in my Appalachian community, formal education has become a central and authenticating element of my recognition as a clergyperson within mainline Protestantism. Both these literacy practices and values coexist.

The biblical literacy I learned in Appalachia has proved to be an invaluable asset to me. Entering Wake Forest University School of Divinity in 2008 after twenty-odd years of Bible drills, Sunday school lessons, and Bible studies in a small Appalachian community helped me go deeper into academic biblical and theological studies than I could have had I enrolled in seminary with much more limited knowledge of the Bible. Moreover, my Appalachian heritage was valued at Wake Forest as an important component in a well-rounded theological education. I was encouraged and given opportunities to reexamine and reclaim my Appalachian heritage by reading and writing about it in dialogue with scholars. I was empowered, in the words of Abrams Locklear, to use the "perilous" literacy practices and values of my Appalachian community to "bear witness to the cultural [and religious] landscape from which [I] come." This very chapter is a result of that empowerment, enabling me to, again in the words of Locklear, "share [my] experience with a larger audience because [I] learned new discursive practices in which [I] can communicate more broadly."[24]

The ability to communicate more broadly while bearing witness to the cultural and religious landscape from which I come also enabled my successful completion of a postgraduate chaplaincy residency with the University of Virginia Health System in 2011–2012. When hospital patients shared with me their questions about theodicy[25] or the Bible's claims and promises, I was able to engage with them in conversation around the biblical text not only because I had three short years of seminary training, but also because I was afforded over twenty years of biblical education in a small Appalachian community. Seminary helped me with new avenues of exploration and interpretation of the Bible, but it was in those childhood and adolescent years in a small Appalachian church that I learned the text and stories of the Bible.

Valuing Literacy

The psychotherapist Bruno Bettelheim has insightfully written: "The acquisition of skills, including the ability to read, becomes devalued when what one has learned to read adds nothing of importance to one's life."[26] Although Bettelheim was writing specifically about the importance of fairy tales in the lives of children, the link between the ability to read and the perceived or actual value that reading adds to one's life can be applied to any demographic or literary genre. In this chapter, it can be seen in my grandfather's stance on biblical literacy. Reading, an act that threatened to take away his daughter, leading her "into trouble," added importance to his life as a central and authenticating element of his identity as a man of God and preacher in mountain culture. Bettelheim's statement also resonates with my own experience as a mountain preacher, as a man gradually coming to terms with his sexuality, and as a lover of reading and writing as acts in and of themselves. But, perhaps most importantly, reading the Bible—the text I learned to read at the earliest of ages—continues to add importance to my life today as a preacher, chaplain, and displaced Appalachian.

On the day of my ordination, I was well aware of the similarities and differences between my grandfather and me. I was also aware that many members of our community viewed my calling as a calling to follow in my grandfather's footsteps. As I stood before that congregation in that small mountain church, I was given big shoes to fill—too big, in fact—shoes that did not seem to fit my feet. My grandfather had performed the traditional masculine activities that set him clearly within the male domain. He married a woman and conceived ten children, the ultimate expectation of any young preacher in the mountains. How could I—a man who loved cooking, playing the piano, and planting sunflowers—fill the shoes of a man who regaled us with stories of his manly history? Could I suppress my love for men enough to follow his path and happily marry a woman? How would I fill the shoes of someone whose ability to read was not learned but a miraculous, instantaneous gift? Given our differences, it would take a miracle. What I now realize is that, like my grandfather's, my ability to read *is* the miracle. It is the miracle that unites our narratives as readers and preachers of the biblical text even as those narratives tell very different stories. Literacy has served as an authenticating component to our identities as mountain preachers even as we both wrestled in our own distinct ways with how to practice and value literacy as men of Appalachia.

Notes

I thank Dr. Bill J. Leonard, Dr. Linda McKinnish Bridges, and the Reverend Pauline Binkley Cheek for empowering witness to the Appalachian religious landscape from which I come.

    1. See Deborah Vansau McCauley, *Appalachian Mountain Religion: A History* (Urbana: University of Illinois Press, 1995); and Howard Dorgan, *Giving Glory to God in Appalachia: Worship Practices of Six Baptist Subdenominations* (Knoxville: University of Tennessee Press, 1987).

2. The theological distinctions between Calvinism and Arminianism can be traced to the historical characters of the Protestant Reformation John Calvin and Jacobus Arminius. While neither of these terms was used to describe the beliefs of the Missionary Baptists or of Pentecostal Holiness in my Appalachian community, those beliefs were nonetheless developments of the ideas of our Christian forebears.

3. Deborah Brandt, *Literacy in American Lives* (New York: Cambridge University Press, 2001), 3; Mike Baynham and Mastin Prinsloo, "Introduction: The Future of Literacy Studies," in *The Future of Literacy Studies,* ed. Mike Baynham and Mastin Prinsloo (New York: Palgrave, 2009), 1–20, 2.

4. Brian Street, "The Future of 'Social Literacies,'" in Baynham and Prinsloo, eds., *The Future of Literacy Studies,* 21–37, 22.

5. Brandt, *Literacy in American Lives,* 19.

6. Deborah Brandt, *Literacy and Learning: Reflections on Writing, Reading, and Society* (San Francisco: Jossey-Bass, 2009), 25.

7. Sara Webb-Sunderhaus, "A Family Affair: Competing Sponsors of Literacy in Appalachian Students' Lives," *Community Literacy Journal* 2, no. 1 (2007): 5–24, 15.

8. Erica Abrams Locklear, *Negotiating a Perilous Empowerment: Appalachian Women's Literacies* (Athens: Ohio University Press, 2011), 2.

9. Sylvia Scribner, "Literacy in Three Metaphors," *American Journal of Education* 93 (1984): 6–21, 9.

10. Kim Donehower, Charlotte Hogg, and Eileen E. Schell, *Rural Literacies* (Carbondale: Southern Illinois University Press, 2007), 55.

11. Webb-Sunderhaus, "A Family Affair," 7.

12. Ibid., 12.

13. See McCauley, *Appalachian Mountain Religion,* 190.

14. Webb-Sunderhaus notes this kind of literacy sponsorship in her study. For example, one student's grandparents sponsored her literacy not through teaching particular literacy practices but by providing study space. Webb-Sunderhaus, "A Family Affair," 11.

15. Snyder, chapter 4 in this volume, 84.

16. Anita Puckett, "'Let the Girls Do the Spelling and Dan Will Do the Shooting': Literacy, the Division of Labor, and Identity in a Rural Appalachian Community," *Anthropological Quarterly* 65, no. 3 (July 1992): 137–47, 137, 139, 137, 138, 143.

17. Ibid., 145, 146.

18. Gary Farley and Bill J. Leonard, "Mountain Preachers, Mountain Ministers," in *Christianity in Appalachia: Profiles of Regional Pluralism,* ed. Bill J. Leonard (Knoxville: University of Tennessee Press, 1999), 153–64, 154.

19. Scribner, "Literacy in Three Metaphors," 13.

20. Ibid., 75.

21. The traditional so-called clobber passages have been discussed by a number of scholars. See, e.g., Daniel A. Helminiak, *What the Bible Really Says about Homosexuality,* millennium ed. (Tajique, NM: Alamo Square, 1994). The phrase *texts of terror* is

perhaps best known from the work of the feminist biblical scholar Phyllis Trible. See Phyllis Trible, *Texts of Terror: Literary-Feminist Readings of Biblical Narratives* (Philadelphia: Fortress, 1984). Both *clobber passages* and *texts of terror* have become common parlance in discussions about homosexuality and the biblical text.

22. Scribner, "Literacy in Three Metaphors," 12.

23. Kim Donehower, "Literacy Choices in an Appalachian Community," *Journal of Appalachian Studies* 9, no. 2 (Fall 2003): 341–62, 344.

24. Locklear, *Negotiating a Perilous Empowerment*, 11.

25. Theodicy has been described as "reasoning about God in the face of universal evil, or human suffering in general, or egregious historical manifestations of evil . . . [or] concrete individual suffering, evil experienced in one's own body or observed in a loved one or a patient, from the perspective of a victim or a survivor or a witness." Margaret E. Mohrmann, "Introduction: Suffering, Medicine and Faith," in *Pain Seeking Understanding: Suffering, Medicine, and Faith,* ed. Margaret E. Mohrmann and Mark J. Hanson (Cleveland: Pilgrim, 1999), 1–9, 1–2.

26. Bruno Bettelheim, *The Uses of Enchantment: The Meaning and Importance of Fairy Tales* (New York: Penguin, 1976), 4.

6

Diverse Rhetorical Scenes of Urban Appalachian Literacies

Kathryn Trauth Taylor

In the late 1940s, my grandma, "Grammy," quit eighth grade and abandoned her home on the rural outskirts of the Appalachian region to migrate to downtown Cincinnati with her daughters—my mother and aunt—in search of better work and educational opportunities. Though growing up we were known by our country cousins as city slickers, our Appalachian heritage carried through the generations in our urban family's strong kinship values, sense of home place, love of music, and respect for the land—not to mention in Grammy's gift for quilting and crafting and her unique ways of pronouncing *fire* and *well*. I was never taught to call ours an *Appalachian* heritage. It was not until I took an Appalachian literature course in college that I first recognized my family as Urban Appalachians, or Appalachian migrants and their descendants. It was here that my English professor, Sherry Cook Stanforth, shared poems that reflected the tensions of owning her Appalachian identity in the academy and introduced me to diverse Appalachian authors, including the group the Affrilachian Poets, whose words carved a space for African Americans to own their Appalachian heritage as well. In reading these works, I became aware of the diverse, quilt-worked identity that Appalachians could create beyond the mountains.

This chapter is shaped by these early experiences. I share here a collage of contemporary Appalachian identity and literacy performances from the

Urban Appalachian communities of Cincinnati, Ohio. Frank X Walker's poem "Affrilachia" highlights the complexities of place and race in Urban Appalachian identity. He writes:

> Anywhere in Appalachia
> is about as far
> as you could get
> from our house
> in the projects
> yet
> a mutual appreciation
> for fresh greens
> and cornbread
> an almost heroic notion
> of family
> and porches
> makes us kinfolk
> somehow.[1]

In the first decade of the twenty-first century, the Appalachian community saw a growing recognition of its diverse members, including Urban Appalachians and Affrilachians—*Affrilachian* being a term coined by Walker in 1991 as a name for African Americans who consider themselves part of Appalachia.[2] In light of these inclusions, scholars, researchers, artists, and community advocates are increasingly encouraging more fluid, complex, and dynamic understandings of Appalachian identity.[3] Today, more than twenty years after the creation of the term *Affrilachian,* Affrilachian art and rhetoric emerge from communities of African American Appalachians both within and beyond the geographic boundaries of the region—complicating traditional, albeit stereotypical, conceptions of Appalachian identity. Within this growing rhetorical ecology—or interactive space of language and culture—researchers in Cincinnati are broadening their methods of identifying Urban Appalachians to include Affrilachians and other minorities. This chapter explores such institutional changes alongside literacy performances by Urban Appalachians, drawing on poetry readings, video documentaries, play performances, writing workshops, and print collections.

I use the terms *literacy performances* and *identity performances* in a rhetorical sense, to mean public language performances that represent, challenge, conjure, or negotiate conceptions of Appalachian identity, community, and culture. How can language choices change people's conceptions of Appalachians? What rhetorical language decisions provide Urban Appalachians with community support and understanding? My project, in other words, works at the intersection of literacy and rhetoric. We often talk about literacy in terms of acquiring or honoring ways of talking, reading, and writing. Alternatively, we often talk about rhetoric as an awareness of the impacts of different language choices. Here, I bring both concepts together to explain how literacy performances are composed rhetorically to negotiate and broaden understandings of Urban Appalachian identity. The literacy scholar Erica Abrams Locklear explains that accumulating new literacies requires social and cultural negotiations that often endanger home relationships and discourse communities. As Appalachian people "learn to juggle entrance into disparate worlds via literate practices,"[4] rhetoric can, I argue, play a strategic role in that negotiation. As a practice of interpreting and generating awareness of language choices, rhetoric offers strategies for harnessing the emotive and symbolic powers of Appalachian literacies—especially for people upholding Appalachian identity in regions that are not geographically Appalachian. In such diverse cityscapes, literacy performances are capable of establishing and generating respect for difference. Public literacy performances—from poetry readings to play productions—invite community members in Cincinnati to grapple with their unique identities and build connections across what were once ethnic divides. Before sharing such artistic literacy performances, I offer an overview of the rhetorical research performances of Urban Appalachian institutions in the city. If we view identity in an interactive, ecological way, then both artistic and institutional performances influence and inspire one another—much like the crowded, busy intersections of Cincinnati's diverse Urban Appalachian neighborhoods.

Theoretical Frameworks

A major goal of this project is to explore the artistic, academic, and institutional ways in which people are resisting static conceptions of Appalachian identity. Before beginning that exploration, I offer Janice Fernheimer's idea of *dissociative disruption*—the practice of complicating or disrupting static or universal identities—as a theoretical framework for viewing the rhetorical power of diverse literacy performances in the city. Dissociative disruption works by bringing about "an awareness of alternative conceptions, even if these conceptions are not immediately embraced by those endowed with hegemonic and institutional power." Focusing on the black effort to be recognized as part of the Jewish community in Israel, Fernheimer explains that through dissociative disruption that effort "reconfigures Judaism to take notice of and account for black faces, which historically have been erased from the hegemonic, visual epideictic of Jewishness."[5] One method for doing so was to create "wreck,"[6] or disruptive spectacle intended to showcase and centralize experiences that are otherwise marginalized.

By encouraging this kind of individualized identity negotiation, Urban Appalachian and Affrilachian art continues to foster diverse voices, claiming them as part of the Appalachian landscape. For example, before Walker coined the term *Affrilachian,* even *Webster's* dictionary defined Appalachians as "white residents from the mountains." Now, after much insistence, both the 2005 revised edition of the *Oxford American Dictionary* and the 2006 *Encyclopedia of Appalachia* include the term *Affrilachian.* By seeking a recognized space for African Americans within conceptions of Appalachia, Affrilachian poetry utilizes dissociative disruption to amplify voices that were previously silenced—working beyond the scope of counternarratives, moving marginalized voices to the center.

The growing scene of Urban Appalachian and Affrilachian art in Cincinnati utilizes wreck and disruption to create a space for multiple identities. Here, I argue that such efforts create a rhetorical scene of influence—an "ecology"—that encourages a multiplicity of disruptions to traditional conceptions of Appalachian identity. Borrowing from Jenny Edbauer Rice's idea of viral rhetorical ecologies, I intentionally use the word *ecology* to suggest the collective and increasingly inclusive effects of disruption.[7] The marginal spaces occupied by Urban Appalachians and African American Appalachians are disrupted through identity performances that move minorities to the center of Appalachian identity and away from the margins—extending former ecological boundaries and creating new spaces for inclusiveness. The experiences of blacks in Appalachia were not circulated until they were named, not meaningful until they were performed, and not rhetorical until their performances inspired new conceptions of Appalachian identity. Affrilachian art, in other words, authorizes and propagates identity through language performances that, when viewed together, create a viral ecology of rhetorical influence that, once institutionalized, becomes socioeconomically, culturally, and educationally powerful. By exploring Appal/

Affrilachian literacy performances like poetry writing and play production alongside institutional changes in support for Urban Appalachians in the city, I hope to reveal how urban spaces open themselves up as places where multiple Appalachian identities can thrive.

Institutionalizing Inclusive Appalachian Identities

Let us begin with a brief history lesson. One of the earliest writings on race relations in Appalachia was published in 1916 by Carter G. Woodson, known today as the father of black history. Tracing Appalachian contributions to the antislavery movement in the pre–Civil War United States, Woodson referred to white Appalachians as "the friends of freedom in Appalachian America." He cited the inclusion of African American students at Kentucky's Berea College in the 1890s as a courageous early example of white Appalachian support of black education and freedom. "In Appalachian America," he explained, "the races still maintain a sort of social contact. White and black men work side by side, visit each other in their homes, and often attend the same church to listen with delight to the Word spoken by either a colored or white preacher." For Woodson, the mountains offered a space of warmth and interaction between races that was rarely felt in urban spaces, where, "in passing from the tidewater to the mountains, it seems like going from one country into another."[8] While Woodson is certainly guilty of overgeneralizing and romanticizing the issue of race in Appalachia, it is true that the passage from the mountains to the city marked a dramatic intensification of race relations. Between 1940 and 1970 in particular, more than seven million Appalachians joined African American migrant communities in cities like Cincinnati, catalyzing new tensions between urban ethnic groups. By 1943, race relations were making news in this city, and in 1944 six pastors wrote a joint statement encouraging community members to exhibit "neighborliness toward both the mountaineer and Negro neighbors who are moving into our part of the West End."[9] In *Uneven Ground*, Ronald D Eller adds: "The migration of millions of young whites from Appalachia and young blacks from the Deep South into the cities of the Midwest added to the congestion and poverty of urban ghettoes, and the shocking scenes of rural blight captured by the media during John F. Kennedy's 1960 presidential primary campaign in West Virginia contradicted popular notions of an affluent America."[10]

By the early 1970s, the Urban Appalachian Council (UAC) was established in Cincinnati to help increase the quality of life for Appalachian migrants in the city. During this early period, Urban Appalachians were recognized because of their surprising invisibility. Because they were a predominantly white minority, their concerns and challenges were often overlooked, made invisible by the assumption that they were merely part of an existing white middle class in the city.[11] Therefore, in the formative years of the organization, the UAC devised a rhetorical strategy to characterize Urban Appalachians an *invisible minority*—drawing attention to their unique struggles, despite their appearance as white mainstream residents.[12] While this strategy continues to fund health, literacy, education, and employment support for the group, it also (historically) restricted conceptions of Urban Appalachians to white people. In addition, owing to the small number of self-identifying African American Appalachians in the city, social needs surveys before 2005 classified counties as Appalachian on the basis of their *lack* of African American residents, further restricting conceptions of the group's diversity.[13] At a recent poetry celebration of Cincinnati's diverse urban neighborhoods called "Our Beloved Community," one older black resident explained that, when he was a boy, Appalachians lived in one part of the neighborhood and African Americans in another. Growing up here, he knew which streets belonged to which groups—and they did not integrate. My mom, a generation younger than this man, similarly recalls racial tensions during the civil rights movement, when her high school grew increasingly diverse. As white Urban Appalachians, her family faced economic struggles similar to those of many African Americans at the time. Our family stories recall how Grammy worked factory jobs, sewed school dresses for her daughters, and kept their small apartment perfectly clean—without the additional help of a man.

It was shortly after that time—in the 1970s—that researchers in Cincinnati began conducting social needs surveys to measure the socioeconomic circumstances of Urban Appalachians in the city.[14] Noting a number of health and wellness concerns, including diabetes and heart disease, researchers began health-status surveys in the 1990s. In the first health-status surveys, conducted in 1996 and 1999, researchers were surprised to find that the health status of the Appalachian population in Cincinnati was poorer than that of any other group, including the African American population.[15] The results challenged community assumptions about disparities between blacks and whites and drew attention to Urban Appalachians as an invisible white minority facing unique health challenges. Owing to their use of race as a way of distinguishing Urban Appalachians' challenges from those of African Americans, these early surveys did not acknowledge the identities of Affrilachians. However, thanks to growing recognition of Affrilachians in literacy performances across the city, Cincinnati researchers began broadening their methods of identification.

Two of the leading researchers behind the health-status surveys, Robert Ludke and Phillip Obermiller, were kind enough to speak with me about how their research methods and survey results have changed over the years.[16] Most recently, Ludke and his colleagues conducted a phone survey of 2,007 randomly selected adults in the Cincinnati area to determine how many were Appalachian. First, they asked participants whether they were first- or second-generation Appalachians, a determination based on county of origin/birth. Then, for the first time, they began relying on self-identification: they asked participants whether they *considered* themselves Appalachian. As a result of this more inclusive research method, about fifty individuals identified as African American Appalachians.[17] Inspired by these results and, no doubt, the growing scene of Affrilachian art in the city and at the UAC, these researchers are also in the process of aggregating data across years in order to gain larger representations of urban Affrilachians.[18]

Broadening research methods to acknowledge urban African American Appalachians has no little consequence when it comes to issues of socioeconomic assistance and program funding. When determining which cities it will provide with financial support and social programming, the Appalachian Regional Commission (ARC) relies on geographic rather than performed definitions of identity. Theresa I. Myadze, a professor of social work at Wright State University, published a study in 2006 revealing that urban blacks living within counties deemed Appalachian are more likely to receive ARC assistance and other resources. As a result, "urban blacks in the selected Appalachian areas are faring better than their counterparts in selected areas of non-Appalachian Alabama in terms of a number of socioeconomic indicators," including poverty, labor force participation, unemployment, median earnings, and educational attainment.[19] In counties within geographically Appalachian borders, urban Affrilachians had an overall better quality of life than did urban African Americans living outside those borders.

One method for broadening such support efforts in Cincinnati—a city that falls one county beyond the ARC conception of Appalachia—is to rely more on self-identification or affiliation with Appalachian identity. In our interview, Obermiller explained that self- and community identifiers are important because they emphasize social networks and associations rather than birthplace. Such social markers help Appalachians channel a "sense of peoplehood" that increases the possibilities for literacy, educational, financial, and cultural support. Obermiller believes that social change comes from saying, "We are Appalachian, and we want *this*—even if we're not in the mountains, even if we weren't born there either."[20] As the term *Appalachian* grows in complexity, researchers in Cincinnati now acknowledge that "convergence to a single identity may be difficult, if it is possible at all."[21] What we can take from these observations is the recognition that a sense of peoplehood is incredibly important in such struggles but that this peoplehood cannot and should not be considered homogeneous or static.

Today, decades after this tense time, the UAC plays host to many ethnic groups and acknowledges that the term *Appalachian* "may consist of multiple identities."[22] A brochure on the UAC's Web site explains that 34 percent of Greater Cincinnatians are of Appalachian descent, despite the fact that many residents either are not aware of their heritage or purposely choose not to identify with it.[23] The harsh stereotypes of Appalachians that still pervade mainstream culture—and the many hillbilly jokes heard around the city—contribute to negative connotations of that heritage as well as narrow definitions of who is considered Appalachian.

As an organization, the UAC today espouses a more dynamic sense of peoplehood, not only in its research methods, but also in its historical materials. A page about "Migration" on the UAC Web site now explains that, in 1974, the UAC began its efforts to "promote a decent quality of life for Appalachian citizens in Greater Cincinnati." By concentrating on issues concerning Urban Appalachians, this historical narrative depicts the UAC as an advocate for other struggling groups, with the goal of "improving the quality of life for the entire community." In its revised description of Urban Appalachians, the organization emphasizes diversity and recognition: "We are your neighbors, co-workers, friends, professionals, service providers, and artists (to name a few). With more than 213,000 first and second generation white and black Appalachians in Hamilton County, you're bound to know one of us. We helped build this community of life in all shapes, sizes, and religions. We are an important part of Cincinnati's history—and its future."[24]

The language here is quite different from the UAC's earlier emphasis on invisibility (the "invisible minority"). Drawing attention instead to diversity within collectivity, the UAC puts forward more inclusive definitions of Urban Appalachian identity and outreach, building connections with other local minorities, such as Hispanics and African Americans. What is most important to Urban Appalachian identity today is a commitment to sharing and respecting diverse experiences. If individual and collective identity experiences are not shared, what it means to be Appalachian becomes lost, and that puts support efforts at greater risk. It is essential in such times to use rhetorical strategies to support diverse Urban Appalachian identity performances and to negotiate the common threads that run through those performances.

Negotiating a New View of Urban Appalachian Literacy

Literacy is one way through which identity performances are realized. As we share and negotiate new views of Urban Appalachian identity, we must consider the following: How do we create respect for literacy practices that receive little to no respect, and how do we justify our teaching of agreed-on practices that are expected to generate respect and professional opportunity? Following a trend in Appalachian literacy studies, most literacy research among Urban Appalachians depicts residents as lacking rhetorical and language tools that will make them successful in school. Perhaps the most comprehensive and potentially damaging of these studies is by Victoria Purcell-Gates, who follows two Urban Appalachians, Jenny and her son Donny, and their difficulty learning to read and write at work and in school. Through her depiction of Appalachian language practices as a kind of *il*literacy in comparison to mainstream literacy, Purcell-Gates's research propagates a stereotyped tension around what it means to be an Appalachian in classrooms and workspaces that often demand middle-class ways of talking and writing. Although residents like Donny and Jenny can face unique literacy struggles because of cultural and class differences, such studies perpetuate negative views of Urban Appalachians as a group always in *lack*.[25]

Kathleen Bennett does a better job of acknowledging this problem and offering a potential solution. She situates cultural assimilation as the conflict site of Appalachian literacy acquisition, observing that students in her study were expected to become school literate by reading stories that depicted city life only from the perspective of upper-middle-class families. "The stories," she concludes, "had little relevance to the lived daily experiences of poor, urban Appalachian children."[26] Despite the stereotype of poverty associated with Urban Appalachians here, Bennett's study does demand an ethical responsibility on the part of teachers to implement culturally relevant curriculum for their students. Both Purcell-Gates and Bennett bring to light important tensions between honoring literacy heritages and at the same time providing resources and skills necessary for work and educational achievement. Because of this tense history between acknowledging versus stereotyping Appalachian Otherness, literacy studies must be careful to examine the ways in which dominant theories of literacy privilege certain cultural, regional, and ethnic groups over others.

One way to pursue this conflict is to encourage, create, and share literacy performances from people who live, work, and learn within Urban Appalachian communities. Rather than begin with the goal of alleviating illiteracy, I begin at the site of performance—reading and writing about the literacy performances of residents as they negotiate their own identities in urban spaces. As Maureen Mullinax writes in her description of community-based arts projects in Harlan County, Kentucky: "Music, poetry, and drama can be used strategically to forge a shared experience and develop a collective identity in social justice efforts."27 In the following section, I share Urban Appalachian literacy performances delivered to the Cincinnati community in a variety of media, from print narratives to documentary films and historical plays.

Performing Appalachian Literacy in Urban Space

The first performance I share here comes from a literacy narrative titled "Looking in the Mirror," published in the 1991 collection *Appalachia*. The narrator, John Russell, returns to his long-unvisited Appalachian home of Wythe County, Virginia, after having lived most of his adult life in a nearby city. When recalling his childhood, Russell explains: "I never realized we were poor, never thought about being black, never felt isolated, never felt inconvenienced, was never hungry but was always confident." Yet, on returning to the county, he identifies the region in these discriminating ways, recalling many of its "indications of despair." Removed from Appalachia, he returns with an interpellating perspective, understanding his past as part of a larger cultural stereotype of poverty and illiteracy: "For me and many more 'ignorance was bliss.' We didn't complain; we knew no other way. We asked for nothing because we knew not what to ask for."28 Russell's narrative compares his childhood identity in the mountains with his current life in the city, drawing sharp distinctions between the two. When I read his story, I cannot help but wish that it featured *more* negotiation—more recognition of the loss that often accompanies such harsh, new perspectives on one's home place. I find myself wishing that, for the sake of many Appalachians who continue to carry the mountains with them into new cityscapes, his story offered our heritage more respect. By offering instead an image of progressive assimilation, Russell feeds into the typical dualism between insiders and outsiders in literacy scholarship on urban Appalachia—and, as a result, ignores possibilities for dynamic, ecological negotiations of his identity.[29]

Yet a different Urban Appalachian literacy performance does foreground negotiation as central to life in the city. The documentary film *Although Our Fields Were Streets* (1991) hosts a series of interviews with urban residents who recently migrated from rural Appalachia. Marlin Wightman, one contributor who moved from Cumberland County, Tennessee, to Cincinnati reflects on his first perceptions of the city. "Cincinnati," he says, "had sounds . . . had smells . . . had Saks. When I got up in the morning I could hear the street bells clanging on Vine Street." He describes one of his preferred activities in his new home near Washington Park as one that extends and negotiates his past memories of home: "We was near Washington Park, and I used to go there, and it was my connection with rural America to sit on the benches and look at the trees and watch the pigeons. I didn't look at them as pests. I looked at them as beautiful birds. . . . Cincinnati had an attraction to me that's hard to describe. It just seemed like home."[30]

For Wightman, the sights of nature—the trees, squirrels, and pigeons—in Washington Park helped him re-create home. "There is no back home to me now," he explains. "When I go back to Tennessee, it's not going back home; it's visiting relatives." Later in the documentary, another community member sings a traditional Appalachian ballad that addresses the pressures of such negotiations:

> Two coats were before me, an old and a new
> I could have either, so what must I do
> One coat was ugly and terribly torn
> The other a new one, had never been worn
> . . . .
> I'll tell you the best thing I ever did do
> I laid off the old coat and put on the new.[31]

Although narratives like Marlin Wightman's are not diverse in a strictly racial sense, they do help us recognize that identity will be reconceived individually in light of new spaces and relationships. Appalachian migrants negotiate new senses of place in the city by both honoring their home spaces (or family roots) and settling comfortably into new cityscapes.

As a current volunteer at the UAC, I hear similar stories of identity negotiation. The "Write to Education" program at the UAC's East Price Hill Community School incorporates weekly poetry- and prose-writing workshops into its GED curriculum. In these workshops, students of all ages, races, and backgrounds—many of whom identify as Appalachian—share literacy performances on topics like home, memory, and community. After writing, almost all choose to read their work aloud, and we all write down lines from other people's poems that we find memorable or inspiring. As we share, voices overlap, emerge, and create chains of lines that connect our poems together. It is a powerful and beautiful experience to hear the lines spoken aloud in a connected way. After hearing of the many challenges facing the Price Hill community, one Urban Appalachian woman recently reflected: "We're all the same. . . . We have the same experiences, but we're just different ages and from different places, you know?"

The indigenous writer and scholar Linda Tuhiwai Smith argues that, without the literacy performances of storytelling, remembering, connecting, creating, and sharing, communities can turn inward and "let their suffering give way to a desire to be dead."[32] Such desires often stem from a people's weariness of both economic suffering and cultural disrespect. Although the stories shared in our writing groups do not reflect a single, historical group event or suffering, they are often connected by shared experiences of struggle. Rather than allowing such hardships to destroy their communities, however, residents in our writing workshops band together and keep community alive in spite of struggle. During a workshop on the topic of memory, one woman with four young children wrote about the very recent murder of her husband. Another man wrote about his experience overcoming an alcohol addiction that kept him from being a better father. Turning such stories into group poems, we wrote that we are from "southern folks who had not much / but all they needed." Other voices continued:

Everywhere I go is home to me now.

Home is where my heart is
not brick
not mortar
nor stone.

Home for us is where raising our children "takes a village." We wrote of "highways dividing up neighborhoods / making it seem like there's no difference between them." We dreamed of safe places where "people who wanna get clean can feel safe / so they, too, can have a chance to be successful." The writers in our group come from diverse backgrounds, and, although we do not all share a common (indigenous) heritage, our struggles and reflections are powerful when they are connected through the act of composing.

By sharing and showcasing literacy performances that negotiate what it means to be Urban Appalachian, residents and artists in Cincinnati take back some of the control relinquished to earlier literacy scholars who depicted their language practices as inferior to school literacies. Institutional standards will continue to play a part in the identity ecology of the city, but there are many other means of expressing and sharing Urban Appalachian language experiences. By analyzing the rhetorical impacts of these literacy performances, we begin to see how different rhetorical choices (like Wightman's re-creation of rural life in the city and our group decision that it "takes a village") shape the possibilities of Urban Appalachian identity. Literacy performances such as those collected in *Although Our Fields Were Streets* and the "Write to Education" program inspire communities to honor diverse and self-sponsored views of Urban Appalachian identity.

Collective Literacy Performances

When brought together, such literacy performances hold special value and generate a more powerful impact in communities. The final Urban Appalachian literacy performance that I share here comes from a young-adult play called *Cincinnati: A City of Immigrants*. The production, which toured through a number of schools in the Greater Cincinnati area in 2012, features German, Irish, Jewish, African American, Appalachian, and Hispanic immigrants who move to Cincinnati in shared hopes of a better life. By weaving together the voices of many immigrants, the play represents the historical accumulation of diverse peoples into the city and the resulting respect that ought to be accorded contemporary people who seem different but who in fact are part of the city's long history of immigration. Yet the project aims to do more than simply create awareness of diversity; it was funded in hopes of reducing the amount of bullying and violence experienced by Hispanic middle and high school students in the city. There are very real material ends to this kind of literacy performance.

Take, for instance, the changes I observed in the audience when the play was performed at Holy Family School, a private K–8 school in Price Hill, Cincinnati. When the German, Irish, Jewish, and African American characters walked onstage and introduced themselves, there was a quiet respect in the audience similar to that expected at a play. However, when the Appalachian immigrant introduced herself as Jenny, she spoke in a rural accent, and the audience erupted in teasing laughter. When the Hispanic man followed her and introduced himself as Javier, a similar strain of laughter repeated. Even from the play's beginning, the more contemporary immigrant groups faced the ridicule and cultural stereotyping that are somehow socially acceptable when directed toward hillbillies and Mexicans. I felt uncomfortable and curious that these more contemporary immigrants were offered less respect by the young audience than were the historical immigrant groups who have already found valid and valued status in the city.

What was (and is) more fascinating to me was the potential of this play to change the audience's views. As the play goes on, the characters' voices begin to overlap, with lines and stage positions weaving back and forth among characters to create a sense of unity in their struggles. The German immigrant shares a story of race riots against Germans in the nineteenth century and the fear she felt trying to find her family during the chaos. The African American immigrant, who had lost her son to slavery, tells of migrating north after the Civil War to rent her own apartment in the part of town that allowed black residents, hoping to see her son on the city streets, but never finding him. The identity performances within the play are emotional; they invite young audiences to empathize with the migrants' experiences. This is especially true of the Appalachian and Hispanic immigrants. While at first I was upset that the children jeered at these characters, by the end of the play they were clapping and cheering for them. The play encouraged the children to view the Appalachian and Hispanic immigrants not as stereotypes but as individuals facing unique struggles, deserving immense respect.

Javier shares an experience of violence he faced during an innocent family dinner at a restaurant in Price Hill when five white men made insulting remarks about how his family should not be at the restaurant—how they shouted, "Go back to Mexico!" Jenny's story overlaps with Javier's by the play's end. After migrating to Cincinnati from the Appalachian Mountains in the 1940s, Jenny takes us through her first day at work as a waitress in Price Hill. Although she cannot read or write, she develops an elaborate system of symbols that she secretly uses to take customers' orders. Eventually, the older woman who hired her recognizes that she cannot read the menu or write out the orders, so she smiles and begins teaching her how to read. It turns out that the restaurant Jenny started working at as a young girl eventually became *her* restaurant—the same restaurant that Javier visited with his family when they were verbally abused. Jenny, an old woman by then, kicks the violent men out of her restaurant and then, on their invitation, joins Javier's family to finish dinner together with them in peace.

Viewing this play as a literacy performance, we see how the playwright's decision to overlap the characters' stories, the director's decision to overlap the characters' stage positions, and the actors' decisions to use authentic accents became a rhetorical argument for an acceptance of difference and a demand for inclusion. Jenny and Javier are different, yet their emotional struggles are similar: both feel out of place in a society that believes them to be less deserving of respect. Although the Urban Appalachian immigrant in this play is depicted as illiterate, her inability to read and write is not an indicator of ignorance; her symbol system is elaborate and shows signs of great intelligence. Because the play relies on emotional connections with young audiences, it makes sense that elementary school students—most still learning to read and write themselves—would empathize with Jenny's experiences. Here, to be Appalachian is to be clever and resourceful, kind and just. The same children who laughed when Jenny and Javier came onstage later cheered when Jenny shooed Javier's attackers out of her restaurant. Such literacy performances make an incredible impact on urban communities like Price Hill, where families from diverse backgrounds visit the same libraries, eat at the same restaurants, play on the same playgrounds, and attend the same schools. "Cincinnati: A City of Immigrants" makes a rhetorical argument about urban identity that wrecks harsh stereotypes and forges new communal bonds.

Implications and Future Work

Contemplating such urban literacy performances in a rhetorical key reveals the ways in which artistic, academic, and organizational efforts can generate more positive conceptions of Urban Appalachian identity. A rhetorical, ecological framework draws our attention to important interactions between art, survey data, individual experience, organizational change, and collective representation. Rather than viewing the UAC's definitions and research methods as separate from poems and songs, such a framework encourages us to imagine how literacy performances interact and influence one another. In these important ways, Appalachian studies can offer rhetoric and literacy scholars a complex context for understanding identity, literacy, collective heritage, community engagement, and spatial politics. In our interview, Phillip Obermiller expressed a hopeful concern that more rhetoric and composition scholars attend the annual Appalachian Studies Association conference, publish in Appalachian studies journals, and explore or contribute to projects at Appalshop.org.[33] Collaborating on local issues can bring our fields' professionals together and offer both groups new methods for supporting and honoring diverse urban communities.

In return, scholars of rhetoric and literacy can offer Appalachian studies understandings of identity that situate individuals within complex frameworks negotiated in terms of language choices and methodological possibilities. As a strategy for making us more aware of the power of our literacy performances, rhetoric can play a critical role in generating more diverse conceptions of Appalachian identity and building networked collaborations of support for communities facing histories of oppression and negative representation. When viewed rhetorically, literacy performances can help advocates, artists, and residents do the kind of work recommended by Fisher and Smith—wielding language to help build "strategic lateral relationships among peoples, places, and ideas that transcend social, spatial, and ideological barricades (such as between . . . rural and urban, white and black)."[34]

If literacy demands confrontation and negotiation of languages, rhetoric provides us with strategies for imagining all the creative potential of our words—and the many material effects of our language choices. By naming minority experiences like those of African American Appalachians, the term *Affrilachian* can be taken up by individuals whose lives and bodies were not recognized before. By broadening its research methods, the UAC can contribute to increasingly diverse and fluid understandings of Appalachian identity and, as a result, serve a larger network of people in the Greater Cincinnati area. By drawing connections between unique immigrant experiences, play performances can disrupt social expectations about minority groups and make our communities safer places to live, learn, and work. It is our responsibility as instructors and writers to engage and encourage diverse literacy performances that shape and reshape what it means to be Appalachian.

Notes

I thank the institutional leaders at the Urban Appalachian Council and the many wonderful residents who utilize its services for their participation in, and collaboration on, this research.

1. Frank X Walker, *Affrilachia* (Lexington, KY: Old Cove, 2000), 92–93.

2. Frank X Walker has published five books of poetry, served as editor of the first journal of Affrilachian art and culture (*Pluck!*), founded the group Affrilachian Poets, helped create the first video documentary of Affrilachia, *Coal Black Voices* (2001), and inspired such advancements as Dwight B. Billings, Edwina Pendarvis, and Mary Kay Thomas, eds., "Whiteness and Racialization in Appalachia," special issue, *Journal of Appalachian Studies,* vol. 10, nos. 1–2 (2004). See also Henry Louis Gates Jr., *Colored People* (New York: Vintage, 1995); Wilburn Hayden Jr., "Appalachian Diversity: African-American, Hispanic/Latino, and Other Populations," *Journal of Appalachian Studies* 10, no. 3 (2004): 293–306; John C. Inscoe, ed., *Appalachians and Race: The Mountain South from Slavery to Segregation* (Lexington: University Press of Kentucky, 2001); Ronald L. Lewis, *Black Coal Miners in America: Coal, Class, and Community Conflict, 1780–1980* (Lexington: University Press of Kentucky, 1987); Theda Perdue, *Slavery and the Evolution of Cherokee Society, 1540–1866* (Knoxville: University of Tennessee Press, 1979); Barbara Ellen Smith, "De-Gradations of Whiteness: Appalachia and the Complexities of Race," *Journal of Appalachian Studies* 10, nos. 1–2 (2004): 38–57; Joe William Trotter, *Coal, Class, Color: Blacks in Southern West Virginia, 1915–32,* Blacks in the New World (Urbana: University of Illinois Press, 1990); and William H. Turner and Edward J. Cabbell, eds., *Blacks in Appalachia* (Lexington: University Press of Kentucky, 1985).

3. See Dwight B. Billings, Gurney Norman, and Katherine Ledford, *Back Talk from Appalachia: Confronting Stereotypes* (Lexington: University Press of Kentucky, 2001); Phillip J. Obermiller and Michael E. Maloney, "Living City, Feeling Country: The Current Status and Future Prospects of Urban Appalachians," in *Appalachia: Social Context Past and Present* (3rd ed.), ed. Bruce Ergood and Bruce E. Kuhre (Athens, OH: Kendall/Hunt, 1991), 133–38; Kathryn Trauth Taylor, "Naming Affrilachia: Toward Rhetorical Implications of African American Appalachian Poetry," *Enculturation* 10 (2010), http://enculturation.net/naming-affrilachia; and Frank X Walker, *Affrilachia* (Lexington, KY: Old Cover, 2000).

4. Erica Abrams Locklear, *Negotiating a Perilous Empowerment: Appalachian Women's Literacies* (Athens: Ohio University Press, 2011), 3.

5. Janice W. Fernheimer, "Black Jewish Identity Conflict: A Divided Universal Audience and the Impact of Dissociative Disruption," *Rhetoric Society Quarterly* 39, no. 1 (2009): 46–72, 64, 65–66.

6. See Gwendolyn D. Pough, *Check It While I Wreck It: Black Womanhood, Hip-Hop Culture, and the Public Sphere* (Boston: Northeastern University Press, 2004).

7. Jenny Edbauer Rice, "Unframing Models of Public Distribution: From Rhetorical Situation to Rhetorical Ecologies," *Rhetoric Society Quarterly* 35, no. 4 (2005): 5–24.

8. Carter G. Woodson, "Freedom and Slavery in Appalachian America," *Journal of Negro History* 1, no. 2 (1916): 132–50, 148, 150.

9. Quoted in Bruce Tucker, "Toward a New Ethnicity: Urban Appalachian Ethnic Consciousness in Cincinnati, 1950–1987," in *Appalachian Odyssey: Historical Perspectives on the Great Migration,* ed. Phillip J. Obermiller, Thomas E. Wagner, and E. Bruce Tucker (Westport, CT: Praeger, 2000), 162.

10. Ronald D Eller, *Uneven Ground: Appalachia since 1945* (Lexington: University Press of Kentucky, 2008), 2.

11. See Robert Ludke, "The Socioeconomic and Health Status of Black Appalachian Migrants in the Cincinnati Metropolitan Area" (paper presented at the Appalachian Studies Association conference, Richmond, KY, March 12, 2011); Phillip J. Obermiller and William W. Philliber, "Black Appalachian Migrants," in *Too Few Tomorrows: Urban Appalachians in the 1980s* (Boone, NC: Appalachian Consortium Press, 1987), 111–15; and Victoria Purcell-Gates, *Other People's Words: The Cycle of Low Literacy* (Cambridge, MA: Harvard University Press, 1995).

12. William W. Philliber, Clyde B. McCoy, and Harry C. Dillingham, *The Invisible Minority: Urban Appalachians* (Lexington: University Press of Kentucky, 1981).

13. Michael E. Maloney and Christopher Auffrey, "Chapter 5: Appalachian Cincinnati," *The Social Areas of Cincinnati: An Analysis of Social Needs,* 2005, http://www.socialareasofcincinnati.org/report5.html.

14. Ibid.

15. Robert Ludke, "The Socioeconomic and Health Status of Black Appalachian Migrants in the Cincinnati Metropolitan Area."

16. Robert Ludke, discussion with author, November 9, 2011; Phillip J. Obermiller, discussion with author, November 7, 2011.

17. Robert L. Ludke, Phillip J. Obermiller, Eric W. Rademacher, and Shiloh K. Turner, "Identifying Appalachian Adults: An Empirical Study," *Appalachian Journal* 38, no. 1 (2010): 36–45.

18. In 2005 and 2010, the researchers oversampled the African American population. Because this research was funded by the Health Foundation of Greater Cincinnati and the foundation has not yet cleared the data for release, the results of these efforts are not yet available. Ludke, discussion with author, November 9, 2011.

19. Theresa I. Myadze, "The Status of African Americans and Other Blacks in Urban Areas of Appalachian and Non-Appalachian Alabama," *Journal of Appalachian Studies* 12, no. 2 (2006): 36–54, 52.

20. Obermiller, discussion with author, November 7, 2011.

21. Ludke, Obermiller, Rademacher, and Turner, "Identifying Appalachian Adults," 41.

22. Ibid.

23. "How Do You Know If You're Appalachian . . . and What Does That Mean Anyhow?" Urban Appalachian Council, November 2011, http://uacvoice.org/pdf/How%20 Do%20You%20Know%20You%20Are%20Appalachian.pdf.

24. "Migration," Urban Appalachian Council, November 2013, http://uacvoice. org/research/migration.

25. See Purcell-Gates, *Other People's Words*.

26. Kathleen P. Bennett, "Doing School in an Urban Appalachian First Grade," in *Empowerment through Multicultural Education,* ed. Christine E. Sleeter (Urbana, IL: Slate University, 1991), 27–48, 44.

27. Maureen Mullinax, "Resistance through Community-Based Arts," in *Transforming Places: Lessons from Appalachia,* ed. Stephen L. Fisher and Barbara Ellen Smith (Urbana: University of Illinois Press, 2012), 92–105, 92.

28. Jack Russell, "Looking in the Mirror," in Ergood and Kuhre, *Appalachia,* 115–22, 115, 122.

29. For an excellent discussion of this conflict, see Barbara Ellen Smith, Stephen Fisher, Phillip Obermiller, David Whisnant, Emily Satterwhite, and Rodger Cunningham, "Appalachian Identity: A Roundtable Discussion," *Appalachian Journal* 38, no. 1 (2010): 56–77.

30. *Although Our Fields Were Streets,* dir. Peter Allison (Cincinnati: Peter Allison Productions, 1991), VHS.

31. Ibid.

32. Linda Tuhiwai Smith, *Decolonizing Methodologies: Research and Indigenous Peoples* (Lillington, NC: Edwards Bros., 2012), 147.

33. Obermiller, discussion with author, November 7, 2011.

34. Stephen L. Fisher and Barbara Ellen Smith, *Transforming Places: Lessons from Appalachia* (Urbana: University of Illinois Press, 2012), 283.

7

Place-Conscious Literacy Practices in One Appalachian College Town

Nathan Shepley

Literacy and education scholars have long studied Appalachian college students, owing to systemic limitations in this population's educational and occupational opportunities and suspicion inherited by this population toward imported education standards. Many Appalachian students maintain tenacious ties to their home environments, see academic knowledge as opposed to their home culture, and distrust non-Appalachians owing to historical exploitation.[1] In one study of Appalachian Ohio students, David M. Dees explains: "Like immigrant sojourners into another culture, rural/ Appalachian college students encounter brief visits into a dominant cultural system that may be very different from their own. The university classroom . . . becomes a cultural system with hidden rules that may be difficult for students to negotiate."[2] Given America's long-standing history of depreciating Appalachian people, evidenced even in scholarly accounts such as James Moffett's *Storm in the Mountains*, research that clarifies the literacy challenges of Appalachian college students risks leaving educators with a dominant impression of the students as culturally disadvantaged individuals who grudgingly engage with college education to become more like mainstream academics or professionals.[3]

As important as it is to document Appalachian students' literacy challenges, I want to shift attention to qualitative research that revises popular notions of how Appalachian students approach college literacy practices. Sara Webb-Sunderhaus furthers such a project when she documents how one class of Appalachian students proactively mentors their peers, thereby using literacy practices for "the betterment of the community" rather than for individual gain.[4] Further, Appalachian-identifying professors are beginning to share their struggles to retain a sense of Appalachian identity while entering new discursive fields.[5] My purpose in this chapter is to build on analyses such as Webb-Sunderhaus's to track occasions when students kept and even enhanced their Appalachian ties in order to succeed in college. Rather than examine one class's work at one point in time, however, I trace several historical moments when college students at one public university, Ohio University, in the southeastern Ohio town of Athens, wrote to deepen their knowledge of their social and physical environs.[6] Focusing on records of students' literacy activities in the decades surrounding 1900, as an Appalachian identity was just beginning to take hold in southeast Ohio, I show how many students found opportunities to produce locally focused writing, guided by the implicit or explicit expectation that college-educated people should connect with their immediate environment. My argument is that these students were not simply praising the local in the tradition of late nineteenth- and early twentieth-century culture workers, as reviewed by Henry D. Shapiro, nor were they merely following an emerging national trend of students writing on local or practical topics.[7] Rather, the students were using writing about their university, town, and surrounding region to publicize and defend hilly, rural southeastern Ohio during a critical period when economic and political centers were taking shape in the central, northern, and western parts of the state.

This argument takes a contextual perspective of literacy, described by the literacy scholar Deborah Brandt as the situating of reading and writing within "broader activities (for instance, working, worshiping, governing, teaching and learning, relaxing)." Brandt explains that "these activities . . . give reading and writing their purpose and point," so studying them foregrounds "the ideological dimensions of literacy," the people who benefit from one's reading and writing.[8] The broader activity that I consider in relation to reading and especially writing practices is past college students' educational activities in and outside the classroom, activities that let the students use their writing to relate to nearby people and places. Not all the writing that I study originated from students' desires; locally aware faculty and administrators initiated and coordinated many of the students' clubs and writing projects. Thus, by focusing on Ohio University students' work in formal and informal literacy activities, we see the many shapes that college literacy programs can take to support students' ties to Appalachia.

Ohio University students rarely produced overtly political tracts, but the writing that they left behind gives us telling clues about the potential of local alliances to create, or at least nurture, defendants of the region now considered Appalachian Ohio. Kim Donehower has argued that rural literacy practices should "bring the struggles for identities and identifications among rural and other constituencies out into the open."[9] The writing that I studied heads in this direction, giving us pieces that resisted emerging narratives of Appalachian abjection and enabled early college students to see that something was at stake in their writing. The students used their writing to discern how they identified and might identify in relation to other members of their university, in turn discerning how their university related and might relate to people of the surrounding area. Though literacy practices of this sort will not necessarily produce Appalachian advocates, they have the potential to enhance current students' involvement in decisions about Appalachia's future. Matters of identification are, after all, crucial to the work of rhetoric, as the theorist Kenneth Burke has explained.[10] But I think that Robert Brooke and Jason McIntosh put the relationship of identification and action best when, in a study of psychological mapping, they write: "Understanding one's personal location within the issues in one's surrounding community prompts an exploration of one's *relationship* to a place, and can lead to the critique and vision that generates writing *for* a place."[11]

Beyond supporting place-based education, which Brooke and McIntosh and others have applied to composition classes, the writing that I study highlights a need to notice where college students come from when they write the local in Appalachia. Early Ohio University students came from counties both within and beyond the borders of Appalachia, as defined today by the Appalachian Regional Commission, with a higher percentage coming from outside Appalachia after 1900. Thus, by tracing this geographically diverse population over time, I show that college students do not have to come from Appalachia or already identify as Appalachian in order to cultivate a kinship with the area and culture, a realization that extends to my own identity as the producer of this research. I moved to Athens, Ohio, to enter a Ph.D. program, but I come from a part of north Georgia just beyond Appalachia's current borders, in an area where most longtime residents identify as southern. Despite my background, the time I spent and the research I conducted in southeastern Ohio enveloped me in interests and concerns shared by many people in Appalachia. At times I felt a kinship with the students whose education I was tracing, a personal attachment of the kind Gesa E. Kirsch and Liz Rohan associate with "the most serious, committed . . . historical research."[12] I empathized with early college students' feelings of distance from commercial and economic hubs, and I felt comforted when studying literacy activities that centralized the people and land that shaped students' college experiences. Given the tenuousness of my own geographic ties, my research introduced me to the possibility of identifying anew, as an ally or affiliate with Appalachian interests, someone eager to make Appalachia visible in discussions about locations and resources.

While the same kind of regional identity may not apply to everyone who lives in the mountainous region stretching from northern Alabama to southern New York, I propose that college literacy practices in Appalachia should treat place-based identification as a becoming, an ongoing process of developing connections and relationships. This fluid conception of location and identity can help Appalachian-identifying students see how issues affecting their hometown or home region pertain to students from elsewhere. For non-Appalachian-identifying students studying in Appalachia, invitations to identify with multiple locations can make Appalachian identity building and regional maintenance the work of *those who take certain actions,* as opposed to those who come from a certain location. Thus, identifying oneself as Appalachian or as allied with Appalachian people becomes a rhetorical move accessible to countless potential supporters of the region, a step toward identification-building practices that scholars today support for the purposes of avoiding rural exploitation.[13] And the fact that the students in my study possessed various geographic ties establishes a need to heed the category *college students in Appalachia* alongside the familiar designation *Appalachian college students.* My addition to existing identity categories highlights how students who gain exposure to Appalachia while in college can prepare to collaborate with native Appalachians in efforts to resee Appalachia's role in academic and cross-regional work.

Site and Methodology

Today, Ohio University, thirty-five miles from West Virginia, serves as a hub of Appalachian studies and lies in an area recognized as Appalachian Ohio. However, in the late nineteenth century, students who studied there found themselves writing themes and speeches and reciting lessons as nearby mining companies organized surrounding settlements, as cities beyond the hilly region emerged as centers of state politics and commerce, and as political leaders from the southeastern corner of the state, once seen as Ohio's center, found themselves treated dismissively by the state legislature.[14] Ohio University and its surrounding area were undergoing an identity transformation as they slowly lost status at the state level. In 1924, former Ohio University president Charles William Super quoted approvingly one nineteenth-century alumnus who wrote: "At the present time the university is with difficulty sustained and its condition is no credit to the State." The alumnus attributed these difficulties to a legacy of "mismanagement and trickery," the latter owing to a state legislature that, since the 1840s, kept the university from generating revenue from its land reappraisals.[15] As the state's oldest public higher education institution and an institution in the earliest-settled part of the state, Ohio University "might have become one of the great American universities" but instead experienced "years of hardship and frustration, limited facilities, enrollments, and equipment" in the late nineteenth century and early twentieth century.[16]

As I consider this context of lost grandeur alongside student writing from the decades around 1900, I inquire into the purposes that that writing served and the geographic allegiances that it showed. The writing that students left behind comes from an array of activities that the students engaged in over time, frequently outside the classroom proper: letter writing, creative writing, literary society membership, and journalistic accounts. Throughout these activities, and supported by pedagogical guidance that stressed local engagement, students demonstrated a tendency to describe and defend their surroundings; this theme persisted despite gaps in the historical record.

In the tradition of historical studies centered on incomplete records, I approach my project similarly to how Cheryl Glenn and Susan C. Jarratt, writing during the 1990s intersection of neosophistic and feminist revisionary histories, described theirs. Glenn noted: "We already take for granted that histories 'do' (or should do) something, . . . [T]hey fulfill our needs at a particular time and place." For Glenn's research, such a need meant reconsidering how scholars perceive the contributions of the early rhetor Aspasia of Miletus when scholars lack her writing. Glenn decided: "Just because [Aspasia] was erased [from historical narratives] was no reason to stop looking for her trace." Therefore, she "read crooked" by privileging secondary accounts of Aspasia's words.[17] Jarratt, meanwhile, used her history of the first sophists to defend "the revisionary historian today [who] will work with an expanded range of materials: not only the pedagogical treatises summarized in traditional histories, but any literacy artifact as it operates to shape knowledge and affect social action."[18] Here, I continue this methodology and add to the recent emergence of local histories of college student writing in understudied locations.[19] Minding Glenn's perspective, I describe my need as locating and understanding the rhetorical work of various student writers at Ohio University, especially as this institution and southeast Ohio saw educational resources and generations of settlers pass them by. Heeding Jarratt, I broaden my selection of evidence from student essays produced for college credit (of which only a few remain) to a range of writing genres and occasions that students came to know at the university. In this way, I notice the significance of where the students came from, what they wrote, and when they wrote it, and I encourage modern-day instructors to resee the value of local writing in Appalachian education contexts.

Voices from the Archive: Recording the Local

To frame my historical evidence, I offer a perspective from 1969, just beyond my primary period of focus; later, I pair this perspective with earlier observations to suggest an enduring theme about writing in Athens, Ohio. In a 1969 article in *The Post*, the Ohio University student newspaper, the English professor Edgar Whan was quoted as saying: "When they first get here [to Athens], students find it hard to see Appalachia around them. But students are changing that." He adds: "They're looking outside. They're trying to make the world better."[20] Whan's words are striking because they suggest value in students' awareness of their surroundings even if the students first struggle to notice Appalachia. His observation centralizes students' perspectives as well as the sociocultural context of their educational sites, emphases consonant with the critical educator Paulo Freire's argument about respecting others. Freire wrote: "We cannot educate if we don't start . . . from the levels in which the people perceive themselves, their relationship with others and with reality, because this is precisely what makes their knowledge." This starting point requires attention to "the political atmosphere, the social atmosphere, cultural atmosphere in which we work as educators."[21] Freire was discussing literacy education with Myles Horton, a cofounder of Tennessee's Highlander Folk School, fewer than six hours south of Ohio University. The kinship between their ideas and Whan's perspective is all the more striking once we notice that historical literacy practices supported by Ohio University did not assume one form and constitute a single educator's push to raise students' consciousness. Rather, generations of Ohio University students found, as part of their overall college experience, diverse opportunities to better see their university's connection to immediately surrounding lands and social issues.

One way in which many late nineteenth-century literacy activities at Ohio University nurtured a state of external awareness was by encouraging (at one point requiring) students to participate in literary societies, which were essentially academic debating groups that doubled as social groups. Although nineteenth-century literary societies shaped the social and academic lives of students at colleges and universities around the country, preparing students to read their writing publically and debate the pressing issues of the day, some of Ohio University's literary societies accentuated factors that bear special notice: meetings that occurred in the homes of faculty members and topics for writing and debate that lent themselves to discussions of local people and places. For example, Ohio University's Columbiad Literary Society, lasting 1895–1901, pushed students to pay attention to their immediate, visible audiences and gave them occasions for sharing canonized literature and their own original, creative work.[22] At a glance, the Columbiads' stated goals seem to make their work revolve around traditional aesthetic standards: "encourage purity of language, creative work, and the development of American literature." Yet a closer look shows that the society did more than appreciate canonized literature. Its members first met at the home of the English professor Edwin Watts Chubb, who would go on to serve as dean and interim president of Ohio University; later years saw the society meet at the home of the English professor Willis Boughton. Further, the society consisted of not only students but also Athens residents, giving students and townspeople the opportunity to write for and critique one another; during at least one meeting, Professor Boughton read from his work as well.[23] Thus, students who participated found themselves negotiating expectations from professors, townspeople, and each other as their writing circulated beyond the classroom. This audience-directed work broadened the traditional activity of college student groups by communalizing literary training.

The topics about which the Columbiads wrote also give clues about students' foci, which included social and intellectual activity around campus and throughout Athens and its environs. For example, at a February

26, 1896, meeting—a date I select because of the group recorder's unusually detailed notes that day—students read poems called "An Arbor," "Cascade Glen," "An Idol," "To Alma Mater," "In Memoriam &[?] in[?] Frieze," "To Dr. F. Cacker [?]," "Beta Theta Pi," "When Greek Meets Greek," and "To John Greenleaf Whittier" as well as a story installment titled "The Pedagogue."[24] These titles suggest an interest in fraternity and sorority systems ("Beta Theta Pi" and "When Greek Meets Greek"), an interest in one's school, college, or university ("To Alma Mater"), and an interest in teaching or teachers ("The Pedagogue" and possibly "To Dr. F. Cacker [?]"). From the remaining topics, "An Arbor" and "Cascade Glen" would have resonated with residents of wooded, hilly Athens, situated between the area now called Hocking Hills to the northwest and the main line of the Appalachian Mountains to the southeast. In this batch of writing, shared orally at an 1896 meeting, we glimpse literary society participants who directed their attention to one another in the same out-of-class venue. Though available records fail to specify who created each topic, we can observe the effects that these topics likely had for various participants. Nonstudent townspeople who attended meetings gained exposure to descriptions and expositions of university social life and nearby rural scenes, and they had time to respond and critique. Students, who probably constituted the bulk of each meeting's participants, encountered diverse perspectives on campus and noncampus life. Meanwhile, professors and administrators saw how students and others imbued locations with new meaning. Through its makeup, meeting locations, and topics of interest, the Columbiad Society allowed students to become mindful of their education's situatedness in a mountain town.

This degree of mindfulness is important when we consider how Athens exerted great influence on early college students, impressing on them that they lived not only in a university environment but also in a broader community. In her 1938 master's thesis, itself an example of locally focused writing, the Ohio University student Elizabeth Irene Smith wrote: "The school and the town were so small that public opinion was an effective means of social control in the students' activities." She explains that the surrounding community's presence was even woven into the university's 1895 code of conduct, which held students to the standards of both the university and the town. At this time, "public opinion" worked hand-in-hand with university regulations to shape student life: "Students were dependent upon the community for most of their social diversion. The school was small and was in and of the community, and the homes were freely open to students. After

East and West wings [sections of the university] were withdrawn as dormitories, all students, men and women, lived in private homes in town until the women's dormitories came in about 1900. Frequent parties were held in the homes of friendly townspeople."[25]

Smith's description casts students as beholden to a community that in many cases supported them when the university could not, a situation that would change only when enrollment grew beyond a few hundred. Smith also reveals that Ohio University of the late nineteenth century and the early twentieth was exceedingly small and easily shaped by norms and needs from the surrounding town: the enrollment totaled 111 in 1839 and even by 1938 no more than 3,000.[26]

It is tempting to assume that students' attention to their immediate surroundings dissipated as their institution began attracting a more geographically diverse group of young people and prioritizing research. However, numerous records from the early twentieth century point to the continuance of a learning environment that encouraged local awareness, though it was an awareness increasingly structured by textbooks and classroom-based writing. In their writing for a three-volume history of Ohio University published in 1950, one class of honors first-year composition students explained that the student population came mostly from southeastern Ohio in 1900 and from all over the state by 1925. Likely coming from Athens and other parts of Ohio, this class of students researched local print sources and interviewed seasoned Ohio University faculty members to describe and preserve their institution's norms and struggles. For example, one student wrote about the university's student clubs, mentioning the "Rural Club" and the "Mountaineers," the latter for West Virginian students who wanted to study their state's history. Another student commented on the university's 1840s debt problems, which she, like historians before her, attributed to the state legislature and which she saw as leading to the university's temporary closing in the mid-nineteenth century.[27] The fact that some of these first-year composition students engaged with past periods of their university's distress, noticing and recording moments of unsavory institutional history, is significant; they echoed and affirmed points of criticism that Ohio University's faculty members and administrators had expressed since the nineteenth century. That is, they brought their perspectives in line with those of people who felt slighted by state legislators' attitudes toward higher education in southeast Ohio.

Less directly, even a composition textbook, *College Composition: A Brief*

Course, published in 1943 by half the English Department's full professors, positioned students to turn to their surrounding town for writing topics. The faculty authors urged students to look to their community for inspiration: "[The student] has only to open his eyes, for there is a world around him so full of interest and tragedy and comedy that he can see and hear enough to provide himself with more material than he could ever use." In the text's early pages, they focus on the community—a community that, while unnamed, looks very much like Athens, Ohio. They encourage students to describe the sight of students in raincoats hurrying to class in the springtime. They present a hypothetical scenario of college themes that an instructor would likely assign, for example, "My Landlady" and "My First Walk under the Elms." They ask students to "conduct an investigation of [their] college surroundings," and they suggest writing topics such as "A College Room" and "My Roommate."[28] These topics reflect the natural climate and likely social interactions in Athens. Students there would almost certainly have worn raincoats in the springtime and walked under American elms—unlike in most, if not all, of the American West. Further, Ohio University students typically lived on campus or in new quarters in town and therefore would have dealt with landladies and roommates.

College Composition: A Brief Course is significant for my purposes because it shows that teaching students to write about and study the local was not confined to the desires of singular faculty members; it was supported by the English Department's educational resources, here a textbook produced by multiple faculty members. Moreover, like the other historical sources that I examine, this textbook cultivates a relationship between college students and the people and places around them. The resulting act of seeing, of looking outward, links the various writing genres and occasions addressed here.

If by the 1920s many students came from urban, suburban, and non-mountainous rural sections of Ohio, then their college experiences gave them opportunities to learn about their local environs and make meaning about the area's past or present identity. If they came from rural, hilly southern and eastern Ohio, then their college experiences gave them opportunities to use their background as raw material for refining their ability to focus on a topic and communicate to an audience. Students from both backgrounds described town-and-gown relations, blurred boundaries between academic writing and the surrounding community, and investigated interregional tensions between the state's earliest settled region and newer, booming regions beyond. Below, I argue that, once we more fully situate Ohio University's literacy activities in the context of southeastern Ohio's transition to a marginalized status, we reveal more about these activities' rhetorical underpinnings, even if their most obvious features—description, explanation, commemoration—seem arhetorical.

Voices from the Archive: Defending the Local

That some early Ohio University students wrote about observable, sometimes tangible subjects from daily life is not as remarkable as the fact that many students used their writing to assert the worth of the university, town, and region while regionally pronounced disputes over funding and educational status symbols threatened to render southeast Ohio invisible from the 1830s to the early years of the twentieth century. When viewed from this angle, college student writing that seems mundane in form and innocent in purpose becomes a "resource" cultivated at least partly "for the opportunities and protections that it potentially grants its seekers," in Brandt's words.[29] Even students' creative writing and journalism, pieces composed to delight and inform, acquire a political undertone, for they commemorate nearby scenes and update local residents during a time when southeast Ohio's leaders and boosters needed impressions of this sort to uphold a recognizable and defensible identity of the area. Thus, we see that, during periods of regional identity construction and discord, writing that describes, celebrates, or informs can resist efforts to hierarchize regions and reallocate state resources.

To illustrate this context of intrastate contestation, I momentarily expand my scope to consider interactions between prominent Athens residents, some of whom were associated with Ohio University, and residents of urban nonmountainous parts of Ohio. For instance, in the late nineteenth century, members of an early heritage society called the Athens County Pioneer Association wrote numerous letters in which they argued bitterly with a Cincinnati publisher about the location of the state's first library: Cincinnati, in southwest Ohio, or Athens County, in the rural and mountainous southeast Ohio.[30] The exchange reveals a fight for signs of educational status that neither side wanted to lose. Additionally, Ohio University presidents such as William Henry Scott and Charles Super spent years traveling to the state capital of Columbus to persuade state lawmakers to increase the university's funding. Scott's work in this capacity is referenced repeatedly in an 1873 student diary, such as when the student noted: "Scott is away attending to the interest of the O.U."[31] Super's efforts are best shown in his own words, particularly when he portrays his institution's trustees as "either inside the fort defending [Ohio University] against enemy onslaughts or on the outside trying to collect the [monetary] tribute which they claimed was justly their due."[32] With images of his university as a "fort" that guarded against "enemy onslaughts," Super casts the university's first century as highly antagonistic, a battle for recognition and resources.

Briefly reviewing this backdrop of local and regional status seeking prepares us to see writing from Ohio University students as more than local color of the kind that historians have blamed for exaggerating ideas about Appalachia.[33] Instead, we see it implicated in larger attempts to gain recognition from Ohio residents who increasingly valued social and commercial centers beyond the mountains. So, when students portrayed their surroundings as beautiful or admirable, we must recognize that, in many cases, they knew about state-level neglect that threatened the university and the town that supported them, connecting them to southeast Ohio's physical places and sociopolitical concerns.

Fear of representational nonexistence permeates early student writing and literacy occasions. Anxiety about the university's physical location appears in literary society records and in previously published student writing. For example, as early as 1837–1838, members of the university's Philomathean Literary Society debated the question, "Is Athens a suitable situation for a literary institution?" and, in 1843, members of the Athenian Literary Society held a debate on the topic "Should the O.U. [sic] be removed from Athens?"[34] That same year, an essay titled "Removal of the College" appeared in a student-run newsletter, *The Echo and University Record*, in which students reported on a proposal from the state legislature to move the university from Athens to the northern part of the state. The student writers suggest locations closer to the geographic center of the state and at the border of the region that now goes by *Appalachia*. Confidently, the students conclude: "Then, and *not till* then will the Ohio University take a rank among the Literary Institutions of the land, consistent with its lofty name and the character of the distinguished men who conduct its affairs."[35]

The Echo and University Record was published for only one year, and the institutional archives contain no other mass-distributed student writing until the 1870s. In one of these 1870s publications, *The Student's Magazine*, a student piece in volume 1 gives a vivid account of how students should see the community: "A word to the people of Athens. *The interests of the Town and College are inseparable; and if the* College is benefited by the publication of a journal, so also is the Town. And so much as the citizens encourage and aid us, just so much do they advance their own interests." Having situated this publication as beholden to both the university and Athens, the writer clarifies how the magazine will benefit townspeople: "We now promise on our part that if we receive fair patronage and aid . . . [we will] use our utmost endeavors to see that the MAGAZINE reflects no discredit on the institution which it represents, and to make it worthy [of] the support of its friends." Later, the writer calls on students to heed the magazine's advertisements for goods and services: "The business men [*sic*] who encourage us by advertising should in return receive the patronage of the students. . . . [Local businesspeople] desire and expect some income from their patronage, and we should do our part that they be not disappointed. Let every student then, who has any interest in the welfare of the MAGAZINE, and of the college, notice our advertising columns, and bestow his patronage accordingly."[36]

Thus, in a new student magazine, the writer calls for readers to act by patronizing local businesses. He or she interprets the advertising of local businesses in *The Student's Magazine* as a prescription for how the students "should" act. Even when discussing the university's education programs, he or she foregrounds public service: "The [Ohio University literary society] student learns to strike out and act more or less independently as he mingles with his fellows in the society hall. He gets a foretaste of actual life."[37] The stress on structured social interaction with opportunities for students to experience trial and error, combined with the request for students to support local businesses, suggests a student body in preparation to contribute meaningfully to the local economy.

The Student's Magazine would publish more overtly glowing pieces about Athens and its surrounding terrain in the coming years, not least of which was its 1880 reprint of a poem by the 1833 alumnus William Dana Emerson, who came from nearby Marietta, Ohio. Emerson's "Athens, Ohio" appears to have been written during or soon after his time as a student in Athens. However, the poem's 1880 reemergence in *The Student's Magazine* and then in President Super's 1924 institutional history testifies to its resonance with the Athens public as the town's advocates, including Super himself, worked to keep southeastern Ohio in the minds of writers and politicians farther west and north. In the poem, Emerson brings an Edenesque pastoral to Athens and its hilly surroundings:

Sweet Athens! The home of learning and beauty,
How I long for thy hills and thy rich balmy air:
For thy wide-spreading green, smiling sweetly on duty,
And the valley beneath, and the stream winding there:
On the north the high rock, on the south the lone ferry:
The ville on the east, and the mill on the west.

In line 1, the speaker links the "beauty" of Athens with "learning," giving readers their first two clues about what he would like them to associate with the town. The rest is a tribute to the natural surroundings of the town and to local conditions that facilitated student growth. The poem ends by associating Athens with a "heavenly plain," using nature to explore the romantic sublime. However, Emerson also describes the university curriculum, the literary societies, and the "fun of the blunders at each recitation!"[38] His poem and, just as important, university students' and other Athenians' decisions to *continue circulating* the poem in the late nineteenth century and the early twentieth gives us an instance of creative writing operating as a defense of Ohio University–Athens–southeast Ohio.

Other instances of creative writing that legitimized the area now called *Appalachian Ohio* surface in the Ohio University history professor Clement L. Martzolff's 1911 publication of William Dana Emerson's poem "To the Ohio River" and the alumnus and Chillicothe native William Edward Gilmore's poem "Lines Written on Mount Logan." In both pieces, Ohio University alumni defend southern and eastern Ohio as preserves of natural beauty that cannot be found everywhere. Such a move contrasts sharply with a long-standing tradition of viewing the mountains and hills as obstacles to happiness, as in the "Settlers' Song" written by early nineteenth-century settlers who traveled from Massachusetts to the just-beyond-the-mountains part of Ohio.[39]

Early students' writing in local magazines and in creative writing collections did indeed focus on exposition or description—on clearly or memorably conveying natural scenes or social and economic relationships. But, by noticing the context in which these pieces were produced and circulated as well as the geographic ties of the students who produced or circulated them, we can also read the pieces as defenses of an area that newer waves of settlers deemphasized in their construction of a state identity complete with a state government's priorities about where to invest its money. Several of the early writings speak to a literacy past that brought students and the region's places and challenges closer together, in some cases allowing students to defend their university and its deep ties to a small town and rural area. Nineteenth-century students from Athens acquired methods for drawing attention to place-based concerns, and students from Ohio towns like Marietta and Chillicothe, and especially from farther away, found opportunities to create place-based subjectivities.

To close this section, I return to the English professor Edgar Whan's 1969 comments about college students, Ohio University, the surrounding area, by that time recognized officially as Appalachia, and the value of external awareness. At one point in his interview with the student newspaper, Whan remarked: "I like Athens. . . . I like it because it's one of the few college towns left—far away from the world. You kind of make your own world."[40] His words contrast productively with earlier observations about the significance of Athens's location in a rural, hilly expanse that is unlike the rest of the state. In a collection of writing celebrating Ohio University's bicentennial anniversary, Charles Carlson, a New York native who eventually joined the faculty of the university, recalled the first time he traveled from the Columbus area to Athens. He remembered thinking: "No one in his right mind would drive to and from Athens. It's at the end of the world."[41] Finally, one of the earliest college student perspectives available, an 1821 letter, shows the new student Owen Evans describing his travels from a town in south-central Ohio to Athens: "I set out alone [sic] a long strange road, that far from home yet going still farther with indeed some tender feelings." After noting that he met a footman, he explained that they continued for eleven miles, stayed the night at "an old Dutchman's house," traveled five miles more, ate breakfast, and then "walked on nine miles further and entered the wilderness": "The people told us that there were bears, panthers, and plenty of deer in it. Here, how glad I was that I had [a companion] with me. It was the most lonesome road that I had ever traveled."[42] Although separated by many years, these perspectives show people applying meaning to the fact of Athens's distance from centers of commerce and politics. For some, particularly outsiders, the location of the town spurred anxiety about the education to be found there. However, equally noteworthy was the tendency for the location and the literacy activities encouraged therein to nudge students toward a willingness to "make [their] own world," as Whan put it. One way students could do so was by aligning themselves with a place that risked becoming invisible as the state's physical, social, and economic identity took shape.

Implications for Appalachia and for College Literacy

The fact that twenty-first-century Appalachia has suffered from powerful stereotyping should not keep us from noticing that some university students in Athens, Ohio, circa 1900 resisted the marginalization of the region through what Deborah Brandt would characterize as "the relational nature of reading and writing," the idea that "people build up and exercise skills through participation with others in particular contexts."[43] Much of the historical resistance that I studied sprang from students' engagement with a small college town, in zones of interaction afforded by semistructured and structured literacy activities that dealt with concerns shared by others in the region. As expanding conceptions of Appalachia began to subsume Ohio University and Athens, some in the town found and maintained counternarratives that cast it and its people as rhetors with voices and interests of their own. In their push to render visible and defendable Ohio University and Athens, some university students affirmed the place of higher education in their depictions of life in the hills and mountains northwest of West Virginia. Today, such writing underscores the importance of framing Appalachian identity as approachable through a practice of situating oneself nearer to a certain land and people than one did previously, an identification practice not unlike that which Kim Donehower describes in her case study of Appalachian literacies.[44] The result is a college literacy experience that promotes affiliational Appalachian identities, as opposed to literacy experiences that sever Appalachian identity from scholarly engagement.

Brandt argues that a contextual perspective of literacy frames literacy within "social postures and social knowledge that begin well before and extend well beyond words on a page." Thus, "serious programs of literacy instruction . . . must teach toward these contextualizing dimensions of literacy if they are to be successful and just."[45] My historical analysis gives us factors to consider as we envision such a program for composition students in Appalachia. Mainly, the program would need to let students of diverse geographic backgrounds explore their commitments to surrounding people, for instance, in the topics that they discuss and research, the genres in which they write, and the spaces in which they share their writing. Whether or not incoming college students identify with Appalachia, they might analyze their current and possible future connections to topics of special importance to Appalachians and to members of neighboring regions. Long before drafting papers, they might examine questions such as, What does it mean that your college or university lies in a particular region? How does the surrounding region get defined and redefined? What in the surrounding town and region is worth writing about and to whom? What regional concerns do members of your college or university share and why? If, as they undertake such inquiry, students learn about the social construction of Appalachian identity over time, they may prove all the more willing to make rhetorical moves that align them with Appalachia.[46]

Locally informed literacy environments of the kind I have discussed invite writers to commemorate people and places and, more importantly, contribute to rhetoric about the region. This process reflects what Katherine Kelleher Sohn has characterized as "coming to voice through education" and its possible result of activism.[47] But, whereas Sohn studied nontraditional modern-day college students who already identified strongly with Appalachia, my focus on students of multiple backgrounds casts the writer's "coming to voice" as a coming to identity, in this case a coming to place-conscious identities through the awareness and cultivation of new affiliations. Even if many past Ohio University students and I cannot claim the descriptor *Appalachian* for ourselves, we can write and use others' writing to challenge nonexistent or otherwise damaging representations of Appalachia; we can interact with residents of the area now known as *Appalachia* to fine-tune our understanding of, and relationship to, the challenges and joys shared by many in the region. Taking such actions and opening up how we identify gives Appalachia more supporters as it adapts to changes in literacies, technologies, ethnicities, and livelihoods. It makes it everyone's concern. In an increasingly networked and interdependent society, the time has come to reread Appalachia with the help of its allies.

Notes

Support for archival visits that shaped this chapter was provided by the Martha Gano Houston Endowment through the University of Houston's Department of English. Additionally, I thank the staff of the Robert E. and Jean R. Mahn Center for Archives and Special Collections, Alden Library, Ohio University, for their generous assistance.

1. David M. Dees, "'How Do I Deal with These New Ideas?': The Psychological Acculturation of Rural Students," *Journal of Research in Rural Education* 21, no. 6 (2006): 1–11; Esther E. Gottlieb, "Appalachian Self-Fashioning: Regional Identities and Cultural Models," *Discourse: Studies in the Cultural Politics of Education* 22, no. 3 (2001): 341–59; Katherine Kelleher Sohn, *Whistlin' and Crowin' Women of Appalachia: Literacy Practices since College* (Carbondale: Southern Illinois University Press, 2006).

2. Dees, "'How Do I Deal with These New Ideas?'" 2.

3. James Moffett, *Storm in the Mountains: A Case Study of Censorship, Conflict, and Consciousness* (Carbondale: Southern Illinois University Press, 1989).

4. Sara Webb-Sunderhaus, "Living with Literacy's Contradictions: Appalachian Students in a First-Year Writing Course," in *Reclaiming the Rural: Essays on Literacy, Rhetoric, and Pedagogy,* ed. Kim Donehower, Charlotte Hogg, and Eileen E. Schell (Carbondale, IL: Southern Illinois University Press, 2011), 207–22, 218.

5. Casie Fedukovich, "Strange Imports: Working-Class Appalachian Women in the Composition Classroom," *Journal of Appalachian Studies* 15, nos. 1–2 (2009): 140–54; Sara Webb-Sunderhaus, "Scholarly Resistance: Appalachians Re-Shaping the Academy" (paper presented at the Conference on College Composition and Communication, St. Louis, March 23, 2012).

6. Officially, much of Ohio joined Appalachia in the 1960s as a result of work by the Appalachian Regional Commission. However, settlement patterns, economic conditions, natural terrain, and other factors have long connected southern and eastern Ohio to other parts of Appalachia.

7. Henry D. Shapiro, *Appalachia on Our Mind: The Southern Mountains and Mountaineers in the American Consciousness, 1870–1920* (Chapel Hill: University of North Carolina Press, 1978). For a fuller look at the rhetoric of early historical culture workers, see Kim Donehower, "Rhetorics and Realities: The History and Effects of Stereotypes about Rural Literacies," in *Rural Literacies,* by Kim Donehower, Charlotte Hogg, and Eileen E. Schell (Carbondale, IL: Southern Illinois University Press, 2007), 37–76, 42; Miriam Brody, *Manly Writing: Gender, Rhetoric, and the Rise of Composition* (Carbondale: Southern Illinois University Press, 1993), 123; Robert J. Connors, *Composition-Rhetoric: Backgrounds, Theory, and Pedagogy* (Pittsburgh: University of Pittsburgh Press, 1997), 64.

8. Deborah Brandt, *Literacy in American Lives* (Cambridge: Cambridge University Press, 2001), 3.

9. Donehower, "Rhetorics and Realities," 76.

10. Burke begins explaining identification by referring to groups that, while different, learn to see their shared interests and describe themselves accordingly, such as Puritans aligning their cultural narratives with those of the earlier Israelites. See Kenneth Burke, *A Rhetoric of Motives* (New York: Prentice-Hall, 1950).

11. Robert Brooke and Jason McIntosh, "Deep Maps: Teaching Rhetorical Engagement through Place-Conscious Education," in *The Locations of Composition,* ed. Christopher J. Keller and Christian R. Weisser (Albany: State University of New York Press, 2007), 131–49, 133.

12. Gesa E. Kirsch and Liz Rohan, "Introduction: The Role of Serendipity, Family Connections, and Cultural Memory in Historical Research," in *Beyond the Archives: Research as a Lived Process,* ed. Gesa E. Kirsch and Liz Rohan (Carbondale: Southern Illinois University Press, 2008), 1–9, 8.

13. Kim Donehower, Charlotte Hogg, and Eileen E. Schell, "Introduction: Reclaiming the Rural," in Donehower, Hogg, and Schell, eds., *Reclaiming the Rural*, 1–13, 9.

14. William E. Peters, *Legal History of the Ohio University* (Cincinnati: Western Methodist Book Concern, 1910); Thomas Nathaniel Hoover, *The History of Ohio University* (Athens: Ohio University Press, 1954).

15. Charles M. Walker, *History of Athens County, Ohio* (Cincinnati: Robert Clarke, 1869), 345–46, quoted in Charles William Super, *A Pioneer College and Its Background (the Ohio University)* (Salem, MA: Newcomb & Glauss, 1924), 29. See also Hoover, *The History of Ohio University*, 78.

16. Hoover, *The History of Ohio University*, 79.

17. Cheryl Glenn, "Remapping Rhetorical Territory," *Rhetoric Review* 13, no. 2 (1995): 287–303, 291, 292.

18. Susan C. Jarratt, *Rereading the Sophists: Classical Rhetoric Refigured* (Carbondale: Southern Illinois University Press, 1991), 13.

19. Patricia Donahue and Gretchen Flesher Moon, eds., *Local Histories: Reading the Archives of Composition* (Pittsburgh: University of Pittsburgh Press, 2007).

20. "Whan Teaches, Innovates, 'Makes His World' in Athens," *The Post* (Ohio University), September 15, 1969, "Whan, Edgar W. Bio," Biographical File, University Archives, Mahn Center for Archives and Special Collections, Ohio University Libraries, Athens.

21. Myles Horton and Paulo Freire, *We Make the Road by Walking: Conversations on Education and Social Change* (Philadelphia: Temple University Press, 1990), 66, 77.

22. Generally, college literary societies consisted of students who met regularly to develop their writing and public speaking skills. The Columbiad Literary Society was unusual for its interest in original creative writing.

23. *The Columbiad* (Athens, OH), 1895–1896, University Archives, Mahn Center for Archives and Special Collections, 1, 52, 84.

24. Ibid., 52.

25. Irene Elizabeth Smith, "A Survey of Student Custom and Tradition at Ohio University" (master's thesis, Ohio University, 1938), 111, 127.

26. Ibid., 30, 41.

27. All three volumes of the university history appeared in 1950, the first two under the title *Ohio University in the Twentieth Century: A Fifty-Year History*, the third under the title *Ohio University in the 1920s: A Social History*. I utilized typescript copies held by the Mahn Center for Archives and Special Collections.

28. Homer J. Caskey, Joseph B. Heidler, and Edith A. Wray, *College Composition: A Brief Course* (Boston: Ginn, 1943), 4, 6, 41–42.

29. Brandt, *Literacy in American Lives*, 5.

30. MS 51, Series II: Correspondence, Athens County Pioneer Association Collection, Mahn Center for Archives and Special Collections.

31. Margaret Boyd, Diary, January 1873–November 1874, MS 15 (1873), ser. 2, box 1, folder 17, Boyd Family Collection, Mahn Center for Archives and Special Collections.

32. Super, *A Pioneer College and Its Background,* 26.

33. Richard B. Drake, *A History of Appalachia* (Lexington: University Press of Kentucky, 2001); John Alexander Williams, *Appalachia: A History* (Chapel Hill: University of North Carolina Press, 2002).

34. Jacqueline Ann White, "An Historical Study of the Forensics Program at Ohio University from 1812 to 1860" (master's thesis, Ohio University, 1969), 38, 57.

35. "Removal of the College," *The Echo and the University Record,* February 1843, Record Group 5, University Archives, Mahn Center for Archives and Special Collections.

36. "Editorials," *The Student's Magazine* 1, no. 2 (1879): 25–26, microfilm, Ohio University Newspapers II, reel 1 (emphasis added to first quote).

37. Ibid., 26.

38. William Dana Emerson, "Athens, Ohio," *The Student's Magazine,* vol. 1, no. 6 (1880), microfilm, *Ohio University Newspapers II,* reel 1.

39. Clement L. Martzolff, ed., *Poems on Ohio* (Columbus: Ohio State Archeological and Historical Society, 1911), 12–15, 17–18, 108.

40. "Whan Teaches, Innovates."

41. Charles Carlson, "A First Visit to Ohio University," in *Ohio University Recollections for the Bicentennial Anniversary: 1804–2004,* ed. Ohio University Emeriti Association (Athens: Ohio University Press, 2004), 18–19.

42. Betty Hollow, *Ohio University, 1801–2004: The Spirit of a Singular Place* (Athens: Ohio University Press, 2003), 20.

43. Brandt, *Literacy in American Lives,* 3.

44. Donehower, "Rhetorics and Realities," 73.

45. Brandt, *Literacy in American Lives,* 4.

46. Drake, *A History of Appalachia;* Williams, *Appalachia;* Andrew R. L. Cayton, "'Separate Interests' and the Nation-State: The Washington Administration and the Origins of Regionalism in the Trans-Appalachian West," *Journal of American History* 79, no. 1 (1992): 39–67.

47. Sohn, *Whistlin' and Crowin' Women of Appalachia,* 151, 164.

8

A Functional Linguistics Approach to Appalachian Literacy

Joshua Iddings and Ryan Angus

Jesse Stuart, a native of Greenup County, Kentucky—the home Appalachian county of Josh—speaks to some of our own frustrations with literacy teaching in our home region when he writes: "Why should a pupil be forced to make low marks because he [*sic*] couldn't *get* Shakespeare? Why should the ghost of this great genius haunt the youth in the high school of a steel-mill city, who were trying to get a speaking and writing knowledge of the mother tongue? . . . I proceeded to teach them on the basis of: *They must control the language regardless of written and spoken errors they made. The language must not control them. They must not have fears. They must enjoy English.*"[1]

Part of the way in which we learn to control language, as Stuart puts it, and succeed in the academy is to learn that we can find value in our language, our ways of speaking. This is well known in the education community when thinking about the ways we teach English language learners;[2] however, this is not necessarily taken for granted when talking about the teaching of native speakers of different regional dialects and cultures such as those typical in the Appalachian coalfields, the primary focus of this chapter.

While reading and writing about authors like Shakespeare gave us a sense of the history and beauty of the English language, it was our sparse exposure to Appalachian authors that gave us real inspiration. In the fifth grade, Dr. James Gifford of the Jesse Stuart Foundation in Ashland, Kentucky, gave Josh and his classmates three of Jesse Stuart's children's stories, and the school based some literacy units on these works. Learning about Stuart's writing, in addition to having an accomplished poet—Mr. Stephen Holt—in an English course in high school, gave Josh the inspiration to believe that he could be a writer, that his voice was important. Ryan had a similar experience in high school when his English teacher—Mrs. Mary Ross—would discuss books with him and taught him how to write about literature. It was not until later in college, however, that he was exposed to, and fell in love with, Appalachian literature. Partly on the basis of this contact with Appalachian literature and our own work in linguistics, we argue that educators can and should use Appalachian literature as a point of departure in helping students gain access to their own voices and to scaffold Appalachian students into the academic writing genres for which they are responsible in school. Starting students where they are—that is, where they have control of their own voices—and learning to read local Appalachian literature helps them see that they can be taken seriously by those within and outside their home region. In our own educational journeys, it was gaining our own voices, partly through our experience reading texts from our region, that helped us see the virtue in literacy education to empower Appalachian students to succeed throughout their lives. Simply seeing local and regional authors' names and faces on books—names that sounded and faces that looked like ours—aided us in seeing our own potential to communicate ourselves through words. In fact, similar stories of the power of Appalachian literature in the lives of Appalachians have been documented, even though each person has his or her own journey toward this sort of consciousness raising.[3]

Appalachia provides for interesting discussion concerning how students are taught to become literate in the classroom. This is partly true because the region is one of the most stereotyped but also one of the least understood areas in the United States. Josh recalls one conversation in graduate school in Indiana where several classmates did not even know where Appalachia *was;* however, many folks had perceptions of who Appalachians *are.* Stereotypes of illiteracy, unkemptness, lack of education, and political passivity abound in the popular depiction of Appalachia. Even within the region, many of us are brought up not understanding our own identity and what it *means* to be Appalachian, even though, as Jeff Biggers shows us, Appalachians have had a tremendous effect on the history of our country.[4] John Williams examines the change in depictions of Appalachians over history, resulting in negative stereotypes of a resourceful people.[5]

In this chapter, we set out to describe an alternative way of practicing literacy in the secondary classrooms of the eastern Kentucky/West Virginia coalfields,[6] from a functional linguistics viewpoint. We do this not because we accept the stereotype of Appalachians being undereducated and illiterate; our purpose is to establish a literacy approach for Appalachian students that fosters a critical understanding of the culture of the region, raises up critical readers of texts, and promotes democratic educational praxis both in the classroom and in the greater society. Thus, this approach utilizes local literature from the region as a way of beginning students' critical literacy and understanding of the linguistic meanings in literature. This approach draws on our own graduate school education in the fields of rhetoric and composition, Appalachian studies, and linguistics and brings together what we feel are effective means of combining these fields in a useful, interdisciplinary way. However, we note that our journey began with our own frustrations that these disciplines did not seem to talk enough to one another; thus, much of our discussion comes out of the desire to see educators make these worthwhile connections across the disciplines, connections we had to largely make for ourselves.

Appalachia, like many colonial and postcolonial regions in the world, is a region of great resources, both natural and human-made. However, local interests are often not considered with respect to the region or the greater needs of the country. Corporatization and exploitation of Appalachia, virtually from its "discovery" by Europeans, has meant that corporate and political interests have focused primarily on stripping the region of its natural resources for the benefit of corporations and politicians, often to the detriment of those citizens who are responsible for the labor by which these corporations make their profits.[7] Coal, steel, and railroad companies, among others, have a well-documented history of exploitation of both the natural resources of the region and the people who live there.[8] While these industries may be on the decline, the region remains one where outside corporations exploit workers owing to economic conditions. For example, during our graduate work at Marshall University in Huntington, West Virginia, several call centers and telemarketing firms were new to the area, offering better pay for many local people but wages far below those offered elsewhere in the country. One company, CACOP, even hired local people to fund-raise for California police departments, presumably because folks in Huntington could be paid less and the police could make more. We are certainly not ignorant of these conditions; however, we—like other Americans—can feel hopeless to intervene in this process.

What is this hopelessness that many feel when they view the exploitation happening around them? The answer seems in part to relate to having a voice. Questions abound in the Appalachian psyche. Whose interests are being considered when important decisions are being made? The answer is typically the interests of those who control the land and its people. This power generally lies in corporate headquarters outside Appalachia and the politicians who serve them.[9] For example, many Appalachians used to enjoy the hard-fought benefits of union representation, as exemplified by the fight for these rights in the Blair Mountain uprising in West Virginia;[10] however, current political conditions and the fear of both political parties to back union representation in this US economic recession have contributed to working-class Appalachians (and others in the United States) having much less control of their own political and economic destinies. With this backdrop, it is educators who are uniquely positioned to foster a generation of students who realize the full potential of participatory democracy in the United States.[11] One way to aid students in changing the conditions they see in their home places is through envisioning a different approach to the ways in which educators view and enact literacy practices in the region.

Theoretical Foundations

Utilizing a systemic functional linguistics (SFL) approach to analyzing texts and the teaching/learning cycle developed by SFL practitioners, scholars have shown how enacting a democratic approach to literacy can increase participation of all students and encourage a classroom structure that mimics the democratic process we want our children to pursue once they leave formal schooling. After all, David Rose shows us that the ability to read and write effectively constitutes the very foundation of a democratic society.[12] This brings us to the question of what a classroom democracy looks like and how it might encourage students' participation in the society outside the classroom. M. A. K. Halliday (echoing Stuart above) has shown that, generally speaking, language is of primary importance to education because students learn language, learn about language, and learn through language.[13] In accepting this premise, we must then consider language to be emphatically important in fostering a critical generation of writers and readers of texts. For it is through texts, both written and spoken, that citizens have made some of their greatest impacts in society. SFL approaches to literacy have proved especially helpful in teaching students how to read and write texts for critical understanding and propping them up into a position where they can actively engage in their communities for change, as controlling language partially determines future possibilities for students.[14] Furthermore, this is the case because SFL is a sociocultural theory of language, meaning that language is intimately related to the culture by which it is used to get things done in the social world.[15] Accepting Halliday's premise means that we cannot ignore the essential role language plays in what and how students learn to become literate.

In this chapter, we describe the SFL approach to literacy in contrast to common approaches to literacy in schools throughout the United States, give an example of an SFL-based pedagogy that has been successful in another marginalized and underprivileged population in the United States and the world, and offer a brief example of how an SFL-based literacy pedagogy can be used in Appalachia. We conclude with some thoughts on the importance of using local texts for classroom reading and writing.

Current School Literacy Practices in the United States

Literacy practices in Appalachia have been a growing concern since formal schooling began in the region. Jesse Stuart spoke often about the importance of teaching students to read and write with a notion of place always in mind. He stated: "When I gave [students] assignments to write themes, I never gave them the topics listed in their books. I told them to write about the things they knew about: people, places, things, and adventures in Lonesome Valley."[16] However, approaches to literacy in Appalachia have typically followed general approaches throughout the rest of the United States. These have resulted from trends that researchers and teachers have found effective mostly in the field of rhetoric and composition, from abandoning current-traditional practices focused on the writing product,[17] to process approaches,[18] to an emphasis on more student-centered approaches, including expressivism.[19]

In 2012, one example of a prevalent literacy approach is the 6+1 Trait Writing Model of Instruction and Assessment (informally known as "Six-Traits" despite the fact that there are actually seven ["6+1"] traits). According to Education Northwest, a research laboratory that helped create Six-Traits, this system is "now used in virtually every state in the country."[20] The traits—ideas, organization, voice, word choice, sentence fluency, conventions, and presentation—are presented as a set of tools based in the process approach that aim to help students improve their writing. These traits are presented, essentially, as those things that good writers do well. In a fashion similar to what occurs in other process-based types of instruction such as a writers' workshop, a teacher explains the trait concept, provides models, and then allows the students time to practice working with that trait. Teachers then break these traits down into rubrics that students and teachers can use to score proficiency. As students are working on their writing, these rubrics aid them in practicing traits and revision.

While still based in the process tradition, this system provides teachers and students with a metalanguage for talking about and understanding writing.[21] However, in Six-Traits, this metalanguage is focused more on rhetorical concerns than on the particulars of language that effective writers control to express themselves clearly. We see this as a serious flaw in Six-Traits—one that seems to be common in other so-called process approaches. Namely, this system allows us to talk about the effects of language (features of writing) without actually talking about the lexicogrammatical features of language itself. For example, Ryan experienced frustration as an instructor of preservice teachers—in a course using Six-Traits—when he noticed that the Six-Traits materials encourage students to consider the voice of their piece without direct instruction as to how they might change their language to represent the voice to be expressed. In such cases, students may be left seeing writing as a mysterious process they themselves cannot control. A writing pedagogy that focuses only on the effects of language without talking about the language itself is like trying to teach different styles of painting without ever talking about the effects of different types and colors of paint. To extend this metaphor, in many classrooms it is as if teachers expect students to paint the ceiling of the Sistine Chapel but all they have is a can of spray paint—and neither the student nor the teacher acknowledges that there is a problem, but both become frustrated with a result not meeting their expectations of effective writing. Without the tools for understanding how effective writers control language for specific rhetorical purposes, students might know when they see good writing but have a difficult time articulating why the writing is well executed. In addition, they may lack the tools to understand their own control, or lack of control, of the writing and language they themselves are using.

What Do Such Approaches Mean for Appalachian Students?

It is often those students who enter schools with language more like that expected in the academy (typically, white and middle class) who find the most success there. This means that students who are marginalized in the society—often nonnative speakers, minorities, and/or working class—may have a more difficult time producing the texts that are valued in the culture of the school context. Although encouraging self-expression and a student-driven classroom, approaches like Six-Traits risk continuing to provide instructions that do not aid students from marginal linguistic backgrounds in reaching the same literacy standards as are reached by their more mainstream peers. We argue that this is the case because these types of approaches provide only context-based knowledge of texts with little or no connection to the language that constructs these contexts and is constructed by these contexts.

When instructors and scholars discuss the ways in which context affects writing and reading practices, they often do so without a shared metalanguage by which to explain and articulate how writers construct language that considers different contexts. We never hear anyone question why our friends in physics use such technical terms as *gravity, force,* and *inertia;* however, the mere mention of *grammar* and *genre* sends shudders through some of our English language arts colleagues. We argue that such specialized terminology allows both disciplines to share a language by which we can discuss the phenomena that we are studying. In addition, because these postmodern approaches focus teachers' efforts on facilitation rather than direct instruction, students without prior knowledge of language expectations of academic literacies may still struggle without the benefit of explicit language instruction.[22] These students may be left feeling as we did in school, that there is a secret code to which they are not privy.

With these negative aspects of such approaches in mind, Appalachian students—many of whom do not hail from mainstream backgrounds—may be left wondering what they are expected to do with discussions of context features of writing and reading.[23] They may understand that their instructors want them to consider their audience, purpose, and voice, but they may not understand how they can manipulate their language to do so. Many Appalachian students do not come to school with the precursors of academic language in their repertoire. This does not mean that they come to school with deficiencies; rather, they come with a home language that is not as highly valued by the schooling context, as seen in the United States in general. As Stuart laments above, one of the roles of instructors is to help all students learn to control language so that they can participate fully in society. Approaches like Six-Traits, while well meaning, do not provide an explicit way for many students to articulate their linguistic choices in writing or the linguistic choices of the authors they read. This could mean that their performance in school continues to show the same achievement gaps. An SFL genre approach to literacy utilizes an explicit pedagogy, based in the connection between text and context, and provides a shared metalanguage with which students and teachers can discuss their reading and writing.

SFL Approaches to Literacy

An SFL approach to literacy finds its foundations in two prominent theoretical notions: genre and the teaching/learning cycle. Here, we focus primarily on genre. The SFL theory of genre is not to be confused with either a literary notion of genre or the notion of genre as conceived by the so-called new rhetoric tradition in the field of rhetoric and composition or the English for academic purposes (EAP) tradition in the field of Second Language Acquisition.[24] As Ann Johns shows us, the new rhetoric approach tends to "start (and sometimes end) with a discussion of the rhetorical situation rather than with a more specific analysis of lexico-grammatical elements within a text,"[25] while the EAP tradition tends to address the needs of second-language learners and also focuses mainly on context. As we noted with the process approach to literacy, the new rhetoric and EAP pedagogies mainly discuss the level of context, not language.

In the SFL tradition, we emphasize the need for balance between students' learning of both texts and the contexts they realize, reciprocally. We root our approach in the notion that texts and contexts share a mutual relationship, where texts realize and are realized by contexts, and vice versa.[26] This is essential to our understanding of literacy because it helps us uncover patterned linguistic resources as well as variation in the ways texts evolve.[27] In other words, when an instructor teaches genre in the SFL tradition, students learn that contexts determine the ways in which linguistic choices are made but also that the differing ways in which we utilize linguistic resources determine the ways in which genres are ever changing. Figure 8.1 shows a common SFL depiction of the relationship between text and context. Here, the level of genre and the register variables field, mode, and tenor are context levels, and below them are language levels.

Our definition of *genre* comes from J. R. Martin and David Rose, who describe it as a staged, goal-oriented, social process.[28] Genre is staged because it generally takes us several moves to reach our goals with the texts we are

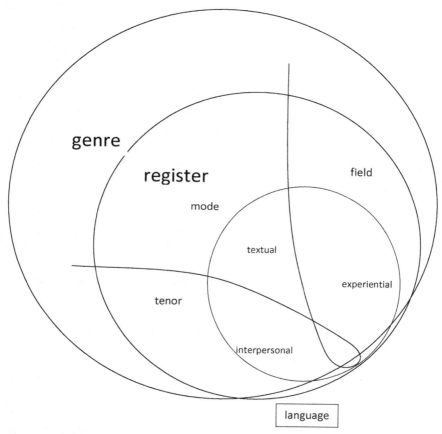

genre

register

field

mode

textual

experiential

tenor

interpersonal

language

Figure 8.1. The SFL genre strata model (adapted from J. R. Martin and David Rose, *Working with Discourse: Meaning beyond the Clause* [London: Continuum, 2007], 17).

writing. It is goal oriented because we typically have something we want to accomplish. It is a social process because we generally have an audience that we must address. Genres are also social in that they are established over time and interlocutors have general ideas of what is expected when reading or writing texts. In discussing genre, we also acknowledge another context notion: register. We discuss register through the notions of field, mode, and tenor.[29]

We also adopt Martin and Rose's description of context and language.[30] First, genre and register (field, mode, and tenor in fig. 8.1) realize the culturally expected schematic and language patterns reflected in each of the stages under which a text unfolds. When we discuss genre, we are concerned with the ways in which texts do or do not develop over the course of their production according to sociocultural expectations. With register, we analyze rhetoric and composition's notions of audience and purpose (among others) and discuss them in more specific ways. We can deconstruct the linguistic choices in the register stratum into three separate variables: field, mode, and tenor, as shown in figure 8.1. In educational terms, field represents the discipline or subject matter about which we are writing. When we discuss mode, we are concerned with how a written, spoken, or multimodal text develops. Finally, the idea of tenor helps students realize the role language plays in the text and how writers interact with their audiences.[31]

While genre and register may at first seem familiar to literacy instructors, the difference between them lies in the connection between these contextual elements and language. More typical literacy approaches—such as Six-Traits—usually account for the same types of contextual factors in their praxis; however, they often do not connect genre and register to language choice. In our praxis, genre and register are intimately connected to language with the concept of Halliday's metafunctions in language.[32] Thus, in our classrooms, we show students the linguistic patterns that realize the genre and register in the text. Halliday and Matthiessen describe language as having three primary functions or metafunctions: experiential, textual, and interpersonal. When discussing the experiential metafunction, we teach students how writers use language to depict the experience they express and how these language choices connect to the field of the piece. We talk about the textual metafunction because here we can uncover with students how language flows to develop the text and how these language choices interact with the mode of the piece. Finally, when we teach the interpersonal metafunction, we discover the role that language plays in the interaction between writer and reader and connect this to the tenor of the piece.

Discussing the metafunctional stratum allows teachers and students to collectively and critically understand the role language plays in the context of the texts they read and write. This is essential for Appalachian students—and all students, for that matter—because, once they engage more with local texts or other texts that describe the people and places they know and love, they can describe what they are reading and writing explicitly. Through an SFL genre approach, students no longer have to guess what writers might be trying to express or, in the case of the typical narrative students write, wrestle with their desire to express their feelings about the struggles and triumphs they have had in their own lives. Through explicit pedagogy, they gain a metalanguage by which they can deconstruct others' writing and construct their own. Students often tell us that they finally understand what an author means and why some texts are more or less difficult for them to read. Furthermore, they claim that their own writing improves because they can make conscious decisions as to how they construct texts for multiple rhetorical purposes.

SFL Pedagogy

Many SFL-based pedagogical approaches have been effective, however, mostly outside the United States.[33] Instructors and scholars have discussed the usefulness of SFL-based approaches to literacy when discussing how students learn to read, write, and understand science, humanities, English language arts, and history, among other disciplines.[34] More scholars have begun to show the effectiveness of this pedagogy in the United States in recent years.[35] In fact, Rose and Martin claim that the approach aids both struggling and advanced readers, with the result that struggling readers reach target reading levels four times faster than expected.[36] However, there are fewer examples of how the pedagogy can aid native speakers of English in the United States. One exception is the work of David Brown, who has described his success in utilizing an SFL-based approach with students who speak African American dialects.[37]

Brown outlines ways in which we can consider students' use of language as a way to introduce the genres and registers of those with more social capital.[38] Academic language becomes another set of linguistic resources for students to exploit, rather than an exploitation of student identity. We accomplish this by working from the linguistic characteristics students have when they enter the classroom, not by treating them like a blank slate as they begin their formal instruction. What this means for Appalachian students is that their own identities and dialects are considered important from the moment they enter the classroom because the instructor can base literacy units on their use of language as a point of departure. The instructor's role is to understand the genres and registers students have and tailor instruction so that it connects to genres and registers that will be needed in the academy and beyond.

In our own work, we have found narratives to be a prevailing genre for most any student since, as Martin and Rose point out, they are universally found across cultures.[39] Story genres, like narratives, are often popularly taught at the beginning of courses. In addition, many students write narratives at each grade level, kindergarten through grade 12. Unfortunately, students often do not learn to move beyond story genres,[40] and those students whose home language might be more like story genres may find difficulty moving into new genres and registers without explicit instruction in how to do so. To further complicate things, the newly implemented Common Core State Standards seem to devalue the role of story genres, emphasizing informational and persuasive genres. This likely will further hinder those students whose home language is more like story genres than other academic ones. David Brown states: "If students understand the complex fluencies they already possess—and those fluencies are not branded as deficient, degraded, or ignorant—they can begin to develop other fluencies without the coercion, whether overt or covert, that many students perceive as part of language instruction."[41] This is the kind of pedagogy we are calling for in those parts of Appalachia where students' home dialects differ from mainstream academic ones.

In our own experiences being educated in Appalachia from kindergarten through parts of graduate school, it generally was the case that many instructors encouraged students to abandon their Appalachian dialect and ways of knowing. For example, Ryan and Josh both vividly remember teachers saying, "*Ain't* isn't a word!" to any peer who would dare utter this common bit of dialect. Such an approach assumes that disentangling our culture from our language is possible in the first place. It also assumes that students cannot be both dialectical and academic—that these two aspects of literacy cannot coexist. Such an approach also does not scaffold students from one point of language use to another because teachers often encourage students to abandon their own voices rather than embrace them as a way toward other language uses. In Brown's approach, students learn a style of language use that is similar to code switching.[42] That is, they learn to effectively control multiple languages, ultimately to their rhetorical, physical, and economic benefit. Students are not limited because of an inability to manipulate Standard English. This ultimately means their participation in a democratic society is determined not by a so-called deficiency in their home language but rather by an efficiency and an ability to understand the contexts under which their linguistic skills can be used in an ever-expanding repertoire of conscious language choices.

Local Contexts, Local Texts

What might an SFL-based pedagogy look like for Appalachian classrooms in their local contexts? Although Appalachia has a rich body of literature and poetry, that work is typically not taught in schools, despite its merits. Appalachian literature is often relegated to the fringes for an emphasis on the literature of so-called canonical authors. This means that generations of Appalachian students are being raised unaware of the great contributions that their people have made to the arts. In their minds, writing is done by outsiders—people from somewhere else. The lived experiences of Appalachian students in their local contexts can become devalued in the language arts classroom, then, because those students fail to see their own lives and people reflected in the literature they read. They may not realize that the land, people, and histories all around them have been the material of great literature for over a century and that they too can participate in controlling their own language. Again, just knowing that folks from our own communities in Eastern Kentucky and West Virginia had published literature changed the possibilities that we saw for ourselves.

Accompanying this blind spot in most curricula is a neglect of the history of Appalachia—particularly the history of the many struggles between people and industry in the area. Students fail to learn about the strength of their people in fighting for better pay, for better working conditions, and against the adverse environmental impact of the many industries of the region, such as those surrounding coal mines. They also fail to gain critical understanding of the many, often preventable industrial disasters that have claimed Appalachian lives. The old cliché that, if we fail to learn from history, we are doomed to repeat the same mistakes is very fitting for Appalachia. For example, just a cursory glance at the history of coal mining in the area reveals a tendency for the industry to sacrifice the safety of miners and the surrounding communities in the interests of increasing profits.[43] We are not taking a stance against coal miners here; we are taking a stance against the way in which such companies do business, exploiting people at the hands of corporate interests.

With this in mind, an ideal text for classroom instruction would be one that is local—meaning that it is written by an Appalachian about Appalachia. It may be about a historical aspect of the area, or it may be about something like the natural beauty of the land. An example of such a text might come from the well-known *Foxfire* series.[44] For our purposes in the context of the coalfields region, we will discuss utilizing a Diane Fisher poem called "Explosion at Winco No. 9."[45] Here, we have a text that looks at one aspect of a historical event in Appalachia: the mine wars that occurred in the early 1920s in Matewan, West Virginia. This particular poem is written from the perspective of a coal miner's wife as she attempts to identify her husband's body after an explosion. In our discussion with students, we contextualize the piece in terms of the historical moment which Fisher presents in the piece.

The poem reads as follows:

Explosion at Winco No. 9
Delsey Salyer knowed Tom Junior by his toes,
which his steel-toed boots had kept the fire off of.
Betty Rose seen a piece of Willy's ear, the little
notched part where a hound had bit him
when he was a young'un, playing at eating its food.
It is true that it is the men that goes in, but it is us
that carries the mine inside. It is us that listens
to what they are scared of and takes
the weight of it from them, like handing off
a sack of meal. Us that learns by heart
birthmarks, scars, bends of fingers,
how the teeth set crooked or straight.
Us that picks up the pieces.
Us that picks up the pieces. I didn't have
nothing to patch with but my old blue dress,
and Ted didn't want floweredy goods
on his shirt. I told him, *It's just under your arm,*
Ted, it ain't going to show.
Ted, it ain't going to show. They brung out bodies,
you couldn't tell. I seen a piece of my old blue dress
on one of them bodies, blacked with smoke,
but I could tell it was my patch, up under the arm.
When the man writing in the big black book
come around asking about identifying marks,
I said, *blue dress.* I told him, *Maude Stanley, 23.*

Our first step in teaching this piece is to discuss the genre with students. We start by pointing out that this poem is from the perspective of a coal miner's wife and that she is telling someone a story from her past. We then ask students what they would identify as the goal of this text. Typically, this discussion leads to the idea that the main goal is to tell a story—a story in which the speaker identifies and overcomes a problem. The specific problem in this case is that the speaker's husband has died in a mine explosion and she must figure out some way to identify his body among many badly damaged corpses. Although the literary genre of this text is a poem, from an SFL genre perspective we would classify it as a narrative because it tells a story with a complication and a resolution. So, even though the word *narrative* typically refers to a type of prose, in the SFL system it can be used to describe the function of any type of text that tells a story with a complication and a resolution.

With the goal of the text in mind, we work with students to articulate the various stages of the text that help the speaker achieve her goals and then give each section a label that describes its function. For this poem, we work with students to make the divisions and labels shown in figure 8.2 (which we have numbered for clarity). The first stage, which we have labeled *orientation,* provides a context for the reader. We know from the poem's title that the *field,* or subject matter, here will be an explosion. Thus, in the orientation stage we find women identifying the remains of their husbands. We also learn about the burden that these women bear, and we end with an episode where the speaker patches her husband's shirt with a blue flowered piece of fabric. Although there are several events described here, they serve to provide a context for the rest of the poem. In a sense, they are not really what the poem is about, but they serve to orient us toward the events that will follow.

In the next stage, labeled *complication,* we learn of the problem faced by the speaker: she and the others at the explosion site are unable to easily identify the miners' remains. Here, we have the true problem faced by the speaker, and some light is shed on events that occurred in the orientation—

Stage	Lines
1. Orientation	1 through 18
2. Complication	19-First part of Line 20
3. Resolution	Last part of Line 20 through Line 25

Figure 8.2. Narrative genre stages in "Explosion at Winco No. 9."

namely, that the other women were identifying their husbands' remains by means of physical features. Here, we point out to students that this stage presents us with a complication that the participants must resolve. In the final section of the poem, labeled *resolution,* we see that the speaker is able to resolve the complication by identifying her husband's body from the patch made from her blue dress.

Applying genre theory to poetry analysis can be a powerful tool to aid students in understanding the content presented in writing. Applying the genre stages to "Explosion at Winco No. 9" gives the piece a structure that would aid the many students who might look at the poem and see a mass of unrelated words. It also moves us away from saying the piece is just a poem, providing more tangible ways to talk about its development. The genre tool makes the relationships between the sections of the poem more explicit, which, in turn, allows students to focus on smaller details in the language of the text.

With the poem divided into genre stages, the teacher guides students through a language analysis using the three metafunctions. In order to conduct a simple analysis using the experiential metafunction, he or she has students identify the participants (typically realized by nouns and their corresponding adjectives) and corresponding processes (typically realized by verbs).[46] These pairings are shown in figure 8.3.

Separating information from the poem in this way allows us to see patterns of meaning in the text's language. In this case, by isolating the human participants and their corresponding processes, we can easily see patterns that relate to who does what in the poem. Subsequently, we can make interpretations about the poem that are based on our reading stance and, more importantly, the poem's language.

Looking at the chart we see that there are three groups of human participants represented in this poem: the coal miner's wives (realized by the various proper names and "us"); the men (realized by "the men," "Ted," and "the man"); and the speaker (realized by "I"). Based on this, we can know that, whatever the poem is about, it involves something between these three groups. Presenting this simple graphic to students, we show the link between participants and processes as the text unfolds. In the case of the women, we can see that the processes most often associated with them are mental processes that happen inside the mind and typically involve some type of thinking or perception—for example, Betty Rose "seen," or you "couldn't tell." The processes that most often pair with the men in the poem are mate-

Stage	Human participant/process
1. Orientation	-Delsey Salyer/knowed -Betty Rose/seen -men/goes in -us/carries…inside -us/listens -us/takes -us/learns -us/picks up -I/didn't have -Ted/didn't want -I/told
2. Complication	-They/brung -you/couldn't tell
3. Resolution	-I/seen -I/could tell -the man/writing -the man…book/come around asking -I/said -I/told

Figure 8.3. Human participant and corresponding process by genre stage.

rial processes that involve a participant affecting an object or doing something for another participant. For our purposes here, the main distinction we want students to grasp is that in a mental clause, the main participant is less physically active, and in a material clause, the main participant is more physically active. Therefore, we point out that the language here describes women as less active and men as more active.

Stage 2 of the poem represents a good summary of this dichotomy between the male and the female participants in the poem—"They" "brung," while "you," representing the miner's wives, "couldn't tell." With this dichotomy in mind, we begin to discuss with students how this fits with our expectations of the explosion event described in the poem as well as our expectations of own culture and gender roles—roles that Fisher calls into question by showing that, because of the great burdens they bear, women are, in their own way, as active as the men who enter the mine. The poem as a whole can also be viewed as making a powerful critique of the mine where Ted Stanley worked. A classroom discussion that unpacks the ways in which this poem works as an effective piece of rhetoric leads to further critical discussions about similar events and circumstances in the lives of students.

For many Appalachian students, these language tools can be an invaluable way to access the rich content found in writing. The added benefit of choosing a text based in the history of Appalachia is that, while students are learning about literature, they are also learning about their history and learning how to look at language critically. The analyses offered above, though brief, illustrate how this approach to literacy can help students move back and forth from a text in their classroom, to their history and culture, and then to their own lives.[47]

One of our ultimate goals as instructors should be to elevate a generation prepared to participate in local, national, and global democracies with voices of their own. Because the Appalachian dialect and the people who speak it have traditionally been silenced in presenting their identity in a way they own, we believe that literacy education provides a way for students to understand Appalachian voices critically and move in and out of more standard academic varieties of English more effectively. Once students and teachers develop a collective metalanguage to discuss the language in, for example, "Explosion at Winco No. 9," they can then deconstruct explicitly the meanings they derive from their reading of the text. Collectively deconstructing texts in this way provides a point of departure for the entire literacy unit. Following the SFL-based teaching/learning cycle,[48] students would then jointly construct their own poem on the basis of their collective understanding of an event based in their local context. Eventually, once students learn to control the genre's language, they could then move into constructing their own independent examples of the genre, experimenting with their own voices and realities. Moving from collective to individual pieces, they can articulate their own experiences using their new understanding of how language works in the genre. In addition, understanding the connection between context and language allows students to read and understand other texts within and outside their schooling experience. They can deconstruct other texts with which they interact throughout their lives, further aiding them in utilizing and working against the texts that claim to represent their various Appalachian voices.

Our view here is meant not to denigrate Appalachian voices but to help students understand themselves and the culture around them in a way that shapes their lives by knowing and explicitly engaging with language in school. Valuing the voices in our classrooms and critically examining them aids students' understanding of their abilities to make positive change in their own lives and the lives of those around them. Doing so with local texts in local contexts means students not only understand the local culture from which they come, but also can make explicit connections between their local situation and larger national and international conditions. In our view, Appalachian children need to critically engage with the language of authors like Denise Giardina, Diane Fisher, Jesse Stuart, and Wendell Berry as much as with that of authors like William Shakespeare and F. Scott Fitzgerald. Using an SFL-based approach allows students to see the linguistic and cultural value first in their region and then outside it.

Notes

1. Jesse Stuart, *The Thread That Runs So True: A Mountain School Teacher Tells His Story* (New York: Touchstone, 1949), 280–81.

2. Guadalupe Valdés, *Con Respeto: Bridging the Distances between Culturally Diverse Families and Schools: An Ethnographic Portrait* (New York: Teachers College Press, 1996).

3. Jane Stephenson, *Courageous Paths: Stories of Nine Appalachian Women* (Berea, KY: New Opportunity School for Women, 1995).

4. Jeff Biggers, *The United States of Appalachia* (Emeryville, CA: Shoemaker & Hoard, 2006). While Biggers's work is controversial because of the positive stereotypes it may express, it does point out positive contributions made by Appalachians. His potential tendency to be too positive does not discount his basic argument that Appalachians have been more than what their negative stereotypes indicate.

5. John Williams, *Appalachia: A History* (Chapel Hill: University of North Carolina Press, 2002).

6. In this case, we are putting forth an approach that assumes that most students in the classroom are from the Appalachian region. However, this may not always be the case in all situations. Thus, our approach is a model for similar approaches that educators can use to teach students from their own geographic region within or outside Appalachia. Additionally, it is possible that students may be from different regions of Appalachia, the United States, or the world; therefore, educators need to carefully select literature that will speak to students' own home culture as the point of departure for such units.

7. Harry Caudill, *Night Comes to the Cumberlands: A Biography of a Depressed Area* (Ashland, KY: Jesse Stuart Foundation, 2001).

8. Williams, *Appalachia*.

9. Stephen Fisher, "The Grass Roots Speak Back," in *Back Talk from Appalachia: Confronting Stereotypes*, ed. Dwight Billings et al. (Lexington: University Press of Kentucky, 1999), 203–14.

10. Robert Shogan, *The Battle of Blair Mountain: The Story of America's Largest Labor Uprising* (New York: Basic, 2004).

11. Ryan Angus and Josh Iddings, "A Social Justice Curriculum for Appalachia," in *Teacher Education for Social Justice: Perspectives and Lessons Learned*, ed. Luciana de Oliveira (Charlotte, NC: Information Age, 2013), 81–90.

12. David Rose, "Democratising the Classroom: A Literacy Pedagogy for the New Generation," *Journal of Education* 37 (2005): 131–67.

13. M. A. K. Halliday, "Three Aspects of Children's Language Development: Learning Language, Learning through Language, Learning about Language," in *The Language of Early Childhood*, ed. Johnathan Webster (New York: Continuum, 2004), 308–26, 308.

14. Rose, "Democratising the Classroom."

15. M. A. K. Halliday, "Language and Socialization: Home and School," in *Language and Education*, ed. Johnathan Webster (New York: Continuum, 2007), 81–96.

16. Stuart, *The Thread That Runs So True*, 72.

17. James Berlin and Robert Inkster, "Current-Traditional Rhetoric: Paradigm and Practice," *Freshman English News* 8, no. 3 (1980): 1–4, 13–14; Richard Young, "Paradigms and Problems: Needed Research in Rhetorical Invention," in *Research on Composing: Points of Departure*, ed. Charles Cooper and Lee Odell (Urbana, IL: National Council of Teachers of English, 1978); Lad Tobin, "Introduction: How the Writing Process Was Born—and Other Conversion Narratives," in *Taking Stock: The Writing Process Movement in the '90s*, ed. Lad Tobin and Thomas Newkirk (Portsmouth, NH: Boynton/Cook, 1994), 1–14, 5.

18. James Britton, "Writing to Learn and Learning to Write," in *Prospect and Retrospect: Selected Essays of James Britton*, ed. Gordon Pradl (Portsmouth, NH: Boynton/Cook, 1982); D. Gordon Rohman, "Pre-Writing: The Stage of Discovery in the Writing Process," *College Composition and Communication* 16 (1965): 106–12; Peter Vandenberg et al., "Critical Introduction," in *Relations, Locations, and Positions: Composition Theory for Writing Teachers*, ed. Peter Vandenberg et al. (Urbana, IL: National Council of Teachers of English, 2006).

19. Richard Kent, "Matthew's Portfolio," in *Teaching the Neglected "R": Rethinking Writing Instruction in Secondary Schools*, ed. Thomas Newkirk and Richard Kent (Portsmouth, NH: Heinemann, 2007), 47–63; Peter Elbow, *Writing with Power* (New York: Oxford University Press, 1981).

20. Mark Workman, "About 6+1 Trait® Writing," Education Northwest, 2011, http://educationnorthwest.org/resource/949.

21. We use the term *metalanguage* here following other SFL scholars to mean language used to talk about language.

22. J. R. Martin and David Rose, *Genre Relations: Mapping Culture* (London: Equinox, 2008), 258; Lisa Delpit, "The Silenced Dialogue: Power and Pedagogy in Educating Other People's Children," *Harvard Educational Review* 58 (1988): 280–98.

23. Shirley Brice Heath, *Ways with Words: Language, Life, and Work in Communities and Classrooms* (New York: Cambridge University Press, 1983).

24. Amy Devitt, "Generalizing about Genre: New Conceptions of an Old Concept," in Vandenberg et al., eds., *Relations, Locations, and Positions*, 84–102; Mary Jo Reiff, "Moving Writers, Shaping Motives, Motivating Critique and Change: A Genre Approach to Teaching Writing," in ibid., 157–69; John Swales, *Genre Analysis: English in Academic and Research Settings* (Cambridge: Cambridge University Press, 1990); John Swales, *Research Genres: Explorations and Applications* (Cambridge: Cambridge University Press, 2004).

25. Ann Johns, introduction to *Genre in the Classroom: Multiple Perspectives*, ed. Ann Johns (Mahwah, NJ: Erlbaum, 2002), 3–13, 9.

26. J. R. Martin and David Rose, *Working with Discourse: Meaning beyond the Clause* (London: Continuum, 2007); Martin and Rose, *Genre Relations*.

27. Martin and Rose, *Genre Relations*.

28. Martin and Rose, *Working with Discourse*, 8.

29. M. A. K. Halliday and Christian Matthiessen, *An Introduction to Functional Grammar* (London: Arnold, 2004).

30. Martin and Rose, *Working with Discourse*; Martin and Rose, *Genre Relations*.

31. Halliday and Matthiessen, *Introduction to Functional Grammar*.

32. Ibid.

33. David Rose and J. R. Martin, *Learning to Write, Reading to Learn: Genre, Knowledge and Pedagogy in the Sydney School* (London: Equinox, 2012).

34. J. R. Martin, "Nominalization in Science and Humanities: Distilling Knowledge and Scaffolding Text," in *Functional and Systemic Linguistics: Approaches and Uses*, ed. Eija Ventola (New York: Mouton de Gruyter, 1991), 307–37; Frances Christie and Mary Macken-Horarik, "Disciplinarity and School Subject English," in *Disciplinarity: Functional Linguistic and Sociological Perspectives*, ed. Frances Christie and Karl Maton (London: Continuum, 2001), 175–96; Luciana de Oliveira, "Nouns in History: Packaging Information, Expanding Explanations, and Structuring Reasoning," *The History Teacher* 43 (2010): 191–203, and *Knowing and Writing School History: The Language of Students' Expository Writing and Teachers' Expectations* (Charlotte, NC: Information Age, 2011).

35. de Oliveira, *Knowing and Writing School History*; Zhihui Fang and Mary Schleppegrell, *Reading in Secondary Content Areas: A Language-Based Pedagogy* (Ann Arbor: University of Michigan Press, 2008); Meg Gebhard, "School Reform, Hybrid Discourses, and Second Language Literacies," *TESOL Quarterly* 39 (2005): 187–210; Mary Schleppegrell, *The Language of Schooling: A Functional Linguistics Perspective* (Mahwah, NJ: Erlbaum, 2004).

36. Rose and Martin, *Learning to Write*.

37. David Brown, "Micro-Level Teaching Strategies for Linguistically Diverse Learners," *Linguistics and Education* 17 (2006): 175–95, and "Dialect and Register Hybridity: A Case from Schools," *Journal of English Linguistics* 39 (2011): 109–34.

38. Brown, "Micro-Level Teaching."

39. Martin and Rose, *Genre Relations*.

40. Arthur Applebee, *Contexts for Learning to Write: Studies of Secondary School Instruction* (Norwood, NJ: Ablex, 1984).

41. Brown, "Micro-Level Teaching," 179–80.

42. Brown, "Dialect and Register Hybridity."

43. Consider, e.g., the April 5, 2010, Upper Big Branch mine disaster, where an explosion claimed the lives of twenty-nine miners. In December 2011, the Mine Safety and Health Administration finished its investigation of the disaster and concluded that the Massey Energy Company's conscious neglect of safety protocols in order to increase profits led to the disaster.

44. See, e.g., Eliot Wigginton, *The Foxfire Book* (New York: Anchor, 1972).

45. Diane Fisher, "Explosion at Winco No. 9," in *Kettle Bottom* (Florence, MA: Perugia, 2004), 7.

46. Every participant can typically be linked with at least one process.

47. While the SFL-based approach may appear similar to a Freirean approach in the way in which the literature is positioned within the curriculum and the idea of "reading the word to read the world," the difference is in the explicitness of the SFL approach to language and its implementation.

48. Rose, "Democratising the Classroom."

9

Rhetorical Theories of Appalachian Literacies

Sara Webb-Sunderhaus

Two years ago, I submitted an article to one of the most prestigious and competitive journals in composition studies. Given that the journal's acceptance rate is less than 10 percent, I was very pleased when the editor asked me to revise and resubmit the piece, which was based on my ethnographic research with Appalachian students enrolled in first-year writing courses. As I read the reviewers' and the editor's comments, I usually found myself nodding in agreement with their suggestions and started planning how to best address their valid critiques.

However, there were a few comments that left me frustrated; specifically, my work was judged to be not "theoretical" enough, and I was accused of being "dismissive of other scholars' work" because I (correctly) noted that, in his *Storm in the Mountains,* James Moffett wrote that the people of Kanawha County, West Virginia, suffered from willful "agnosis"—Greek for ignorance—because they pressured the local school board to ban his textbook.[1] As I wrote in the submitted manuscript: "Moffett does not discuss the literacy practices and beliefs that might have led this community to such a decision, and he fails to recognize the class implications of the conflict as well. Instead, he dismisses this Appalachian community as willfully ignorant." And for that comment—which I felt was rather mild mannered, given some of the blistering critiques of Moffett that I have heard and read by other Appalachian scholars, including my coeditor, Kim Donehower—I was told that I "quickly wrote off Moffett's text" and that I delivered "quick swipes" at another scholar's work.[2]

Though I was irritated by this particular reading of that passage, I understood why the reviewer responded in the way he or she did. James Moffett was known for his efforts in K–12 curricular reform and was one of the leading early figures in the discipline we know now as rhetoric and composition; his book *Teaching the Universe of Discourse* was a text fundamental to this new field,[3] and *Storm in the Mountains* has typically been understood by compositionists as rightfully challenging censorship, religious fundamentalism, and political conservatism. The reviewer's description of *Storm in the Mountains* as "a complex and highly nuanced account of conservative forces in the region where [Moffett] had been living and working" very nicely sums up the prevailing view in rhetoric and composition of Moffett's work.

Given his stature in composition studies and the narrative our field has constructed about *Storm in the Mountains,* I can understand why my reviewer reacted in this way to my brief commentary on Moffett; I am a composition and literacy scholar who, thanks to the Ph.D. program at the Ohio State University, was well trained in the discipline's history and ways of knowing. But, for reviewers to understand how and why I react to Moffett as I do, they would also have to understand that I grew up as an Urban Appalachian in Cincinnati, Ohio, the daughter of parents who were part of the Great Migration out of the Appalachian region in the mid-twentieth century. They would have to understand what it means to grow up in a city where my family's culture was hated and mocked relentlessly and how that experience would eventually shape the way in which I see the academic world. They would have to understand the implications of knowing that, if a fellow scholar wrote about my own family and their neighbors in Lewis County, Kentucky, some of my loved ones—like the people of Kanawha County—could easily be dismissed as "willfully ignorant" because, on the surface, they fit some of the worst stereotypes of Appalachians. For example, there are my (deceased) maternal grandparents, who had eighth-grade educations and who, for as long as I can remember, received some form of government assistance: food stamps, government cheese, Medicaid. Both were toothless, and, during the Depression, my grandpa was a moonshiner. My grandma married her first husband (not my grandpa) at the age of sixteen; he beat her frequently and ruthlessly, resulting in the early births of two dead babies. If there was a list of Appalachian stereotypes, the life history of my grandparents could lead a researcher to check off every box: Poor? check. Toothless? check. Uneducated? check. Violent? check. Lawless? check.

But there is so much more to my grandma and grandpa than these basic facts. Yes, my grandpa ran moonshine for many years, but, owing to his Mormon upbringing, he never drank anything with caffeine in it, let alone alcohol. He never smoked or chewed the tobacco he grew, either. Yes, my grandma was a child bride and a battered woman, but she divorced her abuser at the age of nineteen and married my grandpa two years later, a man to whom she was happily married for sixty years. And, yes, my grandparents had only eighth-grade educations, as did their two oldest children, because the high school was too far away to walk to and the mountain they lived on was inaccessible by bus. But they made sure they moved farther down the mountain so their two younger children would be able to go to high school, a move the family incurred at significant expense, and a sign of just how much they valued education.

These are the facets of life that can go unseen by researchers in the field and be unaccounted for in our theories of literacy. As researchers, we may not have the time, the ability, or the positionality to enter a community deeply enough to learn the complexities of its people, their literacy beliefs and practices. In some cases, we may lack the insider knowledge needed to even know what we should look for, to whom we should speak, and the questions we should ask. Others of us were raised among these complexities and understand them well, but we may have difficulty theorizing what we know intuitively and what we have learned in the field. This is the crux of my chapter: how living through these complexities shaped me as a scholar who studies composition and literacy and made me sensitive to the need for a literacy theory of—and for—Appalachia and its people.

Why Are Literacy Studies Scholars Literacy Studies Scholars?

For people with a background like mine—a first-generation, working-class college student from a marginalized culture—a career as a literacy studies scholar is, in some ways, scholarly destiny because our backgrounds have shaped us to resist typical conceptions of literacy and text. If, as Deborah Brandt argues, multiple generations of a family are "like a delta" in that the family's "environment for reading and writing [is] a repository of accumulating material and ideological complexity," then this multigenerational accumulation of literacy shapes Appalachian students and scholars such as myself in profound ways that go beyond our accepted understandings of the import of literacy and identity.[4]

So what are these "accepted understandings of literacy and identity" that circulate in our field? There are two primary narratives that are typically told: "Here's how my identity shapes what and whom I study and teach," and "Here's how my identity shapes my literacy." We have many examples of these conceptualizations among scholars who study composition and literacy; compelling and moving essays and books by Linda Brodkey, Keith Gilyard, and Victor Villanueva—authors of "Writing on the Bias," *Voices of the Self*, and *Bootstraps*, respectively—are now classic texts that offer beautiful testimony to the power and prevalence of these two understandings of literacy and identity.[5] They are only three among many such scholars, however. I could include the influential work of many others, such as Mike Rose, Vershawn Ashanti Young, Ellen Cushman, and Morris Young.[6] I must include myself in this list as well. As seen in the work of these scholars, narratives of literacy and identity tend to focus on the authors' experiences as students, particularly (though not always) in their K–12 or undergraduate years; their struggles and triumphs with composing, their desires to research and teach people and issues connected to their identity, and sometimes more general career issues they have encountered, such as the difficulty of securing a living wage, getting a job, and earning tenure.

Let me be clear. It is not my intention to criticize the work of these scholars or these understandings of literacy and identity; as I have just written, my own scholarship has perpetuated their influence. These conceptualizations are not misguided, incorrect, or somehow bad; they are just incomplete. Rarely do such scholars—myself included—discuss how our cultural histories, as manifested in our families, led us to composition, rhetoric, and literacy studies in the first place or how our understandings of literacy and identity inform our research methodologies, our relationship with participants, or our definitions of *text*.

When I consider the forces that brought me to study composition, rhetoric, and literacy, it is clear that my Appalachian and Urban Appalachian identities and family played a key role. The conventional narrative that I typically share—one that expresses the most common understandings of literacy and identity in our field—goes something like this. For as long as I can remember, I have felt like an outsider. Whether that be as an Urban Appalachian child in Cincinnati or as a professor who recently received the Indiana University Board of Trustees' official notice of her tenure and promotion, I have never really felt like I fit anywhere. Thus, it is unsurprising that I have been drawn to focusing my teaching and research on other outsiders, such as Appalachians, working-class students, and basic writers—students who historically have been on the margins of the academy. Again, that is the conventional narrative.

But why do I specifically study composition, rhetoric, and literacy? Well, that requires me to tell a different kind of story, one of growing up in a print-rich home even though I never observed anyone I lived with reading a novel. My mother subscribed to magazines such as *Ladies' Home Journal* and *Good Housekeeping,* and my father read two newspapers a day as well as the weekly paper from Lewis County. My maternal grandmother—who moved in with us while I was still in high school—read daily, her texts of choice being the Bible and various magazines, including *the trashies* (her name for the tabloids). I also saw all three of them read for specific purposes. My father frequently referred to *Chilton's Repair Guide* as he worked on cars in our driveway—one of the three jobs he worked—and both my mother and my grandmother had voluminous collections of cookbooks; as master Appalachian cooks, neither of them needed to consult recipes as they cooked, but they both enjoyed reading cookbooks to learn new ideas. Then of course there were the many stories that were read to me, some from books, but many from memory and experience—stories of my family and our history, stories that usually indirectly implied their meaning.

I have always been an avid reader; my parents and grandmother encouraged my love of reading as best they could. They felt that my development as a reader would be key to success in school, so my mother took me to the library and, as I grew older, dropped me off there after school and in the summer. My frugal parents avoided many purchases, but there was always money to buy books for me. These books were certainly not part of the canon of children's and young adult literature; they were usually cheap, well-marketed paperbacks—like the *Sweet Valley High* series—because these were the books that were readily accessible and known to us. In our world, *Little House on the Prairie* was a television show, not a book series. I should add that these books were quite different from the ones I read at the small, Christian school I attended for grades 1–12; there, reading was quite literally salvation, to use an idea inherent in Sylvia Scribner's metaphor of literacy as state of grace.[7] We were required to read and memorize the Bible, and the fiction that we were allowed to read had to be suitably Christian in its themes.

But I continued to read whatever I wanted at home because, while my parents subscribed to a general Judeo-Christian worldview, they did not affiliate themselves with a particular church or theology, especially the fundamentalist dogma of my school. As Loyal Jones has written: "Mountain people are religious. This does not mean that we always go to church regularly, but we are religious in the sense that most of our values and the meanings we find in life spring from the Bible."[8] This separation in my parents' lives of religious belief from church led them to question—and to teach me to question—my school's mandates. This skepticism also meant that any attempts by the school to limit what I read were met with eye rolling and resistance from my mother and grandmother, who strongly impressed on me that I should read whatever I wanted and (in the words of my grandmother) "to hell with what any of the rest of 'em think."

Writing was an important part of life in my childhood home, though it was very definitely gendered female. Grandma wrote in a diary every day until she was no longer physically capable of holding a pen. My mother and grandmother had large recipe collections that they had each written out by hand, and my mother wrote weekly letters to family and friends in Kentucky; writing was how she maintained relationships with the people she loved. Mom's and Grandma's uses of writing were (and, in my mother's case, still are) characteristic of those associated with Appalachian women, as seen in Anita Puckett's "'Let the Girls Do the Spelling and Dan Will Do the Shooting.'" Puckett writes that, in the Eastern Kentucky community she studied, "literate practices are God-given attributes of women's 'nature' . . . providing contexts in which a woman can negotiate her social, religious, and cultural identity." Likewise, my father's literacy practices are in keeping with those of other Appalachian men, according to Puckett, who concludes that, for the Appalachian men in her study, "literate activities are less important than . . . subsistence or business activities," later adding: "Almost all men write almost nothing except their signatures or an occasional price list."[9] Similarly, Gregory E. Griffey describes the invisibility of men's literacy in his Appalachian hometown: "If men had an interest in reading and writing for the mere enjoyment such activities might afford, I never heard them speak of it publicly, especially in the presence of other men."[10] My family bears out Puckett's claims as well as Griffey's experience; to this day, I have never seen my dad write anything at all. I did not even know what his handwriting looked like until after I moved away from home, and that was only because he signed the check that helped my husband and me buy our home.

So like many other Appalachian girls and women before me, I used writing for personal reasons; by the second or third grade, I kept a diary. Around that time, I also started writing short stories as well as letters to friends and other people I deemed important, including fictional characters (such as Big Boy of restaurant fame) and politicians. In the early 1980s, when I was in third or fourth grade and television movies like *The Day After* portrayed the horrific effects of nuclear war, I wrote a letter to then president Reagan and essentially asked him to please not end the world by getting into a nuclear war with the Soviet Union. Several months later, I received a response—personally signed by the president—in which he stated, among other things, that our country would be able to avoid nuclear disaster because of children like me. By high school, I was a prolific writer of poems, personal notes and letters, and stories—some fictional, some modeled on the types of stories that were told to me by older family members, stories full of meaning for my friends and younger relatives. Writing in my diary every day also went a long way toward helping me make sense of the world around me and the contradictions inherent in it.

Writing was one of these contradictions. At home, and in my own personal, private world, the act of composing was highly valuable for a young girl. However, at my Christian school, writing almost exclusively referred to handwriting. Brandt describes how reading is sacred and writing profane in popular memory, and this was certainly the case at my school, where writing was viewed as dangerous because it was an act that could not be as easily controlled as reading. Students' reading material could be and was very effectively limited by the school, but student writing was more difficult to control, for, as Brandt notes, writing has historically been used "for resistance, rebellion, the claiming of voice, and the development of critical consciousness."[11] This fact made writing dangerous, especially in a religious culture that stressed blind obedience and actively discouraged questioning, and as a result I was assigned very little writing in school.

Thus, these are some of the lessons of literacy—at times questionable, at times contradictory—that I learned as an Urban Appalachian girl growing up in Cincinnati: reading frequently and widely correlates with success in school. The reading engaged in at home may be different from, but is not less worthy than, the reading done at school. The opinions of others—whether they be literary experts or would-be censors—should play no role in selecting reading materials; personal interest and enjoyment are the important criteria for choosing a book. There are many different types of texts; while not all are valued widely, all are valuable to the people who use them. Reading serves particular functions (usually, though not exclusively, utilitarian) in adult life. As Kim Donehower has also observed, writing is something women—especially Appalachian women—do as part of a larger responsibility of maintaining relationships with, and caring for, others.[12] Writing is powerful because it can nurture and grow relationships and enable one to reflect on one's life and world. Writing enables one to communicate with—and possibly shape the thinking of—those with great influence in our culture. And, finally, writing is powerful because it inspires fear among those who seek to shape (and even control) others in ways they deem appropriate.

In some of my published work on Appalachian students in first-year writing courses, I have described Appalachians as "living with literacy's contradictions" in a "space where differing belief systems about literacy come into play and blend both institutional and regional contexts."[13] The contradictory models of literacy I have negotiated in my life are also indicative of a wider public/private distinction for uses of literacy in Appalachia. Living with these contradictions is what is normal for many Appalachians. Whether we grow up on a long concrete block in Cincinnati or a holler in Eastern Kentucky, for many of us being Appalachian means living with contradictory attitudes about literacy all the time. At home we learn particular types of literacies, at school we may develop others, and church may bring still others. Sometimes lines between school and home, church and home, or church and school are blurred, as they were in my case. There may also be contradictory literacies within a single family, as I have found in my research and experienced in my own family life.

These contradictions arise because there are multiple, conflicting literacies circulating inside the region owing to the prolific attempts by various missionary and social welfare groups to bring their brand of literacy to Appalachia (a point to which I return later). The sociolinguist James Paul Gee defines *literacy* as "mastery of a secondary discourse" and refers to spaces like home, family, church, and school as discourse communities, writing: "Discourse is a sort of identity kit which comes complete with the appropriate costume and instructions on how to act, talk, and often write." In other words, it is in these discourse communities that we learn not only particular literacies, but also how to use and value them and perform a literate identity: "A way of reading a certain type of text is *only* acquired . . . as a member of a social practice wherein people not only read texts of this type in this way, but also talk about such texts in certain ways, hold certain attitudes and values about them, and socially interact over them in certain ways." When the literacies of different discourse communities come into contact with each other, conflict can emerge: "The conflicts are real and cannot simply be wished away. They are the site of very real struggle and resistance."[14] Appalachia and its people are but one example of this "struggle and resistance," and as a result Appalachians grow up bi- or even multiliterate as we negotiate among various literacy languages at any given time.

However, this resistance is complicated because Gee's conceptualizations of an easily acquired primary literacy (in contrast to more contentious secondary literacies) do not hold true for Appalachians. While I return to this point later, here I contend that Appalachians' attainment of our primary literacy is complicated by our contradictory understandings of literacy as well as by the understandings of our literacies held by others. The contradictions we live with, as well as our awareness of how others conceptualize our literacy, force us to develop the double consciousness of which W. E. B. DuBois writes.[15] We grow accustomed to seeing ourselves (and our literacies) through our own eyes as well as the eyes of others. Those eyes are not often kind, as the literary scholar Erica Abrams Locklear illustrates, writing that resistance "seems unlikely at best if Appalachian people ever hope to change their negative image" because it "would be viewed by many Americans only as obstinate, stubborn, and further proof of backward hillbilly culture." Locklear refers to the process of navigating double consciousness as making identity decisions, using examples from Harriet Arnow's *The Dollmaker* (1954), a book about an Urban Appalachian family named the Nevels, to illustrate how "the residents of Detroit shape the Nevels family's view of itself."[16] As the quote indicates, this process can be especially fierce for Urban Appalachians, who must negotiate an Appalachian cultural identity with other identities we are potentially developing in urban centers near the region—identities that may be constructed in opposition to Appalachianness.

DuBois notes: "It is a peculiar sensation, this double consciousness, this sense of always looking at one's self through the eyes of others, of measuring one's soul by the tape of a world that looks on in amused contempt and pity."[17] He used the term *double consciousness* at the turn of the twentieth century to describe the African American experience, and I realize that it may be problematic for me as a twenty-first-century white woman—a woman with all the attendant privilege of my race and class—to appropriate the concept. While I am utilizing his race-specific term, I am applying it differently than he did as my use is rooted in regional identity, not race. Here, I am influenced by the work of the philosopher Charles Taylor, who has written: "Our identities are formed in dialogue with others, in agreement or struggle with their recognition of us." He added: "The projecting of an inferior or demeaning image on another can actually distort and oppress, to the extent that it is interiorized."[18] Members of an oppressed group can internalize the bigotry that is directed at them, and this lived experience of internalization feels like the double consciousness DuBois describes.

My understandings of my own Urban Appalachian identity were forged in pain. I recall all too well what I endured during childhood: the incessant teasing about the "funny way" my family and I talked, the hillbilly jokes ("Why wasn't Jesus born in Kentucky? Because God couldn't find three wise men or a virgin"), and the constant insults and snide remarks—usually centered on themes of incest—about my family and me. These comments became especially painful after I was molested at the age of seven by a family friend. Like many survivors of childhood sexual abuse, I felt a great deal of shame, and being routinely subjected to bigoted "humor" about Appalachians and sexual abuse led me to feel even more ashamed—not only of my assault, but also of my culture. I feared that what happened to me somehow confirmed all the terrible things people in my city said about Appalachians and proved that I was sexually deviant.

As Katherine Trauth Taylor explains, Appalachians in Cincinnati are certainly viewed with the "amused contempt and pity" DuBois describes,[19] and I wanted no part of that, especially in the aftermath of my molestation. I also did not talk about the assault for many years because I did not want to make my family the target of people's bigotry. Given stereotypes about Appalachians and incest, I feared others would wrongly assume my father or brothers molested me—a fear that was realized in adulthood after I began talking openly about the assault—and I could not bear the idea that the love of my family might be twisted by others into something dirty and false.

Thus, in my child's mind, my molestation and my Appalachian identity became jumbled and mixed together; at that point in my life, I could see my Appalachianness only through the bigoted eyes of others. Using logic twisted by naïveté and pain, I found it easiest to prove to myself and others that my molestation was not my fault by disidentifying as Appalachian; if my family and I were not really Appalachian, then what happened to me could not be blamed on any of us.

My rejection of an Appalachian identity was reinforced by the fact that most members of my immediate and extended family did not—and still do not—explicitly identify as Appalachian. While my family has all the cultural markers of Appalachianness, most of my relatives say they are country or Kentuckians, not Appalachians. The furthest they will typically go toward identifying as Appalachian is to say that they are "from the hills." While all my family take pride in what they would call our Kentucky heritage, some of my relatives—who, like my parents, migrated to Cincinnati during the 1950s—have angrily asked why I focus my research on Appalachians and claim an Appalachian identity when "we are not white trash." *White trash* is one of the most common and hurtful epithets thrown at Appalachians in Cincinnati, and my family's use of the term demonstrates yet again how Appalachians can struggle with DuBois's notion of double consciousness. The aftermath of my molestation and my family's conflicted feelings toward our Appalachianness led me to fight with warring notions of identity for years, unable to "merge [my] double self into a better and truer self," in the words of DuBois, and come to terms with what Appalachianness meant to others, my family, and myself.[20]

I shared the story of my journal article's review at the beginning of this chapter to illustrate how double consciousness and resistance operate in my life as a scholar; like DuBois, I eventually learned how to utilize my double consciousness. My lived experiences as an Urban Appalachian and my family's Appalachian roots gave me the ability to read Moffett in both the accepted ways and in ways that the reviewer could not; to return to an earlier theme of this chapter, I was able to see the complexities. However, this same reviewer noted (correctly, I would add) that the manuscript needed a better theoretical apparatus. The lack of theory in my piece was, in one sense, a result of those same life forces that led me to resist Moffett's reading of the textbook controversy. It is difficult to find an appropriate theoretical framework when theorists have not necessarily developed the complexities, the double consciousness, that this life brings. But this is the very same reason why that reviewer could not see Moffett through my eyes—he or she did not have that lived sense of complexity that comes with being Appalachian and that our current theories do not convey.

My story illustrates some of the ways in which literacy and identity can shape scholars and explain why we do what we do and why we study what we study. This is what I meant earlier when I wrote that my career in literacy studies was, in a sense, scholarly destiny. *Of course* I study literacy; how could I not when some of the issues most integral to literacy studies—reading, writing, identity, culture, power, and text—figured so prominently in my early life and my understanding of the world around me? Growing up as a member of a culture that was not valued and using low-prestige literacy practices and texts went a long way toward making me sensitive to those literacies—and the people who use them. The fundamentalist Christian school I attended gave me hard-won insight into the forming of disparate views of texts and their power. I did not have to read literacy scholarship to understand that the "Great Divide" theory of literacy as expressed by Ong and Goody and Watt—in which literacy is positioned in opposition to orality—was problematic because I lived a more complex understanding, thanks to the stories of my family, texts which were composed as skillfully as any book.[21]

These conceptualizations of literacy, identity, and text have thus shaped my reception of theory and pushed me past some of the field's accepted understandings and definitions, yet—as the comments of my reviewer make clear—at times I find it very difficult to theorize this knowledge. I, like many other scholars I know who come from marginalized populations, do not usually talk about the difficulty of theorizing what I have lived through, of finding a theoretical framework that accounts for the lived experience of marginalization when that is not necessarily an experience that many theorists share. I suspect that one reason why those of us from such backgrounds do not talk openly about these issues is fear; we are all too familiar with the experience of being viewed as deficient, as somehow less than. To talk about the difficulty of doing theory—the stock in trade of the academy—is to open up ourselves, and by extension our people, to what we have heard and felt for years: that we are ignorant, that we do not belong, that we are inferior. Even now, there is a part of me that is silently screaming, "Don't write about this! Don't share anything that could hurt you! Don't betray yourself!" But we need to have these discussions because without them theories that account for the lived experience of marginalization will continue to go undeveloped.

A Literacy Theory of—and for—Appalachia

Most literacy theories do not necessarily translate all that well to Appalachia because they are too general; they do not take into account the specifics of the region; and they come from scholars with different motivations, interests, and experiences. Theories are typically deemed to be successful if they are internally consistent and if they are broadly applicable; theories cannot be generalizable if they are too specific to a particular community or place. Yet, given the contradictory and unique nature of Appalachian identity, a theory that allows for contradictions and that is narrowly applicable is what is needed. Such a theory does not currently exist.

We need a theory of literacy of and for Appalachians that acknowledges literacy's contradictory nature and makes real distinctions among the functions and values of literacy for groups, families, and individuals. While literacy scholars have theorized the influence of group identities and families on literacy, we also need theories that account for the individual and his or her agency. An individual person in an individual Appalachian family may make decisions about literacy that have as much to do with his or her relationship with members of his or her family as they do with the stigmatizing, non-Appalachian world. In other words, we make decisions about literacy in response to not only the non-Appalachian world around us, but also other Appalachians, including our own family members. I am the only woman in my family (i.e., my parents, siblings, and my siblings' spouses and children) with a college degree, and I am the only person with an advanced degree. While I am not the only reader in the family, I am the only one who identifies as a reader, a writer, and an Appalachian. I share an Appalachian and a family identity with all of them, yet I made very different literacy and identity decisions, to use Locklear's phrase.[22]

As literacy scholars, we tend to theorize people's literacy by looking not at individuality but at an individual's group identities and the influence of his or her family. Our theories of literacy lead us to assume that the acquisition of primary literacy is an uncomplicated process that does not require us to make difficult decisions. Gee writes that primary discourses "constitute our first social identity," that they "form our initial taken-for-granted understandings or who we are and who people 'like us' are," including how we value and use literacy.[23] Yet, for many Appalachians, what Gee identifies as primary discourse (which includes literacy) may be hugely contested and contradictory within itself and different within the same family because Appalachian identity is so contested. Appalachians' acquisition of our primary discourse/literacy is not the same as acquiring language because it is not something we simply absorb. It is a process that can be difficult and painful, owing to the conflicted and contradictory nature of literacy in Appalachia, and this conflict is rooted in double consciousness. As Appalachians, we are accustomed to understanding ourselves and our literacies through insiders' and outsiders' perspectives.

If we hope to develop a literacy theory of Appalachia, we must first acknowledge the long history of outside intervention there that has shaped our multiple and seemingly contradictory literacies. Scholars such as Brandt and Harvey Graff have written about how literacy accumulates across generations;[24] given that so many literacy sponsors have directly targeted (and continue to target) Appalachians, there is a tremendous accumulation of different ways to practice and value literacy circulating in Appalachian communities' histories as well as individual families' histories. This is also why it is important for us to develop literacy theories that are specific to Appalachia. *Appalachian* is not a synonym for *rural,* and scholarship on rural literacies will not necessarily help us, due to the specific history of Appalachia that I have identified here as well as other factors: the long history of literacy interventions, the role of the extractive industrial economy, the Great Migration out of the region, and the understanding of Appalachia as an "internal colony" as well as the critiques that have been made of this model.[25]

Thus, Appalachia needs a literacy theory that is grounded in the region and sensitive to its long history of exploitation and marginalization without positioning Appalachians as passive victims or ignorant rubes. We need a theory that recognizes the value of Appalachians' culture, literacy beliefs, and practices without fetishizing them and that acknowledges Ellen Cushman's argument that it is elitist and wrong to dismiss the efforts of marginalized populations to add to their literacy practices as "naïve" participation in their own disempowerment.[26] Unfortunately, this is what Victoria Purcell-Gates does in *Other People's Words,* arguably one of the most well-known works of literacy scholarship on Appalachians. Purcell-Gates fetishizes aspects of her subject Jenny's Appalachian culture, discussing at length the "characteristic traits and customs" that she claims distinguish Urban Appalachians from their fellow city dwellers: a close family network, a love for the land, an emphasis on self-sufficiency and independence, and a "refreshing" habit of straight talking.[27] At the same time that Purcell-Gates uses Jenny's Urban Appalachianness to exoticize her as a strange bird in the urban landscape, she also reacts dismissively to Jenny's desire for phonics-based reading instruction and concern about her Appalachian accent, which was highly stigmatized in her city. Ultimately, Purcell-Gates positions Jenny as a naïve participant in her own disempowerment, to use Cushman's phrase, while ignoring the very real reasons why Jenny may have these concerns.

Purcell-Gates's discussion of Jenny and her son Donny illustrates why current literacy theories are insufficient for understanding Appalachians. Purcell-Gates relies on emergent literacy theory to understand Jenny and Donny's literacy lives; according to her, emergent literacy theory is built on the understanding that "literate abilities and stances emerge developmentally as children observe and engage in experiences mediated by print in their daily lives." She later shares her research questions, which are based on the notion that "the process of becoming literate is mediated by cultural identity."[28] I certainly would not dispute the idea that literacy is mediated by cultural identity, but this conceptualization does not go far enough. Literacy is mediated by many factors, including cultural identity, and cultural identity is not uniform or stable.

I cannot help but wonder how Purcell-Gates would have reacted had she walked into my childhood home—which I strongly suspect was in the same city as Jenny and Donny's residence. What if she had studied my family, with our conflicted feelings about our Appalachian identities, our contradictory beliefs about literacy, and our literacy practices that blended home, school, and church contexts? What would she have made of my mother, who incessantly harped on the value of reading and education yet at other times would say in a mocking voice, "All you ever do is read, read, read"? What would she have made of me when I returned home from college one Christmas and expressed relief to my family that I did not "sound like a stupid hick anymore," then later cried in my room out of shame for what I had said? My family illustrates how many layers of cultural identification and literacy can accumulate among Appalachians, and current theories of literacy are inadequate to describe and analyze them.

Instead, we need a theory that takes into account the multiple, seemingly self-contradictory notions about practicing and valuing literacy that circulate within a particular culture. Yes, literacy is violent, to use J. Elspeth Stuckey's term, but it is highly contested, composed of opposing forces, and fraught with conflict. On the one hand, its power is limited. Contrary to popular views of literacy that position it as one of the necessary tools in achieving the American Dream of upward mobility, scholars such as Stuckey write that literacy "could not be found to produce much of anything useful" and that it is "exploitation."[29] Gee writes that while the quickly changing technological aspects of our society are often used as an argument for the importance of literacy, "increased technology often leads to deskilling people," the impact of which has often been felt quite harshly in Central Appalachia, where some of my family still live and where I have done fieldwork.[30] The closure of many factories, lumber mills, and steel mills in the region bears witness to the conclusion that, far from being a guaranteed ticket to a better life, literacy has become increasingly irrelevant.

Yet these same scholars, as well as many others, position literacy in ways that demonstrate its immense social power. In *Selling Tradition*, Jane Becker discusses the history of literacy workers and social reformers who came to Appalachia at the turn of the twentieth century with a contradictory mission to both venerate Appalachians' "pure" Anglo-Saxon culture and redeem that culture of its "primitive" ways. Literacy instruction was one strategy for Appalachians' assimilation, as the founding of settlement schools gave these workers the opportunity to instruct children in basic encoding and decoding while engaging in what Becker calls *cultural education,* which "entailed selective nurturing and, when necessary, the reintroduction of particular archaic customs."[31] Similarly, Krista Bryson, writing about Cora Wilson Stewart, a native Kentuckian and Appalachian who founded the Kentucky moonlight schools and developed several readers used by literacy workers in the region, notes that Stewart's work in literacy education "contribute[d] to an intertwining of myths about literacy and Appalachians": "More specifically, these publications offer conflicting national narratives about poverty, literacy, and social reform that simultaneously offer both romanticizing and demonizing/pathologizing portrayals of Appalachians."[32]

This is the central contradiction of literacy: its power is simultaneously immense and limited. Yes, literacy is violent in the ways in which it limits the opportunities of those who, like many Appalachians, are outside the culture of power. It has been—and still is—used to dominate and oppress many Appalachians, to romanticize and pathologize our culture, and to ensure the maintenance of a particular social order. It has, in fact, a tremendous amount of power—for good and for ill. Contrary to the lessons we are often taught in school, it is not the solution to all social problems; literacy attainment does not guarantee the achievement of a better life, and literacy is used to deny rights and opportunities. While we must acknowledge how literacy has been deployed in Appalachia as a means of cultural eradication, degradation, and marginalization, we must also identify how Appalachians can use "this piece of weaponry," as Stuckey refers to literacy, to resist these forces.[33]

For some Appalachians—and especially some Appalachian women—literacy can serve as a double-edged sword, one that both inflicts and prevents harm. Locklear notes that for the fictional Appalachian women she has studied, "the new literacies they gain also often introduce or exacerbate already present familial conflicts in their lives."[34] Although Locklear refers to fictional characters here, tensions surrounding literacy and gender roles are often apparent in real-life Appalachia as well. Puckett contends that while some Appalachians conceive of literacy as a "natural" feminine domain, the ways in which Appalachian women can use their literacies are still tightly monitored and controlled: "Ash Creek women walk a literate tightrope, called upon to assert an identity that affirms 'good' reading and writing skills but constrained by cultural norms and social practices in the directions and forms their writing can successfully assume."[35] Typically, "good" reading and writing skills are those that assist women in taking care of home, family, and relationships. Reading and writing recipes, reading bills and other documents to a less-literate husband, and filling out invitations to a baby shower are among the examples Puckett gives of these women's sanctioned literacy practices.

Puckett does not discuss in much detail what types of literacies would be unacceptable for Appalachian women, but other scholarship indicates that literacy becomes contentious when it disrupts adherence to conventional gender roles. Locklear argues that "domesticity and the acquisition of new literacies can function in opposition to one another, particularly when the pursuit of new literacies impedes the performance of duties deemed appropriate by social gender standards,"[36] and my research in Appalachian college writing classrooms provides evidence of her claims. One student's drug-addicted husband blamed her education for his addiction: "He says it's my fault for going back to school. Because as the man, he should be the one to provide for the family, not me." Another female student stated: "[My partner] thinks it's my job to do all the stuff around the house, the cooking, the cleaning. . . . She gets so mad when things aren't clean the way they should be and says that if I wasn't so busy with school I would take better care of the house."[37] Similarly, in *Whistlin' and Crowin' Women of Appalachia*, Katherine Kelleher Sohn introduces readers to women whose husbands resent their development of academic literacies. Lucy must keep her textbooks in her car because her abusive husband forbids her to do homework or study at home, and Sarah says that her husband "felt he should be the breadwinner and felt that [her] being in college was a threat to his manhood in providing for his family."[38]

For these Appalachian women, the attainment of academic literacies was fraught with multiple meanings; social forces such as a depressed economy and traditional gender roles limited opportunities to use their newly developed literacies in the workplace. Yet the women in Sohn's study still strongly felt that their college experience was worth it. Mary, one of Sohn's participants, stated: "I wouldn't be the person I am now [without the literacies gained in college]. I wouldn't trade that growth or the knowledge I've gained. Yeah, I'm glad I did that. I'm glad I did that."[39] The literacy practices and beliefs that these women gained in college were worthwhile and meaningful in their lives. My research with Appalachian college students confirms Sohn's findings; the women quoted above, as well as other women in the study, agreed that, if they had it to do all over again, they would still enroll in college.

My own life and the lives of the contributors to this collection offer further evidence of literacy's import. When I think of my life today in comparison to the lives of many of my relatives—especially those of my mother and grandmother—it would be completely disingenuous for me to claim, as Stuckey does, that literacy did not "produce much of anything useful" in my life.[40] Similarly, Greg Griffey proclaims that "reading and writing saved" him, and Todd Snyder concludes that his college education "absolutely transformed [his] life."[41] In spite of the dangerous power of literacy to establish and enforce oppressive social norms, it can also wield a tremendous ability to improve the lives of individuals. Literacy *does* matter, particularly on the individual level where the benefits may be felt most strongly—but it may not matter as much as we think it does.

Notes

1. James Moffett, *Storm in the Mountains: A Case Study of Censorship, Conflict, and Consciousness* (Carbondale: Southern Illinois University Press, 1988).

2. Kim Donehower, "James Moffett's Mistake: Ignoring the Rational Capacities of the Other," *Changing English: Studies in Culture and Education* 20, no. 3 (2013): 266–76.

3. James Moffett, *Teaching the Universe of Discourse* (Boston: Houghton Mifflin, 1968).

4. Deborah Brandt, *Literacy in American Lives* (New York: Cambridge University Press, 2001), 101.

5. Linda Brodkey, "Writing on the Bias," *College English* 56, no. 5 (1994): 527–47; Keith Gilyard, *Voices of the Self: A Study of Language Competence* (Detroit: Wayne State University Press, 1991); Victor Villanueva, *Bootstraps: From an American Academic of Color* (Urbana: National Council of Teachers of English, 1993).

6. Mike Rose, *Lives on the Boundary: A Moving Account of the Struggles and Achievements of America's Underclass* (New York: Penguin, 1990); Vershawn Ashanti Young, "Your Average Nigga," *College Composition and Communication* 55, no. 4 (2004): 693–715; Ellen Cushman, *The Struggle and the Tools: Oral and Literate Strategies in an Inner City Community* (Albany: State University of New York Press, 1998); Morris Young, *Minor Re/Visions: Asian American Literacy Narratives as a Rhetoric of Citizenship* (Carbondale: Southern Illinois University Press, 2004).

7. Sylvia Scribner, "Literacy in Three Metaphors," *American Journal of Education* 93, no. 1 (1984): 6–21, 13–15.

8. Loyal Jones, *Appalachian Values* (Ashland, KY: Jesse Stuart Foundation, 1994), 39.

9. Anita Puckett, "'Let the Girls Do the Spelling and Dan Will Do the Shooting': Literacy, the Division of Labor, and Identity in a Rural Appalachian Community," *Anthropological Quarterly* 65, no. 3 (1992): 137–47, 139, 141.

10. Griffey, chapter 5 in this volume, 106.

11. Brandt, *Literacy in American Lives,* 148 (and see chap. 5 generally).

12. Kim Donehower, "Reconsidering Power, Privilege, and the Public/Private Distinction in the Literacy of Rural Women," in *Women and Literacy: Local and Global Inquiries for a New Century,* ed. Beth Daniell and Peter Mortensen (New York: Routledge, 2012), 91–108.

13. Sara Webb-Sunderhaus, "Living with Literacy's Contradictions: Appalachian Students in a First-Year Writing Course," in *Reclaiming the Rural: Essays on Literacy, Rhetoric, and Pedagogy,* ed. Kim Donehower, Charlotte Hogg, and Eileen E. Schell (Carbondale: Southern Illinois University Press, 2011), 207–21, 207, 214.

14. James Gee, *Social Linguistics and Literacies: Ideologies in Discourses,* 2nd ed. (London: Routledge Falmer, 1996), 137, 127, 41, ix.

15. W. E. B. DuBois, *The Souls of Black Folk* (1903; reprint, Mineola, NY: Dover, 1994).

16. Erica Abrams Locklear, *Negotiating a Perilous Empowerment: Appalachian Women's Literacies* (Athens: Ohio University Press, 2011), 51, 75.

17. DuBois, *The Souls of Black Folk,* 2.

18. Charles Taylor, *The Ethics of Authenticity* (Cambridge, MA: Harvard University Press, 1992), 46, 49–50.

19. See Trauth Taylor, chapter 6 in this volume.

20. DuBois, *The Souls of Black Folk,* 2.

21. Walter Ong, *Orality and Literacy: The Technologizing of the Word,* 3rd ed. (New York: Routledge, 2012); Jack Goody and Ian Watt, "The Consequences of Literacy," *Comparative Studies in Society and History* 5, no. 3 (1963): 304–45.

22. Locklear, *Negotiating a Perilous Empowerment,* 51.

23. Gee, *Social Linguistics and Literacies,* 137.

24. Brandt, *Literacy in American Lives;* Harvey Graff, *The Literacy Myth: Literacy and Social Structure in the Nineteenth-Century City* (New York: Academic, 1979).

25. For an understanding of internal colonialism as applied to Appalachia, see Henry Shapiro, *Appalachia on Our Mind: The Southern Mountains and Mountaineers in the American Consciousness, 1870–1920* (Chapel Hill: University of North Carolina Press, 1986); and Helen Matthews Lewis, ed., *Colonialism in Modern America: The Appalachian Case* (Boone, NC: Appalachian Consortium, 1978). For critiques of this model, see Dwight Billings and Kathleen Blee, *The Road to Poverty: The Making of Wealth and*

Hardship in Appalachia (New York: Cambridge University Press, 2000); and Herbert Reid, "Appalachia and the 'Sacrament of Co-Existence': Beyond Post-Colonial Trauma and Regional Identity Traps," *Journal of Appalachian Studies* 11, nos. 1–2 (2005): 164–81.

26. Ellen Cushman, *The Struggle and the Tools: Oral and Literate Strategies in an Inner City Community* (Albany: State University of New York Press, 1998).

27. Victoria Purcell-Gates, *Other People's Words: The Cycle of Low Literacy* (Cambridge, MA: Harvard University Press, 1995), 28.

28. Ibid., 7, 204.

29. J. Elspeth Stuckey, *The Violence of Literacy* (Portsmouth, NJ: Boynton/Cook, 1991), 27, 37.

30. Gee, *Social Linguistics and Literacies*, 24.

31. Jane Becker, *Selling Tradition: Appalachia and the Construction of an American Folk* (Chapel Hill: University of North Carolina Press, 1998), 58.

32. Bryson, chapter 2 in this volume, 34.

33. Stuckey, *The Violence of Literacy*, 54.

34. Locklear, *Negotiating a Perilous Empowerment*, 31.

35. Puckett, "'Let the Girls Do the Spelling,'" 143.

36. Locklear, *Negotiating a Perilous Empowerment*, 20.

37. Sara Webb-Sunderhaus, "A Family Affair: Competing Sponsors of Literacy in Appalachian Students' Lives," in *The Norton Book of Composition Studies*, ed. Susan Miller (New York: Norton, 2009), 1600–1616, 1612, 1614.

38. Katherine Kelleher Sohn, *Whistlin' and Crowin' Women of Appalachia: Literacy Practices since College* (Carbondale: Southern Illinois University Press, 2006), 131.

39. Ibid., 37.

40. Stuckey, *The Violence of Literacy*, 54.

41. Griffey, chapter 5 in this volume; Snyder, chapter 4 in this volume, 97.

Afterword

Peter Mortensen

In the spring of 1989, I was a lecturer at the University of California, San Diego (UCSD), where I had defended my doctoral dissertation the previous quarter. By late March, I knew that I was headed to the University of Kentucky (UK) for my first faculty job. I was able to spend about thirty-six hours in Lexington during my formal campus visit and had liked it well enough to accept UK's offer without hesitation.

Prior to accepting the UK position, I had visited Kentucky only once before. In the mid-1980s, a friend and I spent a summer week driving from Washington, DC, to Los Angeles. First day out we followed the interstates west through Maryland and into West Virginia, routing west from Charleston into eastern Kentucky on Interstate 64. We hit Morehead just after dark and had dinner at a Kentucky Fried Chicken not far off the highway. Eating KFC *in* Kentucky! How finger-lickin' clever was that? Then we drove on to Lexington, pitching a tent for a short night in the public campground adjacent to the Kentucky Horse Park. At daybreak we headed west again on I-64. We crossed a high bridge over the Kentucky River at Frankfort, then cut across miles of farmland dotted with dark barns next to tobacco plots. Ninety minutes later we approached the steel bridge across the broad Ohio River at Louisville, where old hotel and office buildings sat hard on the waterfront. Moments later we were in Indiana, having logged two meals, one night, and no more than twelve hours in the Commonwealth. All of this is to say that, in the spring of 1989, I didn't know much about Kentucky, having accumulated all of about forty-eight hours on the ground there and very little in the way of a coherent narrative descriptive of the experience.

Narrative abhors a vacuum. Recognizing this, several people I knew at UCSD began sharing stories about Kentucky. These were the stories that I would carry with me on my journey from La Jolla to Lexington and that would help me settle in a place of interleaved and overlapping identities I am to this day still trying to understand.

Phyllis Campbell was the first to take an interest in my move. She was the office manager in one of UCSD's residential college writing programs. A native of Wayland, in Floyd County, she talked about how higher education was transforming the eastern part of the state. Her brother, Henry, was president of Prestonsburg Community College, not a half hour north of her birthplace. Floyd County was turning a corner, she told me. Times had been hard, but the state was investing in the college, and the college was changing lives—getting people ready for an economy that didn't depend so much on coal mining. She was proud and optimistic.[1]

Not so Moe, who I had gotten to know during the year I was writing my dissertation late at night in a quiet office on campus. A member of the custodial staff, Moe would stop by the office some evenings, and we would talk about the day's events, university politics, and other matters of substance. Once he learned that I was moving to Lexington, he opened up about his family. If memory serves, around the time of the Korean War Moe had been posted at one or another of the military installations in San Diego. Later, the prospect of good work and even better weather prompted him to move with his wife and young son from their native eastern Kentucky to a suburban neighborhood east of downtown. The move had been hard and still was, Moe said. Maybe custodial work wasn't what he had come out west for, but he had few complaints about the hours and pay, and he took pride in working at the university. What worried him most was his son's plan to return to eastern Kentucky. Coal mining there had mostly played out, and big talk about education sparking an economic revival struck Moe as positively "romantic"—his word for the emotion. Much as he might like, he could never see himself returning to "Appalachia"—his word for the place.[2]

Phyllis and Moe introduced me to what would become *my* Kentucky by way of *their* Kentucky. They had little to say about Lexington, except that it was a nice place to visit, what with the scenic horse farms and all. That is to say that they left it to me to discover on my own how their Kentucky had been robbed of wealth by what ended up being my Kentucky. More important, they seeded a bedeviling question: Is there any hope that education, that literacy, can set right the wrongs compounded over more than a century's worth of economic exploitation? The question troubled me because the more I learned about eastern Kentucky—and West Virginia, southwestern Virginia, western Carolina, and east Tennessee—the less I felt able to answer it. Today I recognize how much the question itself advances unwarranted assumptions about how illiteracy is thought to cause the social and economic ills that, at least by metropolitan standards, diminish quality of life in Central and Southern Appalachia. Better to ask who defines illiteracy, why, and what happens when that definition is applied to a place or a population, regardless of the application's motive. Better to ask what a good life is and then look to see how literacy informs that goodness.

Fall 1989, and a thousand miles from home, I felt welcomed in Lexington. Many new colleagues visited my office, stayed a while, and told me about themselves and their work. One asked me to visit him in his office. I obliged, and I spent a pleasant hour chatting with Gurney Norman. At first we talked about the academic year he had spent in my native California as a Stegner Fellow at Stanford University, some three decades past.[3] But this turned out to be merely a pretext for Gurney's inquiries about my life. Who were my people? How did they get to California? When? Why? What did they do? The line of questioning was fairly intimate but somehow not at all intrusive. When we parted, Gurney gave me a copy of *Kinfolks* (1977), his beautiful book of interconnected short stories, published locally by the Gnomon Press.[4] I was grateful for the gift but pressed for time, so I shelved *Kinfolks* for reading over winter break.

Thursday night before the break, I watched *48 Hours,* a newsmagazine that aired in prime time on the CBS television network. The program's title was "Another America," its theme was rural poverty, and its location was Floyd County, Kentucky. The show touched a nerve. The *Lexington Herald-Leader* ran an article about the county having been cast in an "unflattering light."[5] The next time I saw Gurney, he was at once direct and circumspect. Yes, the program was slanderous. But it was hardly the first time the television news had extracted raw Appalachian stereotypes and forged them into spectacular form. Nor, in his opinion, would it be the last. Shame of it was there were other—and better—stories to tell if only people cared to listen. I took the hint and read *Kinfolks* the next week on a flight to see my parents in Los Angeles.

Gurney Norman believed that good narrative displaces bad, given the opportunity. Over the decade we were colleagues at Kentucky, I watched this belief evolve: rather than waiting to *take* opportunities, one should strive to *make* them. I inferred this new attitude from Gurney's response to the announcement in April 1992 that Robert Schenkkan's *The Kentucky Cycle* had won the year's Pulitzer Prize for drama. His criticism was swift, pointed, and in short order amplified in the pages of the *New Yorker* by means of an interview conducted by his fellow Kentuckian Bobbie Ann Mason. Gurney's criticism launched a book project that culminated at decade's end in *Confronting Appalachian Stereotypes,* edited by Gurney, along with Dwight Billings, a sociology professor, and Katherine Ledford, then a doctoral student in American literature. More than a few of the book's twenty-three chapters make mention of Schenkkan's play, which Finlay Donesky reminds us grew out of Schenkkan's ten-hour trip to Hazard and its environs, where he accompanied a local physician on house calls.[6]

Rereading *Confronting Appalachian Stereotypes* some fifteen years after its publication, I appreciate all the more its studied response to the ongoing crisis of representation made spectacularly evident by the critical success of *The Kentucky Cycle.* Some chapters take up the play itself. Others examine the tradition of narrative exploitation out of which the play grew. And still others celebrate literatures native to the place, words of self-definition, self-determination, and self-defense that deserve a broad hearing. What is more, readers drawn to the book would find in its chapters points of departure leading back to "books by a good hundred other writers that any person seeking to understand the Appalachian region must read," as Gurney put it in his capstone chapter.[7] Also to be found in *Confronting Appalachian Stereotypes* are lines of inquiry that scholars in multiple disciplines would choose to develop in years to come. The book's influence courses through the contemporary literature of Appalachian studies and into scholarly literature beyond, including works that are specifically interested in literacy and its representations: Douglas Reichert Powell's *Critical Regionalism,* Katrina Powell's *The Anguish of Displacement,* and Erica Locklear's *Negotiating a Perilous Empowerment* among them.[8] These excellent books notwithstanding, we have lacked a generous and generative accounting of directions future research on literacy in the region might take.

This brings me at last to my reading of *Rereading Appalachia.* If it can be said that *Confronting Appalachian Stereotypes* was provoked in part by *The Kentucky Cycle,* then the provocation that sets *Rereading Appalachia* in motion has to be James Moffett's *Storm in the Mountains.*[9] In bookend chapters, the coeditors, Kim Donehower and Sara Webb-Sunderhaus, prompt us to look again at how Moffett characterized the citizens of West Virginia's Kanawha County, who in the 1970s fought vigorously against their school district's adoption of texts and other instructional resources that Moffett had helped create. We don't hear much about Moffett these days, but it's fair to say that his *Teaching the Universe of Discourse* was among the foundational texts that energized the growth of composition studies in the 1970s.[10] Little surprise, then, that *Storm in the Mountains* was generally well received when it debuted, although there is telling hesitation in George Hillocks's review of the book. Hillocks suggests that Moffett's argument is weakened by, among other things, "his failure to interview Alice Moore and other better-educated protesters," leading him "to ignore, perhaps unintentionally, the religious and philosophical assumptions underlying the protest."[11] Donehower and Webb-Sunderhaus make mention of Moffett's ignorance as well, and they even share something of Hillocks's perspective on the roots of the protest. Yet, unlike Hillocks, for Donehower and Webb-Sunderhaus there is nothing necessarily consequential about the protesters' literacy, "high" or "low." The protesters' purported zeal for censorship is better understood, they conclude, as an assertion of agency in a struggle over who gets to define the form and content of literacy. For more than a century, metropolitans—novelists, researchers, philanthropists—had defined the Appalachian Mountains as a region bereft of letters. Donehower and Webb-Sunderhaus appreciate that the protesters sought to set things straight, on their own terms and in their own words.

So do the contributors to *Rereading Appalachia*. And, in so doing, they have created a book that speaks in the spirit of *Confronting Appalachian Stereotypes*, a book that sets an agenda for a generation of scholarship yet to come. *Rereading Appalachia* is unsparing in its criticism of metropolitans who have held up illiteracy, whatever that might be, as a defining feature of the Appalachian region's inhabitants. At the same time, it looks inward at literacy narratives of regional origin, asking whether they, too, might perpetuate stereotypes that distort how literacy functions in the naming and claiming of Appalachian identities. I use the plural, *identities*, because the book resolutely rejects the imagined homogeneity that is often conjured in metropolitan accounts of the region's culture, politics, economics, and just about any other categorical lens through which people and places can be viewed.

How, then, might we expect to see the intellectual achievement that is *Rereading Appalachia* translated into continued intellectual work in the field of writing studies? Let me suggest some possibilities by pointing to connections with what I take to be related lines of inquiry:

- Krista Bryson's chapter on Cora Wilson Stewart may rankle some readers who object to her questioning of Stewart's progressive legacy. I appreciate Bryson's questions and the criticisms they imply; the questions are pointed, yes, but respectful of context. And I can say from my own foray into Stewart's papers that there is still more worth saying about her participation in national conversations about illiteracy in the 1920s and 1930s. Nevertheless, Stewart's legacy is strong. It continues to survive deep inspection, and she is not about to be erased from the historical record. In this regard, it would be interesting to imagine the trajectory of her reputation alongside figures in writing studies—Mina Shaughnessy comes first to mind—whose pioneering contributions have been reevaluated as writing studies scholarship has matured.[12] The tendency is to discover, as Bryson has, that, in received histories of literacy, the accomplishments of certain individuals, relative to the collectives or networks in which they acted, can be overstated for the sake of narrative convenience.
- Emma M. Howes's chapter on archival practices and cultural memory deepens our understanding of how affective attachments to the past simultaneously enable the preservation of cultural artifacts and limit access to them in consequential ways. Her experience resonates with stories others in writing studies are telling about their time in archives. See, for example, the narratives collected in Alexis Ramsey, Wendy Sharer, Barbara L'Eplattenier, and Lisa Mastrangelo's edited collection *Working in the Archives*.[13] But we should look further. See, too, how colleagues in history narrate their archival encounters, as in Antoinette Burton's edited collection *Archive Stories*.[14] And, considering where Howes situates her research, her work calls to mind W. Fitzhugh Brundage's *The Southern Past*, wherein we learn much about the politics of managing cultural documents that reveal the conditions of labor (and prerogatives of capital) during the industrialization of the American South.[15]
- Over time, the impact of extractive industries on counties in Appalachia has been felt differentially across the region, and the force of these industries' impact can be measured in various ways. Todd Snyder's approach is to link the employment expectations in one industry, coal mining, with the narrowing of literacy education

to a vocational minimum. Snyder's chapter illustrates the value of learning more about the literacy curricula and pedagogies associated with various industries' presence in the southern mountains. Are these curricula and pedagogies wholly captive to nearby industrial operations? If so, what more do we need to know about how school literacy and workplace literacy articulate? We are used to asking this question when the workplace is a factory or an office. We should ask it, too, when the work entails producing the raw inputs that make factories and offices possible in the first place.[16]

- Gregory Griffey's treatment of sexuality and evangelical Christianity reminds us of the intersectional nature of Appalachian identity. The performance of sexual identity in Appalachia is explored in fictional works by Dorothy Allison and Jeff Mann, among other writers, but Griffey's focus is on a kind of everyday "sexual literacy" not explicitly investigated by either writer.[17] At the same time, Griffey's narrative demystifies the religious dimensions of his young adulthood in Central Appalachia in a manner consistent with the varieties of religious experience treated recently in Elizabeth Vander Lei, Thomas Amorose, Beth Daniell, and Anne Ruggles Gere's *Renovating Rhetoric in Christian Tradition.*[18]

- Histories of Southern Appalachia have been written and rewritten and written again in service of white privilege. Against this backdrop, Kathryn Trauth Taylor describes the emergence of Affrilachian identity, which has significance in both urban and rural settings associated with the mountain South. The ethnic compounding of Appalachianness proposed by Frank X Walker and others is a reminder of how literacy learning and literacy practices are intertwined with the racialized and ethnic diversity that has long been present in the region. Ellen Cushman's *The Cherokee Syllabary* is the best current exemplar of why students of Appalachia like Taylor should keep probing the meanings of *race* in a space long imagined to be homogeneously white.[19]

- Nathan Shepley's historical study adds to a growing literature on public higher education in the Appalachian region that includes Douglas Reichert Powell's chapter on Scholar Holler in *Critical Regionalism.*[20] The diverse political motives behind the founding of what have become Morehead State University (in Cora Wilson

Stewart's Rowan County, Kentucky), Eastern Kentucky University, East Tennessee State University, Appalachian State University, Western Carolina University, and other public universities deserve to be scrutinized using the critical stance on literacy that Shepley models so well.[21] Have these public institutions laid a literate foundation enabling of self-determination and local governance? Or have they served as a conduit for the assimilation of local differences into a more easily governed cultural mainstream? Both? Neither?

• Joshua Iddings and Ryan Angus's intriguing functional linguistics approach to literacy in Appalachia recalls how controversial it can be to offer critical commentary on pedagogy that engages ways with words that are perceived to be Appalachian and therefore unsuited for utterance or inscription in metropolitan spaces beyond the mountains. Debra Hawhee felt this backlash when "Composition History and the *Harbrace College Handbook*" appeared in a fiftieth anniversary issue of *College Composition and Communication*. She dared to suggest that the *Harbrace* might have been designed in part to normalize writing that bore the traces of Appalachian contours of speech. The *Harbrace* is a venerable institution, its defenders said, created only to do good. What Hawhee discerned as the handbook's culturally troubled origins was largely dismissed. Given Hawhee's experience, I am interested to see how Iddings and Angus's argument will be received.[22]

In their framing chapters, Donehower and Webb-Sunderhaus are critical of not only James Moffett's *Storm in the Mountains* but also Victoria Purcell-Gates's *Other People's Words,* a study that follows an "urban Appalachian" family as its members navigate daily life in a "print-rich" midwestern city.[23] Purcell-Gates concealed her informants' identities, appropriately per protocol for the sort of ethnographic inquiry she had conducted. Yet the concerns raised by Donehower and Webb-Sunderhaus make me wish that I could hear more from "Jenny" and her son. What are their lives like now, some twenty years or more after Purcell-Gates studied them? A precedent for revisiting ethnographic informants in studies of community literacy was set by Shirley Brice Heath in *Words at Work and Play*, which appeared recently three decades after publication of her landmark *Ways with Words*.[24] It is a good precedent, indeed. No community—no region—exists out of time, and it is especially important to say so about the Appalachian region, often painted from a metropolitan perspective as perfectly changeless. Every page of *Rereading Appalachia* refutes this mistaken idea.

I read the manuscript pages of *Rereading Appalachia* in late July 2014 while visiting family in southern California, some two thousand miles and, for me, fifteen years distant from Lexington. Or maybe not quite so far and long. For just twenty miles north of my childhood home sits the Santa Clarita Studios, where elements of Lexington and the mountains east of it have been re-created on the set of *Justified,* the FX Network drama featuring Timothy Olyphant as a US marshal estranged from, and then returned to, his native eastern Kentucky.[25] Drive north from Santa Clarita another ninety minutes, and you arrive in Bakersfield, gateway to California's San Joaquin Valley, which *The Economist* magazine recently called the "Appalachia of the West," borrowing the comparison from a 2005 Congressional Research Service report by Tadlock Cowan on California's economically troubled breadbasket.[26]

Soon after my return to Urbana, I picked up Rick Perlstein's just-published *The Invisible Bridge,* a book, as Perlstein describes it, "about how Ronald Reagan came within a hairs-breadth of becoming the 1976 Republican nominee for president."[27] I had been drawn to the book after hearing Perlstein interviewed by Dave Davies on NPR's *Fresh Air.* Illustrating a point about the period's emergent grassroots conservatism, Perlstein referenced the "pretty familiar" backlash against school busing in Boston, then turned to a story from 1974 that "a lot of people don't know," a story about textbook selection in Charleston, West Virginia, "and kind of the surrounding, rural areas—kind of the hollers." As Perlstein tells it in his book, James Moffett was simply "a rhetoric scholar from the Harvard School of Education" who had delivered what "members of the cosmopolitan professional classes" of Charleston wanted: the literacy education that would "get their children into schools like Harvard." Such local professionals were arrayed against people "in the hollers surrounding Charleston." Perlstein quotes approvingly from Paul Cowan's contemporaneous reporting in the *Village Voice,* wherein Cowan "read the conflict as, in part, a class war, between educated professionals eager to get their kids into the Ivy League, and plain folk who saw a traditional basic education as a route to upward mobility." Still, perhaps to add local color to his own account, Perlstein describes one of these plain folk, the Reverend Avis Hill, as a man "who ran a combined church, school, and mission out of an abandoned rural store and service station." The description seems anodyne, but it arguably trades on an old stereotype that even Perlstein seems eager to reject, a stereotype that implies that the country preacher's literacy is somehow inferior to that practiced within the city limits.[28] Others might not read Perlstein this way, but it's hard not to after reading *Rereading Appalachia*.

Truly, the idea of Appalachia—and literacy in Appalachia—is always and everywhere on our minds, to improvise on the historian Henry Shapiro's apt phrasing.[29] *Rereading Appalachia* cannot of course change the fact that the ubiquitous idea of Appalachia bears little resemblance to the place and people it is said to represent. No book—or shelf of a hundred books—could do that. But *Rereading Appalachia* will help. As much as its chapters enrich the scholarship of writing studies, so too do they enable us to look beyond that scholarship into a world where impoverished ideas about Appalachia always and everywhere collide with myths about literacy. I trust that readers of this book are now better able to avoid such collisions or at least find themselves equipped to repair damage should damage be done.

Notes

1. I consulted two sources to confirm what Phyllis Campbell shared with me years ago: a posting by her to the Rootsweb online community and a speech honoring her brother delivered by US senator Mitch McConnell. See Phyllis Campbell, "Re: The Pigman Family," Rootsweb, May 14, 1999, http://archiver.rootsweb.ancestry.com/th/read/KYFLOYD/1999-05/0926704511; and Hon. Mitch McConnell, "Honoring the Memory of a Wonderful Kentuckian, Dr. Henry A. Campbell, Jr.," *Congressional Record*, 103rd Cong., 2nd sess., March 9, 1994, http://www.gpo.gov/fdsys/pkg/CREC-1994-03-09/html/CREC-1994-03-09-pt1-PgS13.htm.

2. I know few particulars about Moe's move to San Diego. But it conforms to the pattern of Appalachian out-migration observed during and after World War II, although the destination was atypical. For overviews of Appalachian out-migration that are situated in broad historical narratives, see Ronald D Eller, *Uneven Ground: Appalachia since 1945* (Lexington: University Press of Kentucky, 2008), 20–28; and John Alexander Williams, *Appalachia: A History* (Chapel Hill: University of North Carolina Press, 2002), chap. 5.

3. To appreciate the company Norman kept while in Palo Alto, see "Complete List of Stegner Fellows," n.d., http://creativewriting.stanford.edu/stegner-fellowship-complete-list-of-stegner-fellows. I should add that the California we talked about was somewhat tamer than the state (and state of mind) Norman describes in his novel *Divine Right's Trip* (1972).

4. See also the director Andrew Garrison's film adaptation of three chapters from *Kinfolks, The Wilgus Stories* (2000), http://vimeo.com/24307259.

5. "Another America," *48 Hours*, CBS Television Network (WKYT Lexington, KY), December 14, 1989; Susan White, "CBS Puts Floyd County in Unflattering Light," *Lexington Herald-Leader,* December 14, 1989. See also William Keesler, "Show Gripes Governor; He Asks CBS-TV Chief to Visit," *Louisville Courier-Journal,* December 16, 1989; and Peter Mortensen, "Representations of Literacy and Region: Narrating 'Another America,'" in *Pedagogy in the Age of Politics: Writing and Reading,* ed. Patricia A. Sullivan and Donna Qualley (Urbana, IL: National Council of Teachers of English, 1994), 100–121.

6. Finlay Donesky, "America Needs Hillbillies: The Case of *The Kentucky Cycle,*" in *Confronting Appalachian Stereotypes: Back Talk from an American Region,* ed. Dwight B. Billings, Gurney Norman, and Katherine Ledford (Lexington: University Press of Kentucky, 1999), 288–93, 283. See also Robert Schenkkan, *The Kentucky Cycle* (New York: Plume, 1993); The Pulitzer Prizes, "1992 Winners and Finalists," n.d., http://www.pulitzer.org/awards/1992; Bobbie Ann Mason, "Recycling Kentucky," *New Yorker,* November 1, 1993.

7. Gurney Norman, "Notes on *The Kentucky Cycle,*" in ibid., 327–32, 330.

8. Douglas Reichert Powell, *Critical Regionalism: Connecting Politics and Culture in the American Landscape* (Chapel Hill: University of North Carolina Press, 2007); Katrina M. Powell, *The Anguish of Displacement: The Politics of Literacy in the Letters of Mountain Families in Shenandoah National Park* (Charlottesville: University of Virginia Press, 2007); Erica Abrams Locklear, *Negotiating a Perilous Empowerment: Appalachian Women's Literacies* (Athens: Ohio University Press, 2011).

9. James Moffett, *Storm in the Mountains: A Case Study of Censorship, Conflict, and Consciousness* (Carbondale: Southern Illinois University Press, 1988).

10. James Moffett, *Teaching the University of Discourse* (Boston: Houghton Mifflin, 1968). On the importance of *Teaching the University of Discourse,* see James A. Berlin, *Rhetoric and Reality: Writing Instruction in American Colleges, 1900–1985* (Carbondale: Southern Illinois University Press, 1987), 163–64; and Joseph Harris, *A Teaching Subject: Composition since 1966,* new ed. (Logan: Utah State University Press, 2012), 131.

11. George Hillocks Jr., review of *Storm in the Mountains,* by James Moffett, *American Journal of Education* 99 (1991): 267–70, 269.

12. The comparison I am drawing is well illustrated by reading Jane Maher's *Mina P. Shaughnessy: Her Life and Work* (Urbana, IL: National Council of Teachers of English, 1997) alongside Jeanne Gunner's "Iconic Discourse: The Troubling Legacy of Mina Shaughnessy," *Journal of Basic Writing* 17, no. 2 (1998): 25–42.

13. Alexis E. Ramsey, Wendy B. Sharer, Barbara L'Eplattenier, and Lisa S. Mastrangelo, eds., *Working in the Archives: Practical Research Methods for Rhetoric and Composition* (Carbondale: Southern Illinois University Press, 2010).

14. Antoinette Burton, ed., *Archive Stories: Facts, Fictions, and the Writing of History* (Durham, NC: Duke University Press, 2006).

15. W. Fitzhugh Brundage, *The Southern Past: A Clash of Race and Memory* (Cambridge: Belknap Press of Harvard University Press, 2005).

16. Following this line of thinking, it would be interesting to explore the evolution of the business and technical communication curriculum at the former GMI Engineering and Management Institute (now Kettering University) to discover what the curriculum suggested about managing automobile industry workers who had migrated to Detroit from Central and Southern Appalachia. A good starting point would be the late twentieth-century GMI curriculum detailed in Dorothy A. Winsor, *Writing Like an Engineer: A Rhetorical Education* (Mahwah, NJ: Erlbaum, 1996). Taking another tack, we would do well to understand the literacy lessons of teachers who are challenged to work in locales devastated first by the activities of extractive industries and then by their postindustrial withdrawal. Mike Rose writes eloquently of such teachers. See his *Possible Lives: The Promise of Public Education in America* (Boston: Houghton Mifflin, 1995), 236–83 ("Berea and Wheelwright, Kentucky").

17. Laura Miller, "The Salon Interview: Dorothy Allison," Salon.com, March 31, 1998, http://www.salon.com/1998/03/31/cov_si_31intb; Jeff Mann, "The Mountain Queer Ponders His Risk-List," *Appalachian Journal* 34, nos. 3–4 (2007): 443–47. On "sexual literacy," see Jonathan Alexander, *Literacy, Sexuality, Pedagogy: Theory and Practice for Composition Studies* (Logan: Utah State University Press, 2008). Also of interest are interviews in the University of Kentucky Libraries' Queer Appalachia Oral History Project, http://www.kentuckyoralhistory.org/collections/queer-appalachia-oral-history-project; and Mathias J. Detamore, "Queer Appalachia: Toward Geographies of Possibility" (Ph.D. diss., University of Kentucky, 2010).

18. Elizabeth Vander Lei, Thomas Amorose, Beth Daniell, and Anne Ruggles Gere, *Renovating Rhetoric in Christian Tradition* (Pittsburgh: University of Pittsburgh Press, 2014). But, for a discussion of the rhetorical strategies applied by fundamentalist Christians who aim to shatter the kind of multifaceted identity Griffey wishes to keep intact, see Sharon Crowley, *Toward a Civil Discourse: Rhetoric and Fundamentalism* (Pittsburgh: University of Pittsburgh Press, 2006).

19. Ellen Cushman, *The Cherokee Syllabary: Writing the People's Perseverance* (Norman: University of Oklahoma Press, 2013). See also Frank X Walker, *Affrilachia: Poems* (Lexington, KY: Old Cove Press, 2000).

20. Powell, *Critical Regionalism*, 187–225 ("Scholar Holler: Critical Regionalism and the University").

21. Relevant here is Gordon B. McKinney, introduction to "Issues in Higher Education in Appalachia," special conference issue, *Appalachian Heritage* 28, no. 2 (1999): 3–4. "Issues in Higher Education in Appalachia" collects papers from a 1998 symposium on the subject held at Berea College in Kentucky.

22. Debra Hawhee, "Composition History and the *Harbrace College Handbook*," *College Composition and Communication* 50, no. 3 (1999): 504–23. John Bell, Thomas V. Broadbent, and Winifred Horner responded to Hawhee, who in turn responded to

them. See John Bell, "Why Do We Use English Handbooks?" *College Composition and Communication* 51, no. 4 (2000): 648–51; Thomas V. Broadbent, "An Editor's Response," *College Composition and Communication* 51, no. 4 (2000): 643–48; Winifred B. Horner, "The *Harbrace Handbook:* Changing in a Changing Discipline," *College Composition and Communication* 51, no. 4 (2000): 651–54; and Debra Hawhee, "Regarding History," *College Composition and Communication* 51, no. 4 (2000): 654–62.

23. Victoria Purcell-Gates, *Other People's Words: The Cycle of Low Literacy* (Cambridge, MA: Harvard University Press, 1997). Donehower's and Webb-Sunderhaus's consideration of the rural-urban axis resonates with the call for more dialogue among writing studies scholars who separately examine literacies and rhetorics situated in the city and the country in Kim Donehower, Charlotte Hogg, and Eileen E. Schell, preface to *Reclaiming the Rural: Essays on Literacy, Rhetoric, and Pedagogy,* ed. Kim Donehower, Charlotte Hogg, and Eileen E. Schell (Carbondale: Southern Illinois University Press, 2012), xi–xvi. What might we learn, e.g., if we were to use Jeff Rice's *Digital Detroit: Rhetoric and Space in the Age of the Network* (Carbondale: Southern Illinois University Press, 2012) and Richard Marback's "Detroit and the Closed Fist: Toward a Theory of Material Rhetoric," *Rhetoric Review* 17, no. 1 (1988): 74–92, as points of departure for reexamining the legacy of Appalachian out-migration described ethnographically in John Hartigan Jr.'s *Racial Situations: Class Predicaments of Whiteness in Detroit* (Princeton, NJ: Princeton University Press, 1999)?

24. Shirley Brice Heath, *Ways with Words: Language, Life and Work in Communities and Classrooms* (Cambridge: Cambridge University Press, 1983), and *Words at Work and Play: Three Decades in Family and Community Life* (Cambridge: Cambridge University Press, 2012). One can even imagine that, under unusual circumstances, it would be possible for a researcher to interview Jenny about her experience with Purcell-Gates, just as Gerald Nelms interviewed Susan Gzesh, who was featured as "Lynn" in Janet Emig's *The Composing Processes of Twelfth Graders.* See Gerald Nelms, "Reassessing Janet Emig's *The Composing Processes of Twelfth Graders:* A Historical Perspective," *Rhetoric Review* 13, no. 1 (1994): 108–30; and Janet Emig, *The Composing Processes of Twelfth Graders* (Urbana, IL: National Council of Teachers of English, 1971).

25. For a discussion of why it makes economic sense to film *Justified* in southern California, see Richard Verrier, "Santa Clarita Enjoys Record Year for Film and TV Production," *Los Angeles Times,* July 12, 2013, http://articles.latimes.com/print/2013/jul/12/entertainment/la-et-ct-santa-clarita-film-20130712. The City of Santa Clarita's Film Incentive Program makes a difference, as does the State of California's Film and Television Tax Credit Program. It would be a leap to say that such programs lured filming of *Justified* away from eastern Kentucky, but it is nonetheless worth considering how such incentives shape representations of Appalachia that are produced as mass entertainment. See generally City of Santa Clarita, California, "Film Incentive Program," http://filmsantaclarita.com/for-filmmakers/film-incentive-program; and State of California, "Film and Television Tax Credit Program," http://www.film.ca.gov/Incentives.htm.

26. "The Appalachia of the West: California's Agricultural Heartland Threatens to Become a Wasteland," *The Economist,* January 21, 2010, http://www.economist.com/node/15331478; Tadlock Cowan, *California's San Joaquin Valley: A Region in Transition* (Washington, DC: Congressional Research Service, Library of Congress, 2005), http://fpc.state.gov/documents/organization/59030.pdf.

27. Rick Perlstein, *The Invisible Bridge: The Fall of Nixon and the Rise of Reagan* (New York: Simon & Schuster, 2014), xii.

28. Ibid., 295–96, 299. To his credit, Perlstein avoids much of the condescension evident in Moffett's *Storm in the Mountains.* Perhaps this is so because he sources nothing from Moffett's book, drawing instead on Carol Mason's *Reading Appalachia Left to Right: Conservatives and the 1974 Kanawha County Textbook Controversy* (Ithaca, NY: Cornell University Press, 2009); George Hillocks Jr., "Books and Bombs: Ideological Conflict and the Schools—a Case Study of the Kanawha County Book Protest," *School Review* 86, no. 4 (1978): 632–54, and Trey Kay, Deborah George, and Stan Bumgardner, producers, "The Great Textbook War," *American Radio Works,* http://americanradioworks.publicradio.org/features/textbooks, a radio documentary produced with advice from Mason and sponsorship from the Kanawha Valley Historical and Preservation Society. It is interesting to note that the documentary's lead producer, the Charleston native Trey Kay, was twelve years old and entering the seventh grade at the time of the conflict. See also "How Ronald Reagan Used an 'Invisible Bridge' to Win over Americans," *Fresh Air,* August 5, 2014, http://www.npr.org/templates/transcript/transcript.php?storyId=337917291.

29. Henry D. Shapiro, *Appalachia on Our Minds: The Southern Mountains and Mountaineers in the American Consciousness, 1870–1920* (Chapel Hill: University of North Carolina Press, 1978).

Acknowledgments

We thank Peter Mortensen for his pioneering work bringing composition and Appalachian studies together and for his long-term friendship and support. Beth Daniell has been a scholarly role model for both of us, showing us how to blend critical resistance with personal integrity. We thank the members of the Conference of College Composition and Communication's special interest group on Appalachia for their enthusiasm and fellowship. The contributors to this volume have been wonderful partners in this enterprise, and we appreciate their dedication and willingness to explore their complicated relationships to Appalachia. Ashley Runyon at the University Press of Kentucky has been an efficient and gracious partner in the publishing process. Last, we thank each other for a scholarly and personal bond that has helped us navigate the perils of Appalachian identity, academic careers, family, and motherhood.

I, Sara, had admired Kim's work for many years before having the opportunity to work with her on *Reclaiming the Rural.* I am grateful and honored to now call Kim my collaborator and friend. I thank Beverly Moss for the never-ending support and encouragement that began at the Ohio State University and continues today. Thanks to Morris Young for introducing me to the field of literacy studies, to Harvey Graff for believing in my work and worth and helping me believe as well, and to Pat Mullen for teaching me so much about folklore. Katie Braun and Jason Palmeri, part of my cohort at Ohio State, have been reading drafts of my scholarship on Appalachia for over ten years; I am thankful for their friendship and expertise. It was while working as a professional tutor at the former University College of the University of Cincinnati that I first began developing research interests in Appalachian studies. I thank the faculty and students of University College, especially Stuart Blersch, Floyd Ogburn, and Gary Vaughn, who encouraged me to go to graduate school and taught me so much about the teaching and learning of writing. I thank my Appalachian parents and late grandparents for the many sacrifices they made to ensure I would have opportunities they never could have imagined for themselves. Finally, thank you to my husband, Greg, and my children, Maria and Peter, for sustaining me and giving me a soft place to fall.

I, Kim, thank Sara for reaching out to me to initiate this collection. Many thanks go to Deborah Brandt, whose example and long-term mentorship have kept me rooted in literacy studies. Without the guidance of Robin Brown and Ellen Stekert at the University of Minnesota, I might never have made peace with studying Appalachia. Charlotte Hogg and Eileen E. Schell, collaborators extraordinaire, are models of the courage and tenacity it takes to write and excellent friends as well. Chris Anson and Robert Brooke have been instrumental long-term supporters, and my thanks also go to Michael Corbett and Bill Green for connecting scholars internationally who work on rural literacies. I thank Peter Goggin, Kirk Branch, and the rest of the Western States Rhetoric and Literacy Conference family for more than a decade of scholarly support, great meals, and stimulating conversation. And to my Appalachian family, particularly my aunt Marilee, my parents, and the memory of my grandmother Cordia, my thanks for accepting my choice of career that has taken me so far away from home. Last, my gratitude goes to Jack and Adina, for creating a family in North Dakota every bit as strong as my mountain one.

Contributors

Ryan Angus recently earned his Ph.D. in literacy and language education at Purdue University. His research interests include Appalachian studies, systemic functional linguistics, writing pedagogy, and language in the content areas.

Krista Bryson, a native West Virginian, recently earned her Ph.D. in the English-Rhetoric, Composition and Literacy Program at the Ohio State University (OSU). Her dissertation research analyzes the rhetorics of three Appalachian advocacy programs to propose a new regional rhetoric for advocacy in Appalachia. She is an activist involved with the West Virginia Water Crisis and is producing a documentary on the event with the help of a National Science Foundation grant. She has served as codirector of the Appalachian Project at OSU and has worked with various other Appalachian research groups. Her work on digital literacy narratives has appeared in *Computers and Composition.*

Kim Donehower's research on rural literacy began in the Appalachian town of her mother's family, a town that had seen three distinct waves of literacy interventions by outsiders. Since then, Kim has continued to investigate issues of rural literacy in the Great Plains, but her interest in Appalachia and in the town of her original research is refreshed with every visit home. She is an associate professor of English at the University of North Dakota, where her work focuses on the impact of literacy practices on the survival of rural communities. With Charlotte Hogg and Eileen E. Schell she has coauthored *Rural Literacies* and coedited *Reclaiming the Rural: Essays on Literacy, Rhetoric, and Pedagogy.* Her essays and book chapters have appeared in the *Journal of Appalachian Studies, Women and Literacy: Inquiries for a New Century, Rethinking Rural Literacies: Literacy/Rurality/ Education,* and *Literacy, Economy, and Power: Writing and Research After "Literacy in American Lives."*

Gregory E. Griffey, a self-described "native stranger" to Central Appalachia, holds a master of divinity degree from Wake Forest University, where his master's thesis explored the relationship between mountaintop removal coal mining and local Appalachian theologies. He currently serves as a hospice chaplain in Tucson, Arizona.

Emma M. Howes earned her Ph.D. at the University of Massachusetts, Amherst, and is an assistant professor of English at Coastal Carolina University. Her research and teaching interests include composition and literacy studies, materialist feminism and feminist theory, archival research methods and methodologies, and the histories of women from the Southern Appalachian region.

Joshua Iddings is an assistant professor of English, rhetoric, and humanistic studies at the Virginia Military Institute. He currently teaches courses in writing and rhetoric, Appalachian studies, and language and literacy studies. His research interests include Appalachian studies, writing pedagogy, educational linguistics, and teaching for social justice.

Peter Mortensen is associate professor of English and director of the School of Architecture at the University of Illinois at Urbana-Champaign. His many works on the history of literacy in the United States and on literacy research methodologies include *Ethics and Representation in Qualitative Studies of Literacy,* coedited with Gesa Kirsch; *Women and Literacy: Local and Global Inquiries for a New Century,* coedited with Beth Daniell; and "Representations of Literacy and Region: Narrating 'Another America.'" He is currently at work on a manuscript titled *Manufacturing Illiteracy in the United States, 1880–1930.*

Nathan Shepley, assistant professor of English, teaches undergraduate and graduate courses in rhetoric and composition at the University of Houston. His research focuses on local histories of composition and modern-day ecologies of writing. Whether focusing on history or the present, texts or human subjects, he looks for ways in which writing connects to physical and discursive environments. He sees considerable potential for place-based studies in Appalachia.

Todd Snyder is an assistant professor of writing and rhetoric at Siena College in Albany, New York, where he teaches courses in writing, rhetorical theory, and oral communication. His research interests include Appalachian identity, critical theory/pedagogy, and community literacy studies. His book *The Rhetoric of Appalachian Identity* was published by McFarland in 2014.

Kathryn Trauth Taylor conducts research on and writes about Urban Appalachian communities. Her work has appeared in *Enculturation, PLUCK! Contemporary Legend, Reflections, Trans-Scripts,* and *Computers and Composition Online.*

Sara Webb-Sunderhaus, the daughter of Appalachian migrants, began her research into Appalachians' literacy beliefs and practices in first-year composition classrooms at two universities in the region. Her research broadly focuses on the literacies of marginalized populations, and her current project explores how Appalachians' literacies and identities evolve as they move through various stages of their educations and careers. She is an associate professor of English at Indiana University–Purdue University Fort Wayne, where she teaches undergraduate and graduate courses in writing, literacy, and folklore. Her work has appeared in *Reclaiming the Rural: Essays on Literacy, Rhetoric, and Pedagogy,* the *Community Literacy Journal, The Norton Book of Composition Studies,* the *Journal of Basic Writing, Composition Forum,* and *Open Words: Access and English Studies.* Along with Krista Bryson, she is the cofounder and cochair of the Appalachian Rhetoric, Composition and Literacy Special Interest Group of the Conference on College Composition and Communication.

Index

PLACE MATTERS: NEW DIRECTIONS IN APPALACHIAN STUDIES

SERIES EDITOR: Dwight B. Billings

This series explores the history, social life, and cultures of Appalachia from multidisciplinary, comparative, and global perspectives. Topics include geography, the environment, public policy, political economy, critical regional studies, diversity, social inequality, social movements and activism, migration and immigration, efforts to confront regional stereotypes, literature and the arts, and the ongoing social construction and reimagination of Appalachia. Key goals of the series are to place Appalachian dynamics in the context of global change and to demonstrate that place-based and regional studies still matter.

Appalachia Revisited: New Perspectives on Place, Tradition, and Progress
Edited by William Schumann and Rebecca Adkins Fletcher

The Arthurdale Community School: Education and Reform in Depression Era Appalachia
Sam F. Stack Jr.

Sacred Mountains: A Christian Ethical Approach to Mountaintop Removal
Andrew R. H. Thompson

Rereading Appalachia: Literacy, Place, and Cultural Resistance
Edited by Sara Webb-Sunderhaus and Kim Donehower

CPSIA information can be obtained
at www.ICGtesting.com
Printed in the USA
LVOW03s1719271117
557738LV00001B/45/P